Slack Worthington

Politics and Property or Phronocracy

A compromise between democracy and plutocracy

Slack Worthington

Politics and Property or Phronocracy
A compromise between democracy and plutocracy

ISBN/EAN: 9783743413511

Manufactured in Europe, USA, Canada, Australia, Japa

Cover: Foto ©Suzi / pixelio.de

Manufactured and distributed by brebook publishing software (www.brebook.com)

Slack Worthington

Politics and Property or Phronocracy

POLITICS AND PROPERTY

OR

PHRONOCRACY

A COMPROMISE BETWEEN
DEMOCRACY AND PLUTOCRACY

BY

SLACK WORTHINGTON

———

G. P. PUTNAM'S SONS

NEW YORK   LONDON
27 WEST TWENTY-THIRD ST.   27 KING WILLIAM ST., STRAND

The Knickerbocker Press

1891

The Knickerbocker Press, New York
Electrotyped, Printed, and Bound by
G. P. Putnam's Sons

PREFACE.

DISCONTENT and strife, to a greater or less extent, have always existed in the world and doubtless always will exist. It is believed by many that the higher the degree of intellectual development in mankind as a class, the greater this discontent, for the reason that objectionable conditions can be more keenly appreciated. Notwithstanding this ever-existing unrest, whether aggravated or assuaged by intellectual development, the causes which produce it are as essentially a part of the great whole,— of the earth and its operations,—as are man's members a part of his physical being ; and these causes can never be entirely annulled, hence their effects must, in a measure, always exist.

It is claimed in the following pages that *poverty* can never be eradicated from society any more effectually than disease can be absolutely prevented in the human body ; but since the latter can be relieved by the proper application of scientific remedies, so likewise can the former be ameliorated by the timely enactment of intelligent laws. The object of this work is to urge strenuous opposition to both plutocracy on the one hand, and socialistic tendencies of all kinds on the other, and advocate a reasonable middle or conservative position between the two, which for convenience is termed " Phronocracy," which signifies the rule of reason, prudence, and understanding.

Heretofore writers opposing the alarming concentration of wealth into the hands of the few have urged against these accumulations conditions that are too violent, and for poverty systems of relief that are utterly impracticable.

This work seeks to avoid both these extremes by acknowledging that the property rights of men shall, to a reasonable extent, be fully recognized and sedulously protected, but that the masses have grievances that must not be ignored. Nothing is proposed that is to the slightest extent visionary, impracticable, or revolutionary, but, on the contrary, only measures are recommended that can be adopted by law within the bounds of prudence, reason, and justice. It also advocates the curtailment of the elective franchise by the only proper and feasible manner possible, viz. : by property and educational qualification.

CONTENTS.

CHAPTER I.

CHAPTER VIII.

CHAPTER IX.

CHAPTER X.

DIAGRAM I.

ILLUSTRATING THE AVERAGE BURDEN OF TAXATION IN PROPORTION
TO PROPERTY UNDER THE PRESENT SYSTEM.

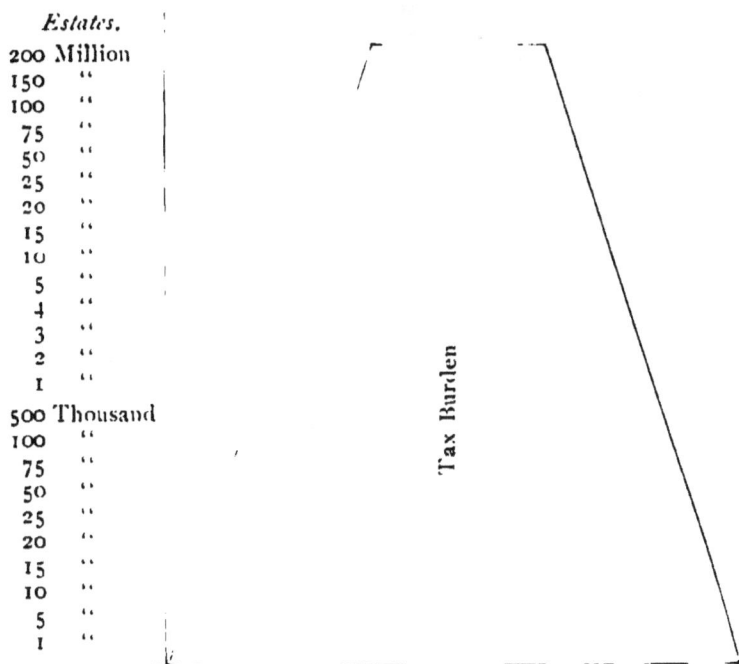

Estates.

200 Million
150   "
100   "
75   "
50   "
25   "
20   "
15   "
10   "
5   "
4   "
3   "
2   "
1   "

500 Thousand
100   "
75   "
50   "
25   "
20   "
15   "
10   "
5   "
1   "

Tax Burden

By the closest obtainable data it is found that very large estates do
not, *on the average*, pay tax on more than one third their value, and
that small estates are usually assessed in full, or pay three times as
much *in proportion* as large estates.

xi

DIAGRAM II.

ILLUSTRATING THE EXACT RATIO OF TAX BURDEN TO PROPERTY

UNDER THE

PHRONOCRATIC CUMULATIVE SYSTEM.

Estates.

5 Million
4 "
3 "
2 "
1 "
900 Thousand
800 "
700 "
600 "
500 "
400 "
300 "
200 "
100 "
80 "
60 "
40 "
20 "
10 "
9 "
8 "
7 "
6 "
5 "
4 "
3 "
2 "
1 "

Y ———————————————— Z

Tax Burden

X

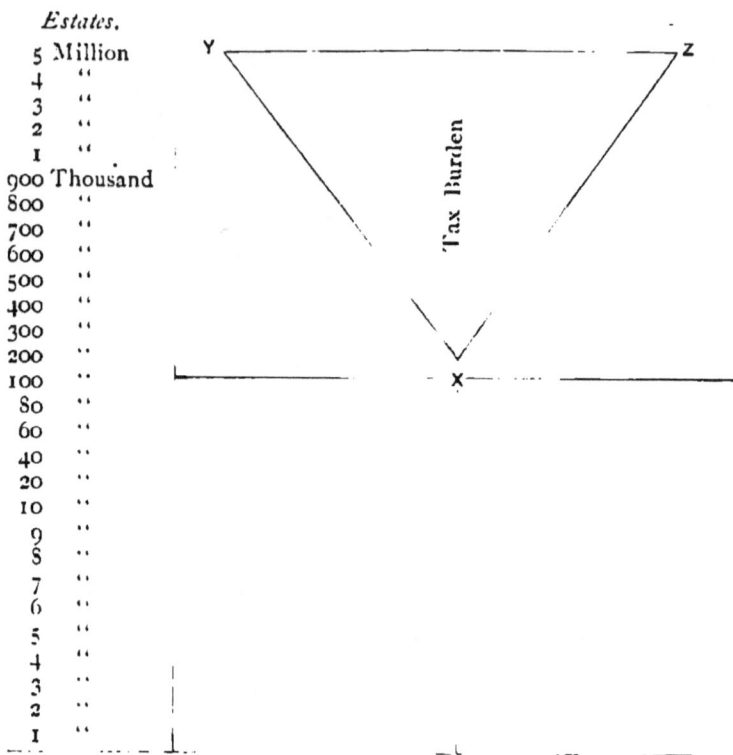

X is supposed to be one-fiftieth of YZ.

The burden on a five-million estate is shown to be just fifty times as great per M. as on a one-hundred-thousand estate, and on smaller estates the burden is so light as to be inappreciable on the above scale.

DIAGRAM III

ILLUSTRATING THE BURDEN OF PROTECTIVE TARIFF.

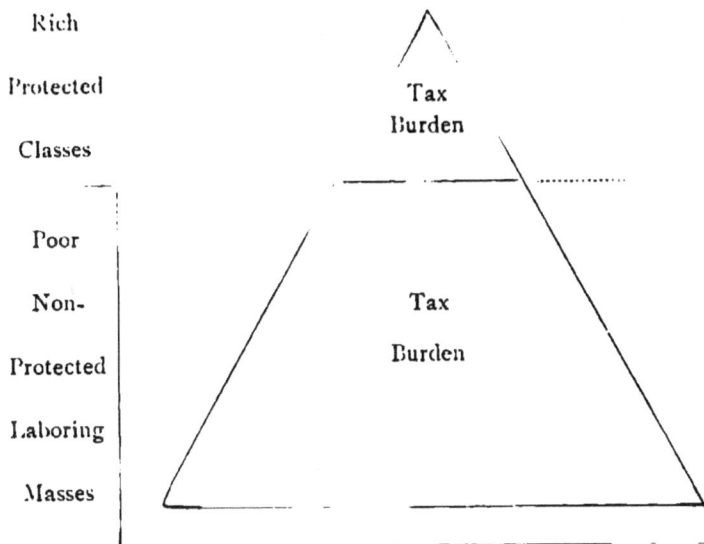

Rich

Protected

Classes

Poor

Non-

Protected

Laboring

Masses

Tax Burden

Tax Burden

DIAGRAM IV.

ILLUSTRATING THE RELATIVE BURDEN OF U. S. REVENUE UNDER PHRONOCRATIC CUMULATIVE TAXATION.

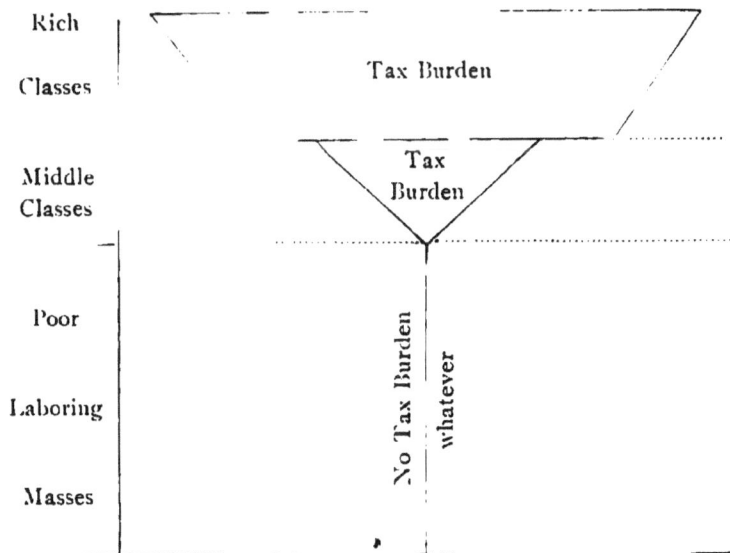

Rich

Classes

Middle
Classes

Poor

Laboring

Masses

Tax Burden

Tax Burden

No Tax Burden whatever

POLITICS AND PROPERTY;
PHRONOCRACY.

CHAPTER I.

Man : his original state ; his advance toward civilization ; his acquisitiveness—Individual property : man's right to same—Government : its origin and progress—Popular strife and energy—
Diversification of civilized wants—Trade and exchange : compromise between wealth and poverty—Phronocracy : its meaning
and purpose.

It is evident to mankind in general, that the earth on
which we reside—an infinitesimal portion of the material
universe—exists. Whence it cometh or whither it goeth
is beyond the ken even of the most profound and erudite
of men. It is likewise apparent to the same general class
that the animal called the human being exists on the surface of the earth ; but whence he cometh or whither he
goeth is likewise veiled in mystery and shrouded in darkness. It is most reasonable to conclude that man began
his existence within the tropics, whether on the Eastern
or Western hemisphere, or whether at the date of his beginning the landed portion of the earth was co-extensive
and conterminous is unknown and inconsequential. It
is likewise evident that the primordial man existed in
a state or condition which, as compared with the en-
vironments of what is properly denominated modern
civilization, was absolutely barbaric. As time passed

he progressed ; or, in other words, he began to exert his
inherent power upon the existing inanimate matter that
surrounded him ; and to use his force to such an extent
as gratified his inclinations in the destruction and utilization of co-existing animate objects within the scope of
his ordinary powers for purposes best suited to his wishes
and wants.   He ran the lion into his lair, he pursued the
antelope into the jungles of the forest, he caught the
fishes of the brooks and estuaries, he multiplied his own
species, and as the population became more numerous,
individuals thereof began to travel the surface of the
earth, and in rudely constructed boats to navigate the
landed confines of the unknown seas.   Later, when
entering into lands and climes in which the rigors of the
weather demanded other and altered appliances from
those required for ordinary comfort in the sun-lit regions
of his primitive abodes, he began to clothe himself in the
skins of the inferior animals that he subjugated and destroyed, and to burrow holes in the ground for the purpose of constructing rude habitations, and to fell trees
with which to construct primitive huts for shelter from
the uncongenial and discomforting winds of his unac-
customed country.   Finally, advancing into a state or
condition from the standpoint of the present, properly
demonstrated progress, he began to comprehend that he
possessed, and proceeded to exercise, supreme dominion
over things animate and inanimate around him.   Com-
measurably with his progress, or rather with his approach
to that state or condition that most fittingly represents
our present civilized life, there began to be displayed
natural acquisitiveness prompted by a realizing sense of
the absolute necessity for provision against want.   He
was able to fully comprehend that a hole in the ground
was a more comfortable abode than the open landscape,

and, later, that a rudely constructed log-hut was more suitable to his wants than a hole in the ground ; also, that the skin of a bear, a weasel, or a mink, could be so constructed as to be of much value in insuring that comfort which he desired and that contentment which he sought ; hence, he naturally began to possess himself of all of these that he could secure, and to use them at once, or to secrete them for the future. Naturally, therefore, the possession of individual property followed closely behind the approach of man to his present condition, and as civilization advanced the varieties and diversification of individual possessions multiplied. The furs of the animals he captured, the fish he caught, and the the trees he felled were naturally and rightfully the property of the man who secured them, and he cherished a natural unwillingness to divide with another. They were the fruit of his toil ; and, since they possessed originally no value, he acquired title by the effort expended in reprisal, and he had an unquestioned right to exert that effort ; and, having so done, would not now willingly become dispossessed without adequate compensation.

Having, therefore, progressed until individual property became an important element in human existence, it became necessary to institute some means of protection against attacks for the possession of that property upon the part of those of his fellow-men who possessed more dishonesty and less industry than himself. It soon became apparent that all men were not equal either in size or intuitions ; neither had they the same identical desires. They differed from each other as radically, though originally perhaps not more so, than the trees of the forest, and less so, doubtless, than the fishes of the sea. Why some grew to be stronger than others, or why some could combat successfully with the most ferocious beast and possess himself of its skin, if he desired it for clothing, or of its meat, if he wished it for food ; and why others could not, or at least were less forcible in this quality than the most favored, was and still is unknown : it is the natural condition, that is all.

Continuing to advance nearer to the condition to which civilization has attained, that faculty of the human being called intelligence began to assume a wider scope and more comprehensive range.

Hitherto, scarcely mindful of the energies and forces of nature, he now began to realize that the wind would blow, that the lightning would flash, that the thunder would roar, that the sea would toss, that the seasons would change, and that Nature would wear continuously an altered aspect, and be subjected to changed conditions that he could not fathom or in any sense control ; hence he began to conclude that there must be some power that did control all these, that could exercise dominion over same, and so he ascribed to the sea its god, to the north wind its god, to the forces of Nature, or, in other words, to the agencies around him, and to personal attributes inherent in his kind and in things in general, their god or controller—hence, doubtless, the idea of a Supreme Being. Since the powers ascribed to the gods were insufficient to regulate and control individual passions, to insure peaceable possession of individual property, to protect the weak against the strong, or to regulate the ordinary affairs of life, there began to be established schemes and systems of government. At first the most forcible of a certain tribe or community would assert, and, by his physical and mental power, maintain, a supremacy over the balance of his fellow-men ; which, by reason of the inherent predisposition of men, caused by their observation of natural forces, to look to a power higher than themselves, crystallized into what was considered a *right to rule*. The chief seemed greater than the masses ; hence he must be nearer to the power that caused the winds to blow, the sea to toss, and the elements to be in action. The desire for gain and for the manifestations of individual prowess would cause strife and contention between the chiefs of various tribes, until the strongest would subjugate the weakest, resulting in greater extensions of the rule of the successful individual ; and thus, as time rolled on, states and nations were builded up by the subjugation and absorption of smaller tribes and communities ; and, as their chieftains and rulers attained glory and renown, they were thought to be endowed with supernatural attainments consequent upon the belief that otherwise they could not so successfully, if at all, have achieved their greatness and power ; hence, perhaps, the idea of the "Divine appointment of the King." The ruler, once established in his kingly state, whether by force or otherwise, succession had to be provided for, and was, in earlier days in most cases, determined by force ; but more recently and in some parts of the world is in this day actually regulated by inheritance, as if any man could inherit, possess, or transmit the right to rule over his fellow-men. When, in 1776, the American colonists of King George III. conceived the idea that "all just power came from the consent of the governed," a great stride was made in the progress of the world. It was a radical departure from the idea of "Divine right," and hence more in keeping with progressive thought.

The attainment by man to that state of civilized life which suggested the advisability of or necessity for any system of government, was coeval with the development of man's acquisitiveness and the possession of individual property. In other words, the idea of government was suggested, and the institution in its most primitive form was established chiefly for the purpose of protection to property and life ; and the proper functions of government are to this day fully exercised, when protection to life and property have been secured and peaceful and uninterrupted possession thereof established and maintained. The numerous and varied manifestations and the unwarranted and non-essential exercise of governmental power can and should be limited to these simple agencies. Admitting, therefore, what appears to be self-evident, that the human being is so constituted that, apace with that progress which he has manifestly attained, he must have wants, and that his wants must prompt acquisitiveness, and that this attribute of his nature prompts accumulation, it is obvious that individual property is as much a natural condition as individual life ; hence that property, to the extent that its aggregate is reasonable and can be available to its possessor, should be held or possessed by him in uninterrupted enjoyment.

To a certain extent, man in the abstract has a natural right to possess the earth and its belongings ; and, since all men are constituted, in the main, of the same kind of matter, and possess, to a greater or less extent, the same ability to enjoy pleasure, comfort, and ease, and have the same general disinclination to endure pain, discomfort, and toil, he should possess it ; yet it is no more possible to institute that condition in society which will render the equal possession of property possible, than it is possible to make all trees absorb from the earth and air the same amount of moisture, or cause all plants and animals to grow to the same uniform size—such is not the natural condition, that is all. The tree appears to have a natural right to that part of the soil from which

its roots take nourishment, and to that share of space
over which its branches ramify ; and so, in the enjoyment of that natural right, does it accreate and grow,
bear its fruit, its seed, and carry out its apparent purpose
and mission on earth, unless by the interference of some
stronger power, as a cyclone or a storm—both as natural
a consequence as the existence of the tree itself,—it
is uprooted or destroyed, or unless, by the hand of man
or by the teeth of a beaver or otherwise, it is hewn down
and converted into something suitable for use. The
stronger, whenever suitable to its wishes or purposes,
will destroy the weaker ; the fittest, all things considered,
will survive.

Society, from the time of early civilization, has, to a
certain extent, acknowledged man's right to live, to
maintenances from the resources of the earth ; and,
in conformity with the acknowledgment of that right,
has established and supported houses for the maimed,
the decrepit, and, furthermore, for the poor. It has
maintained hospitals for the sick, it has supported
public parks and public roads — furthermore, it has
supported public schools—in fact, it has in many cases
recognized fully the agrarian and socialistic principle.
To have extended this indulgence further—that is, to
have opened all such recognized institutions to all who
wished to become inmates—would be to place a premium
on idleness, and thus paralyze the world's affairs.

The natural inclinations of men to possess and retain
property has never been denied. The assertions of a
few misanthropic agitators that, though natural, it should
never be allowed ; that all the world's effects should be
considered common property has never gained much
support, because such views are not only irrational but
unnatural. Men always have had and always will have

wants, they always did and always will strive to supply
those wants, and he who is sufficiently energetic or sufficiently fortunate to acquire the means of gratifying
those wants never did and never will consent to an
equal division with his fellows, who have been either
less energetic or less fortunate ; hence all ideas looking
to the abolition of government which has been established for the protection of this personal property and
life should be absolutely abandoned, and the thoughts of
men directed towards the institution of some social
or governmental system, by virtue of which the personal
accumulations of men cannot become so colossal as to
be useless and unwieldy to their possessors and a detriment to the well-being of communities ; and, at the
same time, towards providing for every individual increased opportunity for acquiring a reasonable competency and an increased security of its peaceful
enjoyment after having been acquired. For years a
constant and unrelenting strife has existed between
employer and employé, which, with disagreeable and
finally with alarming frequency, has interrupted the
trade and business of the world ; has caused distrust
and insecurity to become rife in all moneyed centres,
which has pervaded the body politic, permeated every
enterprise, and stifled the progress of the world's affairs.
So great and so irremediable appears to be the discontent
of the masses that, in 1890, the Emperor of Germany,
whose predecessors and compeers had never hitherto
vaguely dreamed of recognizing or countenancing the
cogent force of popular unrest and intrigue, called a
conference of laboring men for the purpose of considering the cause of the prevailing universal complaint,
and, if possible, to provide a remedy.

   In keeping with the influences and conditions that

usually prevail where no definite plan is proposed—no definite end at which all could aim, suggested,—this and many other conferences of similar character and import resulted in nothing save to aggravate rather than to assuage the manifest grievances under which the masses groaned. In America, Russia, and France, incipient manifestations of anarchism have been from time to time displayed, but such is the force of prudence and good sense that no great upheaval of the people with an unconquerable spirit to burn, pillage, and rob, has yet occurred.

Civilization has reached such a condition that, though the whole of Europe is armed for the purpose of maintaining national autonomy, thwarting foreign aggression, and suppressing domestic insurrection, yet most contentions and differences, whether national, social, commercial, or individual, are settled by the arbitraments of peace, not by the sword and cannon in the ghastly throes of bloody war.

Discussions, even in the iron-ruled and tyrannically oppressed empires of Europe, are prevalent, both on the hustings and in the prints.

No direct effort has been of late years made at the dethronement of governments ; but murmurs of discontent are uttered by the people of those countries where the popular voice, though capable of being uttered, cannot be made effectual, by reason of the oppression of the military and the divine right of the king.

In America the difficulty has existed not in the ability to change or modify existing conditions, but to devise some plan that would receive the support of a sufficient number to make its purposes effective. Some orators and writers have maintained that the people are suffering from no grievance that legislation can mitigate, much less relieve ; that the gulf between Dives and Lazarus always existed, and always would exist ; that civilization requires that there should be a master and a slave, or rather an employer and an employé ; that we must have scrapers for our streets and stokers for our ships ; that we can never more effectually eradicate poverty than we can extirpate disease ; and, in fact, that the world would be no better if all were in affluence, or even possessed of a reasonable degree of comfort, than if a few were opulent and the many in rags.

Others, however, maintain that the earth belongs in usufruct to the people, which in a measure is true, and that all men are entitled to its benefits and rewards; that the fact that the wealth of the world is being so rapidly concentrated into the hands of the few, and to an extent that does not benefit but actually burthens its possessors, is an unnatural condition, and should be changed.

A few individuals now become possessed of a property that is monopolistic in its nature ; and, by reason of the rapid increase of population and consequent increased demand, there arises an increase in value—"an unearned increment,"—for which the owners are in no sense responsible, and of which they should never be possessed, *beyond certain reasonable limitations.*

Labor organizations combine so as to curtail the supply ; demand shorter hours for work, so as to give occupation to more individuals or to lessen the burthen upon those who are engaged. Capital will concentrate into trusts and associations, so that it becomes a matter of serious doubt whether or not all capital will not eventually drift into one grand monopoly and labor into one discontented mass.

Among the extremists of both sides who are capable

of considering, and who possess inherently the candor to confess, there seems to obtain a concurrence of opinion that possibly the present conditions are not as good as they might be made, nor yet as bad as they have been pictured. Anarchy having been absolutely abandoned by thinking men, there remains only those who recognize man's right to property, hence the necessity for some kind of government. The first class maintain that the existence of wealth and poverty are natural conditions, essential to the progress of civilization, and cannot be altered ; the second claiming that there must be a more equitable distribution of wealth, and consequent alleviation of the pangs of poverty.

The first class insist upon the curtailment of the ballot and the vigorous enforcement of property rights and class distinctions. Many of the second class, after having attempted by various schemes to equalize man's condition and estate, finally concentrated upon the principle that government should own all and operate all the enterprises of life to which man's energies could be devoted ; because by this means alone could the fruits of industry be equitably distributed ; or, in other words, that if every individual labored for the state, the result of that labor would be the accumulation of wealth in the aggregate to about the same extent as now, when the accumulation is placed into the hands of fortunate individuals, and that the state having received these accumulations could in turn distribute the same fairly and equitably among the people, who in either case contributed them, but who under existing conditions failed to receive any distributive share, save a paltry sufficiency for life's actual needs, frequently not even that, and never any of its luxuries.

Others of the second class propose various schemes of taxation, prominent among whom are the single- or land-

tax advocators ; others, the control by government of
the enterprises of greatest magnitude that are claimed to
be in their nature monopolistic, such as railways, highways, canals and waterways—in a word, all enterprises
relating to transportation and communication ; others in
America oppose foreign immigration.

Others argue that the policy of national protection
against the products of human labor in all countries
would surely operate as a panacea for all ills in any
country ; others, that close competition of the products
of all by unconditional free trade will effect the desired
result—that is, alleviate the condition of the masses.

Thus to an endless multiplicity are plans and schemes
proposed until there likewise exists a chaos of objection
of difficulty and doubt.   In America, where every human
is a king, or where at least every individual participates
in the creation of the king and in the policies that shall
control his reign, the discussion is of course more universal and widespread, and it is commonly admitted that if
any decided alteration in existing social condition is to
be inaugurated, it will most likely begin in the United
States.

There the idea of individual liberty from the thraldom
of the king first had its birth and there the experiment
was first inaugurated, the success of which, though
scouted at and scorned by the sages of the civilized earth,
has become, after a century of experiment, universally
acknowledged ; so that the States now stand united, and,
with an ever increasing effulgence, blazing forth the
brightest stars in the galaxy of nations—the pride of
their people and the envy of the world.

In America naturally should be conceived, and if possible executed, the idea of individual liberty from the
thraldom of concentrated wealth, and there, after many

discouraging vicissitudes and trials, may be achieved, ere long, the most glorious civil triumph that has ever been recorded in the history of nations.

That triumph will be the result of a compromise between the most liberal and progressive of the advocates of the old system of unlimited individual property accumulations and rigid and imperious class caste and aristocratic distinction, and the most conservative of the advocates of socialism of all varieties ; the two absorbing, as it were, the very essence of manhood itself, that is, the progressive middle classes—the central portion of the arch in which is always found the keystone of the structure. It is observed by statisticians that in America the increase of wealth is proportionate to the increase of population, but that the possession of that wealth is concentrating with alarming rapidity. In other words, the average wealth per capita has usually been somewhere in the neighborhood of one thousand dollars—the American standard coin. In 1880, when the population was forty-five million, the aggregate wealth of the country was about forty-four billion and in 1890, when the population was sixty-four millions, the wealth of the country was sixty-one billion.

It was estimated in 1880, that the world was growing richer to the extent of about ten million dollars per day, of which the United States of America contributed about one fourth. Now, therefore, it becomes apparent that if the possessors of property diminished in anything like the same ratio that property itself increases, there must come a time when the world and all that is in it might practically be owned by one single man.

What good could such possessions be to any individual ? Or what use could the wealth of the world be to a million individuals ? Great fortunes accrete with an accelerated

velocity, whilst the requirements of life remain practically the same. One man can eat only so much food,
though he possess the means to buy food for ten thousand.
One man can wear only a certain amount of clothing,
though he be able to supply raiment for the civilized
world ; he can only sleep in one bed and under one
roof at one time, though he be able to supply both for a
million of his fellows. What use, therefore, to any individual is the possession of property ten thousand times
greater than he actually requires or can possibly use ?
Why should a man gather into his storehouse ten million
blankets when he can only use one, and permit them to
be there till they are moth-eaten and useless, when a
million of his followers are shivering with cold ? Why
should any man by any system that is recognized by the
civilization of the world be permitted to gather into his
garner food for one million souls and permit it to lie
there till it rots, when thousands of his fellows are
starving ?

The abandonment of anarchism, which is offensive to
all good citizens (for all such recognize the fact that
until the human being has reached absolute perfection,
laws must be instituted for his protection and restraint),
aids much the cause of the approaching reformation.
Threats of violence cause more rigid discipline, whilst
appeals to reason prompt mutual discussion. When the
possessors of several million dollars (of which class there
are several in the world) are confronted with the question, as they now are with much frequency and force,
even by the most conservative of daily prints, " What
good to yourself and family is so much wealth ?" they
are at a loss to reply. If you cannot possibly use it,
then your only desire is glory, or the personal satisfaction
of excelling someone else. You have reached a point

where accumulation is in excess of the desire for provision against possible want, and you have acquired a fortune beyond the point which is thought reasonable to stimulate exertion. Each thousand dollars will earn about fifty dollars per year, which is more than the average human being can earn in excess of his support.

In a word, the millions who toil are in but very few instances richer at the end of a year even to the extent of fifty dollars than they were at the beginning ; whilst every man who owns one thousand dollars can safely rely on an income of fifty dollars or more.

Disassociated from technical definitions, all wealth is the result of labor. The world grows richer year by year because its inhabitants are adding to Nature's possessions, their labor.

What is not consumed in sustenance, and consequently destroyed, represents accumulation.

Money is simply an agency for facilitating exchanges, and represents but a very small portion of the property of the world. Primarily and, it would appear, very justly man is entitled to the products of his own labor ; in other words, to the wealth that he himself creates.

The wants of the civilized man are many and various. Without attempting to name or classify, it is safe to assume that he who can supply, surrounds himself with at least one thousand different articles—all produced by labor from the earth and its belongings ; hence, each man being entitled to the products of his own labor, would, in order to live in a civilized state, be obliged to produce these one thousand different articles or remain unprovided unless some other scheme of procurement could be suggested or devised. As it is not within the limit of one man's capacity to produce what he wants of each of the said one thousand articles, and as different men are adapted to different avocations, and have preferences and capabilities differing from each other, some will naturally drift into one thing and some into another. The man who produces shoes naturally wants clothes, and he who produces hats naturally wants spoons, and so forth, and so on throughout the entire list of individual requirements. The bootmaker will voluntarily exchange boots for clothes ; in other words, both willingly exchange their respective products ; hence there arises the system of barter and exchange. In this exchange, some must get more value than others, and so in the work of production some will produce more than others, some are more frugal and fortunate than others, and some are sick less frequently than others ; hence from causes entirely natural and unavoidable, some will become richer than others.

Increased riches enable the possessor to provide increased facility, and increased facilities either increase excellence or cheapen production ; hence some more fortunate bootmaker, from causes entirely natural, can produce a better boot, which he can exchange for the product of another man's labor, than the less fortunate can produce, or he can produce the same quality under conditions and circumstances that enable him to exchange it for less value, resulting inevitably and yet naturally in driving the less favored out of business, who must engage in some other occupation or sell his labor to the other man at an agreed compensation ; hence, employer and employé, and it must, will, and should be so to the crack of doom.

The employer will not of course pay the employé the full amount of his value, but must reserve for himself a profit on his labor, and if this profit is ten per cent., he has but to employ ten men to gain the labor of one individual complete, and so on till a vast fortune has been amassed, and each step in the procedure has been reasonable and natural and consented to voluntarily by the less fortunate man.

Ten thousand different civilizations might be begun on the earth and whilst men are men—whilst we are what we are—the result as above briefly outlined will in the end be substantially the same, because men are not all equal ; if equal, they are not all favored with the same fortunate conditions ; hence some must advance, some must accumulate—it is unavoidable so long as human beings are a part and parcel of, or an incident to, the earth and its operations. To repeat : conditions are not the same, and men are not the same ; if conditions were the same and men, as all admit—*must admit*—differ, as they do, in energy, frugality, shrewdness, and perspicacity, then no law or social restriction that applies to *all men alike* will ever prevent one man from being lord and another his slave or practically that. The only solution, it must be finally agreed, is to institute a system of laws that *do not* apply to all men alike and under circumstances reasonably just and equitable.

To devise some scheme by which individuals may be permitted to reap the benefits of their energy, their shrewdness, their brain force, or their good fortune to such an extent as will provide adequate remuneration,—such as will enable them to acquire not only a competency for provision against want, but a sufficiency for indulgence in any moderate, or even, if desired, extravagant luxury, and at the same time secure a barrier against excess, is a problem difficult of solution. Still greater is the difficulty in instituting a practical barrier against excessive accumulation, and at the same time

2

avoiding any interference with the legitimate progress of commercial enterprise. It having been admitted generally that men are not equal, it is obvious that gradations must exist in society, and it is not improper that they always should exist. In order that life itself shall continue, it is and will be absolutely necessary that certain menial and degrading occupations be engaged in. Some men are willing to pursue these trades, and are by nature and inclinations suited to the same, while others are not ; hence, each individual being unable to perform all the services for himself that civilized life requires, in the natural turning over and sifting out of affairs, those best adapted to and most contented with certain avocations usually drift there by natural causes, such as would result in the course of time were all civilization to be begun anew, unless the conditions, characters, attributes, appetites, propensities, and adaptabilities of mankind should be altered—a result not in keeping with Nature, nor likely to occur.

The Republican and Democratic parties in America have practically ignored the questions of excessive accumulation, of universal suffrage, of foreign immigration, of territorial annexation—of the great and growing evils of concentrated capital and the widespread discontent of the masses of the community. They have been devoting all thought to protective duties, legislation relative to the coinage of silver, the race question in the South, and to pension monstrosities. Between the respective organizations there has ceased to be any great difference on questions of principle. The Republicans claim to be, in fact are, protectionists ; yet, they recognize the necessity for a reduction of import duties. The Democrats are really in favor of tariffs for revenue only, but are afraid boldly to assert and vindicate their belief,

and continue to temporize and dally with trivial and unimportant details of a tariff reduction measure until it is
simply a question between Republicans and Democrats
whether or not the duty should be taken off this and
placed on that or taken off that and placed on this—
whether sheep's wool 'shall be free or taxed or whether
sugar should be free or taxed, and after the labor of the
mountain the mouse is produced bearing a placard on
its back proclaiming to the world that certain grades of
sugar shall be free, but for a period of years bounties
shall be paid to producers, and that wool shall be taxed
so that the voice of the sheep can be heard in the land
and the shepherd's crook preserved in all its primitive
beauty, even though in cheaper lands and in more
favored climes wool can be produced and sold to the
consumer at a largely reduced figure. The Republican
party, in which properly belongs the plutocratic sentiment of America, has failed to deal successfully or at all
with the alarming concentrations of accumulated wealth ;
and the Democratic party cannot countenance the curtailment of suffrage in any form, so that between the two
neither question is treated, and in fact no questions at all
are discussed of any great importance on which there are
any decided differences of opinion.

This condition of things will continue, and the people
remain in a state of disquietude and unrest till the
" Phronocratic " or " Conservative " party promulgates
its platform, which, in brief, is as follows :

1st. No taxation shall be imposed except for revenue.

2d. That revenue shall be derived from a source that
is least burthensome to the people and most certain to
the government, which source is *"from property accumulation,"* not from imposts, nor from the existing system
of internal taxation.

3d. Taxation shall be so applied as to produce the necessary revenue and at the same time check the alarming concentration of individual wealth.

4th. A man to be a voter shall be able to read and write English and pay tax on a certain amount of property.

5th Foreign immigration of all Caucasian races of self-sustaining capabilities shall be encouraged.

6th. The jurisdiction of the United States shall as soon as possible and consistent with civilized methods be extended over the whole of North America.

7th. "Nothing shall be done by the General Government that the local authorities are competent to do, and nothing by any governmental power that individuals can do for themselves."

These are the seven cardinal principles, of which number four should become the shibboleth of a new and progressive organization to be called the " *Phronocratic Party*," viz. :

1st. Cumulative Taxation.

2d. Electoral Qualifications.

3d. North-American Annexation.

4th. Anti-Centralization.

The party's insignia should be a four-leaf clover, with one of the above principles written on each leaf, and the white clover-blossom in the centre of all.

Its principles on being promulgated will at first be shouted at as hostile to both property rights and agrarian preferences, but conservative men of all parties, and especially those cherishing views hitherto more radical, will come to the conclusion that some sort of a compromise between the extreme conditions in life are necessary and proper.

Property has rights that must be preserved ; and mankind has complaints that must not be ignored. *All men should be permitted to possess property to the greatest amount consistent with a proper and just compensation for their ability, their energy, and their opportunity, and should contribute to the support of the governmental system that protects that property in the ratio of their ability to contribute.*

All men should be permitted to participate in government who have attained that standard of excellence and acquired that amount of property necessary to a proper appreciation of the purposes of government; but not otherwise.

The name " Phronocratic " is derived from the Greek words φρονέω, I think, I consider, I reflect, or φρονίς, understanding, prudence, knowledge, and κρατεῖν, to be strong, or κρατος, strength ; and is intended to express an idea midway between excessive Plutocracy — from πλουτος, wealth, and κρατος, strength, into which state or condition it appears as though the machinery of government is rapidly drifting —and excessive Democracy—from δημος and κρατος, the former signifying " the people in the mass," and the latter " strength," or rather " socialism," towards which, in natural hostility to the control of the rich, many conservative minds and many good citizens are drifting It appears that by the concentration of wealth the government will become irretrievably plutocratic, or that by reactionary violence or lawlessness it might become excessively democratic or socialistic.

As both extremes appear useless, the compromise is suggested which shall be neither all plutocratic nor all socialistic ; that the former shall be checked by the institution of a barrier against unreasonable and useless individual wealth, and the latter by a prohibition against the exercise of useless and ridiculous individual ˙

suffrage ; hence, no name can with greater propriety be applied to the advocates of the proposed compromise, and of the reforms and features incident thereto, than " Phronocrats," signifying that party which holds to the belief that *understanding, prudence,* and *knowledge* are the proper foundations on which the government should rest, and that neither Plutocracy nor Socialism are for the best interests of the people as a whole.

The plutocratic portion of the Republican party can not accept the wealth-curtailing feature of the phronocratic creed, nor can the Democratic party countenance the qualified ballot. *Both these extremes are ruining the country.* Unrestricted wealth is quite as reasonable as unrestricted suffrage—both being wrong and altogether unreasonable. There seem to be natural and vital obstacles in the way of regulating both through either of the two great parties, hence it appears impossible for Phronocrats to ally themselves with either and accomplish anything whatever. Democrats must always favor universal suffrage and Plutocrats must always cling to wealth. Phronocracy is more democratic than Democracy in its antagonism to *excessive wealth*, but less so in its equally reasonable opposition to *excessive suffrage.* The practicability of these views and the elaboration and explanation of same in connection with other propositions for the betterment of social conditions will be discussed in the following pages.

CHAPTER II.

No reasonable argument having ever been adduced against the rightful possession of individual property and the maintenance of a governmental system which would guarantee its possession in peaceful and uninterrupted enjoyment and control, some people are disposed sneeringly to ask, "What do the masses want? What would they have? Is there any cause for complaint? Have they any grievance whatever?" "Is it," in fact, many ask, "a detriment to society that a few individuals should own the property of the world? Do not the masses receive their per-diem for their toil, and with that compensation can they not secure the actual needs and requirements of life?"

All men possess a natural right to breathe the air, to drink the water, and, if need be for argument, to occupy the land. However, civilization and the occupation by man of lands and climes not suited to his primitive conditions create needs and wants of great diversification, and, in man's labor to supply these wants, by reason of the inequality that exists in the physical and mental organization of man as an individual and of the varied

and unequal conditions to which he is unavoidably subjected, the possession of the products that supply these
wants becomes unequal, and, as has been shown, by
causes entirely natural and in conformity with the consent of the less favored individual.

The weight of public opinion must, however, finally
settle down to a recognition of the fact that the masses
have a grievance—that the greatest good to the greatest
number is not subserved when the wherewithal to secure
the desirable things of life is possessed by the least
possible number, as is the inevitable result of things as
they are controlled by existing conditions.

The most cogent agent in producing excessive
accumulations is the wealth represented by the "Unearned Increment." Where enterprises are monopolistic
in their nature—that is, such as are practically exempt
from the effects of competition, as is the case with most
railways and highways, canals and waterways, the unearned increments grow to colossal proportions in any
prosperous state ; but in such enterprises as represent
the ordinary trade and traffic of the world—that is, the
butcher, the baker, and the candlestick-maker, where
competition is spirited and universal, the unearned increment is of no considerable importance. This element
of increase resulting from the stimulated patronage or
demand of the people, is caused by increasing population,
and is especially noticeable and striking in the United
States of America, where towns and cities grow up as
rapidly as the flowers of the tropics ; where the iron rail
is close in the wake of the buffalo's trail, and where the
hoot of the owl and the screech of the wildcat scarce
cease to echo in the jungles of the forest till the whole
is ablaze with electric illumination. To deny man's
right to become possessed of the value resulting from

uncarned increment is tantamount to a denial of man's right to property in the abstract; for, if entitled to possession at all, he has as just a right to the good, or such as will and does profit by unearned increment, as to the bad, which might and does become still worse by abandonment and decay. Before any party for the furtherance of any of the proposed systems of reform can assume any magnitude, the question of Free Trade and Protection, in America, must be thoroughly threshed out. For years, party lines have divided on this all-important issue. America has progressed beyond the wildest dream of its most enthusiastic citizens. It has grown in population, in wealth, and in power faster than the fires of its prairies can sweep the autumnal grass from its limitless plains; there seems to be no bounds to its possibilities, no limit to the ambition of its citizens, and no measure to their vanity—no shrine at which they will consent to worship and no king before whom they will bow. They appear to be ready to wrestle with the angels and to command the lightning of the sky, and should one of Glory's brightest suns that ever shone in the meridians of heaven descend from his lofty eminence arrayed in all his celestial attire, they would be anxious to contest and contend with him for the superiority of their plans and the excellence of their systems.

Though owning, in 1890, that part of North America, from the Mexican Gulf to the northern lakes, and from the restless waters of the Atlantic to the golden shores of the Pacific, yet the grand old American Eagle, the emblem of liberty and power, is fancifully pictured at no far future day to stand with his feet perched upon the ferruginous mountains of Missouri—soon to be the centre of population and power—with his pinions outspread, lash-

ing the billows of both oceans, his beak plunged into the
frozen waters of the Arctic Zone, his tail winnowing the
waves of the Carribbean Sea, with a hundred million
people marshalled in the holy cause of liberty, pursuing
countless diversified occupations in fraternity and peace.

All this is by some attributed to that policy of protection to home industry that has been instituted from the
necessary imposition of an almost prohibitory tariff as a
means of securing a revenue for the suppression of the
Rebellion of 1861, and the liquidation of the debts incurred by reason thereof—*a most stupid error.* The
country has progressed, not by reason, but in spite of,
protection, as has been maintained, pending the exhaust-
less controversies and debates on the subject, and as will
be proven when, after a material reduction, and finally
the complete extirpation of the fallacy, things still move
on as they will move. The delay in the destruction of
the system is prolonged by the foolish persistence of the
laboring classes, in spite not only of theoretical but
practical demonstrations, in the belief that therein is a
remedy for their grievances ; in other words, that a system that causes food and raiment to be dearer, and
which tends to increase and centralize the wealth of the
country, can and will alleviate their pangs. That such
monstrous and appalling stupidity could obtain in the
minds of the masses is beyond the ken of the few who
fully appreciated the enormity of the error.

That designing politicians should prey upon the ignorance of the people, or that corrupt and inordinately
vicious propagandists should become the mercenary
tools of the few who have been profiting by the system,
is not especially surprising, but is baneful and pernicious.

Figures and statistics have been piled mountain high by
the advocates of both sides in the controversy. The fact

that the country has progressed results to the advantage
of the protectionist, and to such an extent that for many
years the other party, that really favors throwing off the
yoke, has been obliged, either from motives of policy or
has consented from promptings of timidity, to appear
before the country in a false and ridiculous attitude.
One side cries protection for the sake of protection, and
consistently maintains its position by so-called arguments directed to its support, thus perpetuating its
ascendancy and the continuance of the system ; and the
other party, composed of men utterly hostile to the principle of protection, and who know that its effects are
injurious and necessarily discriminating—who are in favor
of no tax, save for revenue, and that from the source least
burthensome to the people and most certain to the government, for want of bold and vigorous leadership mildly
pose before the public with dulcet muttering,—sweet,
sugar-coated pellets, to the effect that they are not free-
traders—oh, no,—but " Tariff Reformers " ; that protection is a good thing, but we want just a little less of it.
If it is a good thing, the people naturally conclude that
they wish not less but more of it, and if a bad thing,
then they want none of it at all, save for such a period
as would be prudent to effect the speediest conservative
change. The country requires, of course, a certain
amount of revenue, and even the outspoken free-trader
cannot for some time advocate the total abolition of
imposts, for the reason that he cannot conceive of any
other source from which to derive the much-needed
revenue, and from which more than half that now collected is obtained ; *but Phronocracy points out the
source.* Finally, revenue will again begin to be collected largely in excess of the wants of the government **prudently administered.** The public indebtedness

will become greatly reduced—even brought in at a premium—pensions will begin, after the most unreasonable
and astounding increase, also to decline, and it will be
found to be absolutely imperative that taxation should
be reduced, or the earnings of the country will be needlessly absorbed by the government to lie dormant in its
treasury, a temptation to extravagant and vicious legislation, or be by some means redistributed among the
people.   It appears to be idle folly to collect a fund
simply that it may be again distributed.

The best distribution is that which exists before there
is any contribution.   Finally, even the strongest protectionists will be obliged to yield to popular clamor for
reduced taxation.   They will doubtless begin by curtailing internal revenues, then by small reductions on such
articles as it is thought cannot be produced in the
country—a ridiculous condition of governmental stupidity.   An article that cannot be made at home can be
bought by the consumer in the world's cheapest markets ;
but if there is a remote expectation of domestic production, the consumer must pay tribute to some favored
manufacturer.

The question of free trade and protection, unvexed
by statistical information, finally resolves itself into the
following :

Shall governments, like individuals, pursue and encourage such avocations as are most fittingly suited to
their natural adaptabilities and conditions, or shall they
not ?   It has been long since determined that the price
of labor is and can only be regulated by supply and demand ; that if labor could be consolidated into trades
unions and assemblies, none of the individuals thereof
consenting to supply his labor for less than a certain
compensation, a certain price could be secured, or by

reason of a demand in excess of supply an increase could be demanded and obtained, but not otherwise, and this temporarily only. The thinking portion of laboring men have begun to understand that legislation cannot supply what legitimate demand does not warrant ; that the only way they can maintain a high rate of wages is to curtail the supply, not to increase the duty on the products of labor. If ten thousand men should be engaged in the manufacture of clothes, and the industry in which they were employed was the only one in the country in which they lived, is there any laboring man so daft as to conclude that if the tariff on cloths was doubled the price of their wages would be doubled if their employer could possibly secure operatives for .ess ? All such conclusions are unnatural and preposterous, and it will soon be obvious to all wage earners that the price of labor is controlled, like the price of everything else, by supply and demand only. It is useless, therefore, to expect from legislation any alleviation of the condition of labor that does not control the demand and supply of that labor. It is likewise useless to expect to curtail the supply save by that questionably efficacious method—organization. Tariffs will never reach it.

How ridiculous is the proposition that seeks to maintain the price of labor by instituting a prohibition against the products of labor, and yet invites that labor itself, freely and without restraint.

Is a laboring man any the less formidable and competitive because he works directly at the elbow of another, than he is if he labors three thousand miles away ? Is he not rather more competitive to the extent of the cost of the transportation of the article he produces ? Then why should a laboring man argue for protection against

the products of labor ? It is a barren ideality, it is simply
illusory and absurd.

Protection, therefore, against the products of labor
tends only to increase their cost to the consumer, giving
the increased price as an item of profit to the protected
manufacturer, not as a means of increasing the price of
labor, which, be it again asserted in defiance of disproof,
can be effected only by curtailing of supply or increase
of demand.

Why is the relative price of labor, in 1890, in the Empire of Germany—a highly protected country—less than
the same in *free-trade* England, unless because the demand for labor in proportion to the supply is less?
These facts will be, as time progresses, fully appreciated
by the laboring masses who have for years been misguided by the enticing and pleasant sound of the cabal-
istic word " Protection."

It will finally be admitted by the advocates of the
system that there never was any justification for their
policy save in " national independence," that is, as the
free-traders always affirmed, there is one argument and
only one—national independence. Statistics and figures
are produced and information obtained to show that
certain benefits have resulted in certain periods during
which the policy has prevailed, but never has man been
able to prove that the same or greater results might not
have been achieved had the contrary policy been adopted.
Volumes have been and may yet be written, but finally
it will be admitted that there never was any good argument for protection save that of national independence. All others have a retro-active effect. If the same
protection be granted to every individual in a country,
that is, say for example, twenty per cent. on everybody's
products, the result would be that in fact no one would

be protected, because he would be obliged to pay as much
more for everything he used as his protection amounted
to ; hence, he had as well, in common with his fellows,
exist without any. Therefore, if universal protection
would be tantamount. to no protection at all, how can
partial protection be anything else than rank discrimination ? In other words, if out of one thousand pursuits,
in the prosecution of which the population of a country
is engaged, one hundred are protected, it follows necessarily that the price of the products of these favored few
will be enhanced to the extent of that protection until
domestic competition reduces the said price to within a
reasonable limit of gain. Then, during this interval, the
consumer has paid a premium for his goods that he might
otherwise have saved. What has he received in return
for that outlay ?—an industry or say ten industries. Is
there any absolute proof that the United States would
not have secured these industries in any case, even had
the protective duty not been imposed ?

There is no possible argument in favor of developing
an industry at home if the cost of that development is
greater than the value of the industry to the country.

If the United States of America were so constituted
by natural position, agricultural conditions, and climatic
influences as to be able to produce Indian corn, cotton,
and wheat only, and that they could produce these articles cheaper than any other nation, would it not be a
wise and frugal policy for the population to engage in
these productions and exchange their crops for the various other articles of human requirements, or rather to
sell and then to buy, than to tax their people for the importation of these articles, so that an unnatural industry
could be developed at home ? Certainly this would be
economy, frugality, and general good policy, provided

there was an absolute assurance that the various needs
of human life that were produced by outside countries
could always be obtained. If a man can always buy
boots from a bootmaker, why should he bother about
learning to produce them himself at a greater cost? If a
country cannot naturally produce grapes by reason of
the rigors of its climate, why should it tax its people so
that some individual should be enabled to produce them
under unnatural and consequently more expensive conditions, making the price more than they could be bought
for from lands and climes where their cultivation is in
conformity with natural and consequently cheaper production?

For years protectionists have supported their policies
by presenting to the people an endless array of statistical
information going to show that from 1860 to 1880 the
population had increased to such and such proportions,
and that since only a certain part thereof has been derived from immigration, it necessarily follows that protection also gives a marvellous stimulus to the fecundity
of American wives. They have submitted data to show
that factories have increased and multiplied; that railways have been extended into remote sections of the
country—in a word, that the sun has cast his benign and
life-giving rays upon their continent, that the clouds have
wept over their three million square miles of arable
land—all attributable to protection. Such high-sounding platitudes, however, will ere long spend their force
and the populace will begin to inquire, " Would it not
have been so under any other policy?"

From statistics the other, or free-traders-under-the-
bushel party, are able to show that during periods ante-
rior to the great internecine struggle, when comparatively
no protection existed, a greater amount of territory was

added to the public domain, an equal, and in some respects a greater, proportionate augmentation of both wealth and population was secured, and an equal labor remuneration paid, than under any era of high protective duties. So that the votaries of each policy must substantially assume the following diametrically opposite position without any evasion, conciliation, or compromise :

1st. That if protection is good then prohibition, which would be the perfection of protection, would be better.

2d. If reduced duties on imports is good, then free trade, which is the perfection of said reduction, would be better.

Hence, therefore, the people may soon be obliged to choose between two ultra alternatives, the one of complete commercial isolation from the outside world, or the Chinese-Wall policy, as it should be called, and the other unrestricted contact with the entire outside world, or the "World" policy, as it should be called. Tersely presented to the people, there will be the "Wall" policy and the "World" policy. There is no argument that can be presented in favor of the "Wall" policy except that of national independence ; all others are sophistical, easily refuted, and almost absurd.

They react upon each other and, of course, render null any effect. We must tax our people, it is urged, to build up within our wall industries that will supply all our civilized and daily increasing wants ; for, notwithstanding the great improvement in facilities for the navigation of the sea, and the increasing sources from which people can buy, yet, there may come a time when the supply will be cut off and we will be left in a state of lingering chagrin, with a redundance of wealth but no opportunity to exchange it for our diversified wants.

The "World"-policy advocates claim that such argu-

3

ments are jejune and visionary; that it has long since been demonstrated that wherever there existed a demand there would come a supply; that when conditions are ripe, fitting, and appropriate, all industries would come without the artificial and unreliable stimulus of prohibitory legislation, and even if not that, there are two essential elements of profit or gain : one is to buy cheap and the other to sell high—goods well bought are half sold,—and that there is no more reason or sound sense in instituting a system under and by reason of which the people are excluded from the cheapest markets in which to buy—one of the essential elements of gain,—than there would be in the imposition of a similar prohibition against exportation, thus excluding them from a good market in which to sell—the other essential element of profit and gain.

It is an undeniable principle of nature that one thing cannot be artificially builded up unless another thing is correspondingly torn down. Hence, in protecting the classes there must be oppression to the masses.

If, therefore, natural competition is interfered with, and by schemes of legislation one man or one set of men are enabled to acquire for their product 20 per cent. more than the price at which it could be secured in the world's open market, it is a direct gain to him or them ; but must be a corresponding loss to some other man or set of men, or nature has gone crosswise and twice two have ceased to be four. The only undetermined link in the chain is, in what respect has the second man been recompensed for his loss ? If to the full extent of the other man's gain, then the conditions are equalized and there was never any use for the protection originally—the books balance. If he has not been adequately and fully recompensed, then an injustice has been forced upon him, and the system that forces it is wrong.

It has been discovered that all the masses receive
consequent upon the protection to the classes is a kind
of mushroom growth of industries. Those that are
sufficiently well founded could have existed without it
and will exist when it is abolished. The fungus growth
will soon perish, but on their ruins will soon be erected
sufficient of every description to compete successfully
with the producers of the world. It is found that the
consuming masses pay in increased prices to the protected classes fully ten times as much as the industries
created are worth to the country, and in all cases until
home competition forces prices down to within a reasonable limit of gain, which usually requires years, the
protected classes pocket the major part of this excess.
It is found that a rolling-mill or foundry that can
produce 10,000 tons of merchant's iron per year can
easily be erected for $200,000. The average price of
its product for the twenty years intervening from 1870
to 1890 is found to be about forty dollars per ton, representing a business of $400,000 annually, or $8,000,000
for the entire twenty years. By comparison, the price of
the product to the domestic commoner above that which
he would have paid in competitive markets of the outer
world has been fully 25 per cent., representing $2,000,-
000 outlay for a plant costing only $200,000. For years
the laborer has been misguided into the belief that this
tremendous excess was paid out to him in increased
rates of wages, but recently the scales have fallen from
his eyes, and he sees that his employer obtains operators
wherever he can get them cheapest ; that whilst the
product of the manufacturer is protected the laborers of
the world can come in free ; that the only way he can
succeed in maintaining a higher rate of wages is by
organized unions and consequent avoidance of competi-

tion, which for years, while skilled mechanics were scarce, has worked to good advantage, but now and for the future, by the very stimulus that the protectionists claim is making the laborer rich, there is and will be allured from continental Europe, from China, from India and Japan, hoards of competitive operators that would otherwise have remained in the lands of their sires. So that the very thing that is falsely claimed as a protection to labor, by prohibiting its products, results in the virtual ruination of good wages by bringing to the country thousands of competitive operatives.

Looking at the case from the standpoint of reason, it appears incredible that the laboring men have been so long gulled and betrayed by so palpable a delusion.

Why could they not see that protection against foreign products could only result in keeping out these products, consequently causing the price to be high, and that inviting, as this allurement does, the labor of the world, could only result in increasing labor competition and in making wages low ?

Such protection is like holding a glittering tinsel before the eyes of a baby ; it stretches out its arms and cries for it, even though you tell it that it is hot, because a baby has not sense enough to know that a hot thing will burn.

So with the laborer and protection. Equally senseless, and if possible more thoroughly inexplicable, is the position so long persistently maintained by the American farmers, who, in 1890, numbered nearly one half of the population of the country. This class of citizens, usually prudent and frugal, are supposed to consider and support measures tending to the public good, but for years, whilst being compelled to sell their wheat and their corn in competition with the producers of the world, they have blindly supported protection in many localities, apparently preferring to pay an increased price for their implements rather than to be able to secure them in the markets in which they are forced to sell their crops ; in other words, they sell in the competitive what is necessarily the cheapest, and buy in the protected which is necessarily the dearest market ; hence, as an inevitable result, the mortgages on farms are in many cases thicker than the soil itself—almost as thick as the skulls of the mortgagors. However, it is not so much stupidity as prejudice that causes such anomalous associations in political affairs.

A Northern farmer had been a Republican during the war when he favored the preservation of the Union ; how could he now march under any other banner, it matters not how much opposed to his interests present Republican policies may be?

Opinions and associations are oftener the result of prejudices and passion than of reflection and reason ; hence great reforms are more frequently accomplished by the thunder of guns and the glistening of swords than by the peaceful processes of reflection and thought. However, the days of bloodshed consequent upon political or religious differences have long since been past ; yet many men who honestly believe that the continuation of protection principles and policies are prejudicial, if not almost fatal, to the good of the greatest number of the people, act as though they would rather face the muzzle of a dynamite gun than to affiliate with the party calling itself Democratic, even though the position of that party and the propositions of its platforms should be identically harmonious with their personal opinions as to present federal policies, and it will not be until the new organization called " Phronocratic or Conservative " possesses men's affiliation and support that the hitherto Republicans of anti-protection sympathies will begin to vote at all for their individual interests. To this organization also should be subsequently added the most progressive and liberal of the plutocratic class and the most responsible and conservative of the rankest Democratic or socialistic class.

The growth of the organization may be as slow as its methods are conservative, but its foundation will be as solid as its professions are sound. The changing opinions of the country as to the principle of protection will result simply in uprooting an old and worn-out prejudice, and will be a step in the direction of the greater reforms that may follow. Its most valuable effect, aside from its influence on commerce, which will be shown by its results, will be to pave the way for the victory that will finally establish ineradicably the principle that all paternalism in government is baneful and pernicious and hostile to the perpetuity of republican institutions, except that interference and safeguard which will prevent an unreasonable and unwarranted concentration of individual wealth and vouchsafe to property moderately possessed increased security, stability, and force.—*Such is Phronocracy.*

CHAPTER III.

THE questions of free trade and protection having been briefly discussed, and the inadequacy of the prevalence of either theory for the proper adjustment and regulation of social affairs and wants being admitted, it is clear that other and greater remedies must be applied to bring about that improvement in social affairs that appears to be suggested in the interest of humanity and demanded as a check to monopolistic power. The proposition that the government should own and operate the enterprises of the country that are by nature monopolistic, such as railways, highways, canals, and waterways, now comes up for consideration.

The principal reason for the advocacy of this proposition appears to lie in the fact that out of these enterprises has been derived the most colossal accumulations, and that the only possible remedy is to absorb those accumulations by government or to so cheapen the price of the service they render as to make them simply self-sustaining, as one of the parts of the governmental machine.

Ab initio, there need never exist any government whatever if the passions and propensities of men could be otherwise controlled.

If all human beings were philosophers of the intellectual depth, breadth, and scope of the most erudite and profound of the existing sages of the earth, there would be no possible need of government—all would exist in peace and harmony without ; but each individual might be obliged to perform his own manual labor, his equally cultured compeers being unwilling to serve. The fact is, however, and, fortunately, always will be, that all men will not become philosophers ; that if all were at birth capable of becoming such, accidents, incidents, and occurrences of human life will absolutely prevent.

Hence, there will be, as there should be, hewers of wood and drawers of water, unless the world and its belongings are entirely changed. The most trivial circumstance will frequently change the current of a man's whole life, so that he who by heredity might have possessed the material and intuitions for a philosophic development may have been diverted by an unfortuitous combination of human events into some channel that would cause him to be a border-ruffian, a barbarian, or the cook of a ship.

Government is not the most desirable institution of which one could conceive, for its very existence depends upon a certain sacrifice of the inherent rights of the individual to the state for the well-being of the whole—for the better guaranty of social order. A thing or an institution, therefore, that in itself involves a sacrifice is not a thing the influence and scope of which we should desire to enlarge and extend to the utmost possible limit, but such as we should wish to diminish and curtail to within the narrowest possible sphere. Not the greatest possible restraint consistent with human endurance, but the greatest possible liberty consistent with social order is the true principle of government ; and the greater the social order and domestic tranquillity that naturally pervades the social institutions, the less the necessity for government and the more liberal its functions may become.

If, therefore, government is an incubus on society, a thing to be shunned not sought, and which is tolerable not because of its attractiveness, but of its necessity, why should the scope of government be unnecessarily enlarged ?

People yield to the state certain of their individual liberties, and by so doing cramp their individual freedom and desires, yet it is thought better to yield something so as with greater certainty to retain the rest. That policy, therefore, which seeks to yield the most is much more in conflict with domestic civil liberty than that which yields the least. Governments are administered by human individuals, and in times gone by those individuals were thought to be akin to the Divine.

Now, however, when all just power is believed to be derived from the consent of the governed it follows as a necessary corollary that those who are governed least are governed best. Formerly a potentate or king, for motives and desires wholly his own and for his personal aggrandizement and power, could levy imposts and collect taxes—even confiscate private property for individual gain. Now there exists no civilized state in which the powers of the king are not in a manner prescribed, and ere long, as in America, the king will be simply a creation of the people—an instrument to perform certain duties in conformity with their will. Since the evident tendency of civilized life is toward the system which yields the least possible prerogative to the state or the king, how could the grievances of the body politic be in any degree assuaged by enlarging the scope of governmental power?

The argument in its support is that thus the government would become the distributor of accumulated wealth and would deal it out to the people either directly by the apportionment of so much to a certain locality or state, or by operating enterprises monopolistic in their nature at comparatively no charge. Here very naturally arises the question, what are monopolistic enterprises and what are not?

If the government is to own and operate railways throughout the country at large, why not the tramways in the municipal streets? If the telegraphic, why not the telephonic, wires; if the canals, why not all country roads; if waterways in general, why not municipal water-work systems? If wires for the transmission of electricity for intercommunication, why not for light, heat, and power; if water mains, why not gas mains, and if gas and water mains, why not oil mains; and if operating all systems of communication and transportation, why not the steamships on the ocean, the boats on inland rivers and lakes; and thus, with a precedent once established, what might the government not do with equal reason and justification? It is obvious that the matter would ultimately resolve itself into a multiplicity of opinions as to what the government should do and what it should not do, so that from this chaos of controversy order can only be reached by the universal admission that the government must do nothing that can possibly be done by individual enterprise, or it must convert itself into a gigantic workshop and do everything that individuals might do. It is either all government or no government in effect. The determination of what should and what should not be operated by government could not be reached by the magnitude of the enterprise, because it is found that many municipal tramways are of greater size and scope than many overland railways, and that telephonic operations for localities reach in the aggregate a sum equal to, if not greater, than the overland telegraphic lines ; that many steamboat lines are of greater proportions than corresponding railway lines ; in fact, great monopolistic trusts have been formed in various lines of ordinary mercantile trade that assume vastly greater proportions and are more avaricious and grasping, more hurtful to the interests of the masses, than are many of the transportation companies. Is the government also to absorb and operate these because they have become "by nature monopolistic"? To extend its ramification to all pursuits that could just as reasonably be considered within the power of the government as those relating to transportation would deprive individual enterprise of more than a moiety of its occupations and make government attachés of most of the people. To go this far would be worse than not to begin at all or than to absorb everything by government.

It would create an immense and unwieldy governmental machine, performing much of the labor that could be more expeditiously and cheaply performed by the individual ; would create an irresistible power in patronage that would forever perpetuate the "ins" in office, which, as to the ordinary trusts involved, might not be so hurtful or disastrous, but would be sufficiently cogent in its influences to control legislation and convert that grand principle which maintains that the people shall rule—that laws are for the people, not the people for the laws—into a hollow mockery and a sham ; in a word, it would result in the perversion of the very objects of self-government and a subversion of popular rights. If half the people of a country were the employés of the government how much better contented or better conditioned would the country as a whole become ? Furthermore, how much better or cheaper would the business be transacted ? All experience in civilized life goes to show that enterprises operated by the government are invariably more inefficiently or more expensively conducted than are the same classes of business under private management and control, which if not demonstrated by experience would be almost an inevitable conclusion from ordinary deduction, for in the one case they are operated by employés whose labors are perfunctory, and in the other by employers under rigid discipline for individual gain. There exists not this day, nor did there exist at the time of the greatest popular interest in governmental control, a single enterprise of any description or character that private individuals could not have taken at any fair basis of valuation and performed the service at ten per cent. less and gained to their stockholders ten per cent. more than accrued to government in its loose and disjointed control. How few municipal water-works systems yield to the city a revenue above interest on their cost, aye, how many never pay the interest on cost, yet where does or did there exist a single water-works plant that private enterprise would not gladly have taken at a disinterested valuation and agree to supply water to the community at ten per cent. less than the price previously paid ? In fact, it is said that a European syndicate has proposed to buy every single water plant both in Europe and America that is operated by the public on these identical terms.

Water-works in general have been owned by municipalities, and in general they have lost money. Gas plants in general have been operated by individuals, and in general they have doubled their capital stock every few years. A water-supplying system is far more monopolistic in its nature than a gas-supplying system, for there is no substitute and can be no competition in water, and there can be and is in gas. Water is a necessity and gas is a luxury ; gas must be manufactured, hence involves much detail ; water is simply pumped and involves no detail.

The price of gas has been relatively as cheap to the consumers as has been the current price of water, which is proven by the fact that spirited competition has not materially reduced rates ; one goes up and the other goes down, because one is well managed, the results affecting the pockets of private individuals, and the other is controlled by everybody and is no benefit to anybody. The government's business is necessarily everybody's business, and everybody's business is nobody's business, and the only sensible course to pursue is to keep out of the hands of everybody everything that it is possible to give to anybody. But one solitary example of consequence can be produced that affords the slightest possible argument for governmental enterprise on the score of economy, and that is no example at all—to wit, the federal post-office system of the United States, which, to 1890, never paid expenses, never was self-sustaining ; yet, when it was suggested that the business be transferred to private express companies, the aggregate operations of which at that time, in small parcels, extended to almost as many localities as the post office itself, any company doubtless could, in consideration of a long contract, do the business at a less price than the government has been charging, and would make much profit where the government has been losing. On the score of efficiency there is no argument, for both are performed by men, and a man is usually *less, not more*, efficient when he works for good old Uncle Sam than when laboring for the directors of a soulless corporation. Furthermore, a conclusive demonstration is found in the efficiency of the express and telegraphic systems—both equally and almost relatively as cheap as Uncle Sam's letter system.

A more widespread opinion favoring the control of the telegraphic lines of the country by government exists than for most any other enterprise; but then if telegraphs, why not telephones, and so on throughout the list?

However, since it is thought best to retain the transmission of mail matter in the hands of the government, it might be proper that the postal telegraph should also be made a part of that particular department. Whilst it cannot be doubted that both could be as effectually done by private enterprise; yet conditions might arise when the government, in the administration of its functions, might require control of this part of the country's business. This, however, could about as reasonably be urged regarding transportation in general and many other enterprises, so that virtually it may be continued only because it has heretofore existed and had done reasonably well.

Much objection, however, is urged to the necessary employment by government of the army of postal clerks and general attachés, which puts prestige and patronage into the hands of the party in power, thus tending to deprive the individual of his natural right. In fact, it will soon become almost a fixed principle of popular belief in America that the general government should only protect

the country from foreign aggression ; preserve the peace,
and regulate the commerce between, not within, the States ;
provide and maintain a uniform and stable circulating
medium ; then provide and maintain collectors of revenue necessary to carry out these purposes ; and, having
done this, that the general government will have performed the major part of its whole duty, leaving to
States the regulation of all domestic affairs and to cities
the employment of police ; or, practically and in short,
that the governmental functions are simply to protect
life and rightful ownership in individual property, maintain peace, and regulate commerce, obtaining its revenues to do this from the extraordinary accumulations of
individual property ; that this and this alone is the rightful function and prerogative of government, and why
should free men yield more ? So great and irresistible
may yet be the popular outcry against concentration by
governments and to the patronage and power exercised
through federal employés, that postmasters may soon be
elected by the people of the city or locality in which their
duties are performed, and all collectors in the districts
and by the people whose property they assess, taking all
this patronage out of the hands of the President and
placing it with the people where it belongs, until this dis-
tinguished functionary will be shorn or rather relieved
of many of his duties in the matter of appointments to
office, which would be far more satisfactory to the incumbent as well as to the people, and being relieved of this
arduous and unpleasant duty he would devote more time
to affairs and matters of state. His chief remaining
appointments would be simply the members of his own
cabinet, foreign diplomats, and consuls, territorial governors, and judges of the federal courts.

Everything should tend towards retaining in the hands

of the people every possible governmental function, and when the ballot has been purified by the only effectual method—curtailment,—or by the disfranchisement of the unworthy, greater safety and security will rest with the people than ever before, and there will be less inclination to delegate their powers to officials.

Governmental control of the leading enterprises of the country can be productive of no good result, being alike unnecessary and ineffectual ; so likewise is the proposition to *absorb all* business by the government for the same identical reasons and for others of greater moment and objection, to wit, uselessness and impracticability.

This proposition involves primarily the employment of the time, energy, and ability of all individuals for each other, or, in other words, for a kind of a government, the duty of which is to be the equal distribution of the products of human labor ; in a word, all are to produce and all are to divide—a Utopian dream, the principal merit of which lies in its utter impracticability —a scheme suitable either to the gods or to the fishes perhaps, equally applicable to both, but of no use to man. It will never be seriously considered by any whose opinions are worthy of notice.   It is a virtual denial of man's right to property in his individual capacity, but admits an incidental or sort of reversionary right to a share in everything.   In fact, writers on social questions have ceased to deny man's right to property individually, which is as unquestionable as his right to breathe air ; they have ceased to maintain that he is not entitled to the fruits of his labor and to enjoy those fruits however he may, in conformity with social restraint ; likewise it is admitted that there must and always will, and in fact always should be, gradations in society : that it is utterly impossible to effectually eradicate poverty, which, to a certain extent, is a necessary result of the operating forces of nature.

The earth's axis inclines 23½ degrees to the plane of the ecliptic, hence there are variable seasons in certain zones.

In the winter some men will be stricken with pneumonia, and in the summer some will be overcome and prostrated by the heat ; both conditions are the inevitable result of nature and its operations, the fault of no man nor set of men ; both conditions will incapacitate some men for duty, hence some more favored men can pass them in the race. But, says an objector, there should be no race, no contention, no strife between men ; all should exist in fraternity and love, no selfishness, but a general acquiescence in the rights of each to all. No race, no strife, no contention means no exertion, or universal idleness, in which case all would starve. Many would rather work than starve, hence they naturally object to a division with those who would rather starve than work. And thus in ten thousand ways and from ten thousand conditions, all natural and unavoidable, to say nothing whatever about the inherent qualifications and attributes of man as an individual, some are bound to fall below the level of the average and some rise above it ; and to seek entirely to remedy, or in any considerable extent to alter this result by legislation, is tantamount to making the world anew. Man can, however be obligated to contribute to the support of society and to the maintenance of government in proportion to his ability to contribute ; he can be so taxed that when his fortune reaches an abnormal excess his payments to the state will be equal to the income from his estate, thus preventing the useless individual accumulations of the

4

favored and increasing individual opportunity of the
oppressed. This is all that can be done consistently
with man's natural right to a reasonable reward for his
energy, his ability, and his industry; in fact, it is all that
justice demands and all that the community should wish.
Man usually accumulates property in proportion to his
ability; it is not therefore unjust that he should contribute to the support of that governmental institution
which protects that property in proportion to his ability
to contribute; aye more, betimes man's accumulations
are the result of fortuitous combinations of events, not
to his skill or energy. These conditions, however, are
natural, and he should be entitled to a reasonable reward
therefrom, and since much accumulation is the result of
these fortunate agencies, less is the discrimination against
the successful individual when the state interdicts against
useless excesses, and says that from this excess will I
support my authority. Tax excess excessively, medioc-
rity moderately, and poverty not at all, is the correct
principle of government and of taxation to support it.
On the other hand, all mankind have the natural right
to live, by which we mean, to the possession and consumption of a certain portion of the earth's products,
essential to the continuance of life. He has this right
as against the efforts of his fellow-men to the same extent that he possesses it as against the contending forces
of nature, and no more and no less. He cannot exist
against the contending forces of nature, especially if he
chooses to inhabit a part of the surface of the earth subjected to the rigors of an uncongenial clime, without
effort, and often the most strenuous effort will not avail,
and he perishes, consequent upon the fault of no man
or set of men, but by reason of the natural order of
things. So, likewise, must he exert his efforts in the

strife against the opposing forces of his fellow-men, and likewise as in his contest with natural obstacles, he sometimes perishes, and consequent upon the fault of no man or set of men ; and he has asked much of his successful rival when he combines with the less successful and says to the former : "*So far shalt thou go and no farther.*"

He has demanded in this, however, no more than the successful rival can well afford to grant ; in fact, to the extent of his comfort or his happiness he is in no sense oppressed ; his cupidity and his greed alone are circumscribed.

Men being entitled to a reasonable compensation for their efforts, does not carry with it the admission that they are likewise entitled to an unlimited reward for avarice and greed, for much of that gain results from the increment forced upon them by the requirements of society, and this increment should, after certain limitations, inure to the benefit of as many individuals as possible, consistent with public good.

In keeping with the impracticability of accomplishing any practical good to society by the merger of all enterprise into the hands of the government, which is but an aggregation of agents of the people to perform certain duties, is the legislation that is continuously being enacted looking to the regulation of freights, traffics, and the like, by governmental authority. The general government can regulate commerce between the States, that is, it can prevent any embargo being placed upon the products of one by another in transit over their respective boundaries ; it can prevent States from instituting any sort of prohibitory conditions as between each other, but it cannot regulate the traffic within the boundaries of the State itself. This duty or privilege is

reserved to the State legislators, and their enactments
are sometimes unwise and detrimental to the public
weal. It would not answer in all the States to prescribe
a certain fixed rate beyond which no charge should be
made, for in some localities a price equal to five cents
per mile for each and every first-class passenger would
be cheap, and in some others a price in excess of two
cents would be high ; hence if any limitations are made
they must usually be so high as to effect no practical
good, and had as well not exist.   The construction of
railways and highways, canals and waterways, in some
sections of the country is comparatively cheap, and in
others very high.   Many times in different sections of
the same State the cost would be more than quadrupled,
so that a legislative enactment to the effect that the price
of all traffic within the State must not exceed a certain
stipulated rate would be in excess of what one company
might desire to charge, and not sufficient for the actual
maintenance of another.   The average cost of railway
construction in Nebraska or Kansas is much below that
in Colorado or Nevada, for the former are located in a
broad and level country, and the latter in the precipitous
rocks and crags of mountain gorges.   It has usually been
the custom to prescribe a maximum, but this is frequently
above the actual charge for transportation.   People resident in any section must have facilities for transportation,
otherwise their land is valueless and their unconsumed
crop will rot ; hence it is that in nearly all sections the
socialistic principle of maintaining public wagon roads
prevails, not because the people believe in socialism
in the abstract, or would be willing to have their
land taxed for many other schemes in the nature of a
general divide, but because it appears to be to the interest of the property itself to have it so—that is, by sub-

mitting to a tax to maintain a public road (which is about the same in principle as submitting to a tax to maintain a public hotel), their land appears to gain more in value than the tax really costs. The road, therefore, being supported or rather operated by government, and individuals who have no property and pay no tax being permitted to use it as freely as those who pay the most, seems to be a great concession to the socialistic senti- ment, yet it appears as though the tax-payer is more than recompensed by the increased valuation of the land con- sequent thereon. Well, say, the government absorption- ists, if it be to the interest of the tax-paying landowner to maintain the public road, why would it not be more largely to his interest to establish lines of free carriages on said road, so that the socialistic principle as to trans- portation could be carried out to its fulness ? And if to his interest to maintain highways and establish carriages thereon, to be supported by taxation on his property, and for the free use of the public, why with equal reason might it not be to the interest of the landowner to con- struct and maintain a line of *railway*, and establish free carriages *thereon*, which condition rendered to its ulti- mate end would mean governmental control of all trans- portation ; and if of transportation, which in value amounts to about one fifth of the whole and employs about one tenth of all the people, why not of everything else ? In other words, why should the people not create agents to do the business of the country and distribute the profits if there be any, and, if none, then give to each man so much food and raiment and let him go on his way rejoicing ? Thus there appears to be some enter- prises in which the socialistic principle does operate to advantage, such as the maintenance of free wagon roads and streets, free parks, free schools, free poorhouses, hospitals, and the like, and the reason why it should appear to work well to within their limitations—in fact, appear to be necessary to this extent—and yet iniquitous to any extent beyond, is because further governmental control thwarts individual enterprise. The fact is that society is obliged to recognize the socialistic principle to some extent, but this offers no argument for its universality ; but it is clear to the minds of far-sighted men that if something is not done to check the colossal and useless accumulations of individual property, the socialistic principle may be very largely extended, and it is best to meet the issue at once and favor the said principle outright to the extent of annihilating all *excesses*, and curtailing it as much as possible as regards all *mediocrities*, with sedulous care not to stifle enterprise.   To impose a limit on traffic or to create other restrictive conditions is in fact to a certain extent a barrier to enterprise, and it is really questionable whether or not to permit the matter to regulate itself would not result in the end in greater development and consequently greater competition, hence better and cheaper accommodation, than to attempt to protect the people by controlling even the maximum of charges.

In some sections of country the residents would gladly agree to pay ten cents per mile for ordinary railway passenger traffic rather than to have no line of road ; in fact, it is questionable if the residents of any country would dispense with same altogether if the rate should be double that sum.   In America in 1890 there existed about 167,coo miles of railway—more than all the world besides combined,—yet crops could not at times be properly transported.   Now, by permitting capital to construct roads and charge for the use of same their own stipulated rate (being common carrier the same, of course, to all under similar condition), granting no privileges and imposing no restraints, it might be that in every belt of country in America twenty miles wide there would be a line of road running both north and south, east and west. The distance between the oceans averaging, say, for a short calculation, 3,000 miles, and the width north and south is 2,000 miles, there would be on the 20-mile basis, 100 lines of road 3,000 miles long, or 300,000 miles, running east and west; and 150 lines 2,000 miles long, or 300,000 miles, running north and south; or in all 600,000 miles of road, and none nearer to the other than twenty miles apart, which would be ten miles from the central tracts of land to the nearest road—which, with a loaded team, is a fair average distance to haul a load of produce and return the same day over a fair highway in good repair. Since access to facilities for communication appears to be the great promoter of values, it is a question whether or not, all things considered, as much good would not result from the multiplication of those facilities, superinduced by the ability to regulate their own rates, as by a diminution of same consequent upon legal interdictions, thus permitting the laws of trade to regulate the price of traffic.

Who can say that it would not be better for an entire country to have two lines of railroad twenty miles apart, charging ten cents per mile, than one line, charging but five cents per mile, forty miles off. Perhaps both could comfortably live at ten cents, and one would grow very rich at five, but the average haul over the highway which in the case of the two would be, say, ten miles, in case of the one is twenty miles. If wagoning over country roads cost fifty cents per mile (about a proportionate rate), it is clear that a haul of but ten miles to a ten-cent road would enable the goods to be transported some distance at even that rate before the actual outlay from farm to market would be much greater than on the five cent road, where the goods were wagoned twenty miles at fifty cents per mile.

These matters should be fully discussed, as also social- istic highways, socialistic schools, parks, and the like, and it may be determined that it is best to let natural conditions, not in conflict with the general plan of cur- tailing excesses of individual estates, prevail at least for a while till it can be demonstrated whether or not in adopting generally and fundamentally the principle and policy of governmentally regulating the extremes of for- tune, there would not be interference sufficient to enable the people to dispense with some of the other features long existing in communities and recognized as valid. Relative to all socialistic tendencies and all schemes for the absorption by government of individual enterprises, it may be safely said *that the least possible is the best.* Socialism as applied to individual excesses is the most reasonable and least oppressive of any, and that alone should prevail in lieu of all that can possibly be dis- pensed with. Absorption of enterprise by government is not only impracticable, but is in fact simply the turn- ing over by the people to the people and then turning back by the people to the people, or, by the people to their agents (the people) and by the agents (the people) back to the people, the usufruct of labor, making no allowance for individual excellence, energy, opportunity, or desire, which is as much in conflict with nature as it would be to say that all trees shall grow to the same uni- form size. Let the tree expand reasonably, but if it gets so big as to be useless in itself and threaten destruction to the forest it would be wise to trim it up a little.

Then comes on a great and apparently endless discus- sion as to the maintenance of public schools.

It is urged that this exercise of the socialistic princi-

ples is useless ; that, in fact, it is injurious ; that it
creates an artificial equality that is hurtful rather than
beneficial to society ; that it unfits many for occupations
that must be pursued by some ; that it creates in these
an increasing discontent, and enables them to more
keenly appreciate and more deeply to lament the gradations in society which must exist until everything assumes a different footing, or, say, until the world begins
to turn the other way and the sun to revolve around the
earth ; but that whilst things are as they are gradations
cannot and should not be prevented, and that to educate
the masses is a step in that direction which on the whole
is not proper ; that in fact and in truth,

> From ignorance our comfort flows.
> The only wretched are the wise.

It is maintained on the other hand that education
makes men less passionate and vicious ; that they are in
consequence more easily controlled ; that it prevents
crime and outrage by enabling people to understand the
enormity of it ; that on the whole it is worth more to
property to have an educated populace than an uneducated one ; that the tendency towards disqualification
and unfitness for certain occupation will be offset by increased compensation ; that professors of colleges will
clean the streets or remove the garbage for a certain
compensation ; that menial occupations would command
high prices rather than degrade workmen, and so on *ad
infinitum.* The other side maintains that a little education is worse than none at all ; that it makes of what
would otherwise be a mild pilferer in the street a bold
and defiant counterfeiter and forger—a character more
difficult to control and, by reason of his greater ability,
more dangerous to society ; that if you would keep the
people in subjugation you must keep them in ignorance ;

that ascendancy in all institutions will flourish most where the masses know the least.

Thus by these divergent views the free-school system may be in some sections abandoned according as the majority in · localities, by which alone the institution should be governed, should decide. However, in most States and counties of the United States and later on in other countries which have intermittently encouraged and abandoned it, the institution will likely be supported to such an extent as will enable the attendants to learn to read, write, and cipher, or what may be considered the "citizenship course," and nothing beyond. It should become law that man must both possess something and know something before he could participate in government—(strange that he should ever have participated in it otherwise) ; and since the opportunity would be before him to possess the requisite amount of property which he could do in a few years by frugality and economy, especially since the main contributions for the support of government are proposed to be taken from accumulated property and are by reason thereof scarcely perceptible to the poor or the intermediacy, so likewise is it thought best, all things considered, to give him an opportunity to acquire the other requisite, to wit, a certain amount of knowledge, so that he who should become a citizen might if he would.

Beyond these limitations, however, there should be the most rigid scrutiny and the closest possible guard against the extension of delegated powers or socialistic operations, the former confined essentially to security to property, and the latter to the actual and self-evident needs of the social state and to the limitation of excesses caused by the increase of population and the utilization of those excesses for the support of the state—rather " Conservative Socialism or *Phronocracy.*" " *Aut Phronocracy aut Nullus.*"

CHAPTER IV.

Single or land tax considered : sincerity of its advocates—" The world belongs in usufruct to the people," correct in the abstract—Original possession : how acquired — Right of original possession— Land the product of labor—Impracticability of "uninterrupted access to natural opportunity"—Tax to full rental value tantamount to confiscation, and less fails of the object sought—Not justified by simplicity ; generally impracticable and void of good effect—Relief only secured by laws oppressing the favored and assisting the oppressed.

BEFORE entering into detail as to the means, methods, and circumstances under and by virtue of which the " Phronocratic-Conservative " alliance is proposed to be formed and the discussions of the principles supported by same, there arises for consideration another and by no means unimportant propagandism that has been promulgated and supported by men of intelligence and thought—to wit : the Single or Land Tax proposition,

This class of reformers aim, as do all, at the greatest good to the greatest number. They recognize to the fullest extent that man is entitled to the fruits of his own labor ; that he possesses a natural right to own and enjoy any property that results from the labor of his hand or his brain, and that he is entitled to an effectual guaranty to the peaceful and uninterrupted possession of that property. Hence the single-tax advocates can by no means be classed among those who in any way seek to institute a condition of anarchy in society, or to forci-

bly dispossess any man of the fruits of his toil ; and, consequently, as a party that aims by the enactments of law
and by methods peaceful and persuasive to institute certain changes in human affairs that would, in their opinion,
ameliorate the condition of the masses of human beings,
they are entitled to and should receive the utmost consideration and respect.   Their views are discussed and
their pronunciaments elaborated ; in a word, such has
become the condition of society that no sect or class that
tends toward revolution and force will be in any sense
tolerated.   The intellectual development of the world is
such that all who seek to dispose have first to propose,
and any proposition affects no disposition unless it is
supported and upheld by the most forcible and reasonable arguments—or, in other words, brain rule, not brawn ;
there is no force except that of convincing and irrefutable
arguments.

The single-tax advocates, with great reason, claim that
the " world belongs in usufruct to the people " ; that all
men are entitled to " equal access to natural opportunity " ; that natural opportunity is the earth and its
belongings.

When jocosely asked, " What do you want ? " they
appropriately reply, " We want the earth—our natural
inheritance."

Land is considered the gift of God to the people, as is
water and also air.   Since the natural right of access to
water and air have not as yet been denied, why should
access to land, an equally important element of human
existence, be withheld ?   Man cannot live without earth,
air, and water ; in fact, some individuals of the materialistic faith espouse the belief that man is nothing else
than a combination of material forms—a highly-developed protoplasm, a mollusk, a fish, a bird, a mammal, a

monkey, a man—animate yet wholly material, *a result
and not a design;* that the earth is inhabited, why? because the sun's heat, the land and water, all co-existent
if not ever-existent, aided by action, motion, force (which
implies energy), all of which exist as an accompaniment
of the great whole (but why or how no man knoweth),
produces something, and that something is the vegetable
and animal life of which man is but a part. We ask,
"Are the planets of our own system similarly inhabited?" Certainly not, if by inhabitants we mean
things and beings identical to and in keeping with our-
selves. The actinic agencies of nature there may—
doubtless do—produce something, just as similar agencies here may have produced what we see all around us,
but who knows what, how, or in what shape it has been
manifested? It is by no means the same as here, because the conditions are radically different. Who knows,
or is prepared to absolutely prove, that man is not a
result of the actinic forces of nature and has assumed
the form he has and the attributes and characteristics he
possesses, because such form, such attributes, and such
characteristics are the fittest, most appropriate, and
most reasonable, all things considered. But why di-
gress? Our object is to delineate what is happening
in the world among its people, come or originate and
ultimately end howsoever they may. The single-tax
advocates seek to place all tax on land values, reliev-
ing every other kind and class of property from any
contribution whatever to the support of government;
they seek in effect to make the amount of this tax equal
to the rental or productive return of the property. They
confine all assessment to land values essentially, to the
lot on which the house is erected, not to the house itself
or its belongings; to the farm directly as soil and dirt

only, not to the houses, the fences, and the barns. The reason why everything save land is to be exempt from taxation, is because improvements of all kinds are the product of labor, and that to tax labor's product is, they say, to discourage and oppress the exercise of its energies, to place an incubus on development, and correspondingly hamper enterprise.

They also maintain that any man is entitled to hold land in use ; that to tax land to its full rental value would make it undesirable, yea, unprofitable, if not utterly impossible, to hold it out of use at all, and that if no one held, then all who wished could occupy and use ; hence, the means would always be at hand by which man could exert his energies, or, in other words, he would then have uninterrupted access to natural opportunity—the consummation not only devoutly to be wished, but the remedy for all wretchedness. If a man could not obtain employment in a shop at a satisfactory remuneration he could become independent of the shopkeeper by entering in upon and cultivating any patch of land which would be open to his exertions, unless actually in use by some of his fellows ; if a man wished to build a house he should be permitted to enter upon and possess any vacant city lot not actually utilized, and so on to the end ; land not in use could be used by any one, just as water not drank and air not breathed could be used by any one—a happy contemplation, but a remote and impracticable realization, with nothing in it save a barren idea, nothing save a Utopian dream—a wild phantasmagoric vision, that vanishes ere it 's fully seen.

To begin at the beginning : How did man become possessed of landed estate ? We will assume for illustration that the ancient and presumably sunken island of

Atlantis, alluded to in Bacon's allegorical fiction, (rich in
productiveness by reason of its long inundation) should
suddenly emerge from the bottom of the sea. Supposed
to have been located somewhere north of the equitorial
Atlantic it would be in easy position of access, and,
being fertile and productive and located 'neath friendly
skies and surrounded by balmy air, it would naturally
become the modern Eldorado—the promised land, the
haven of untold wealth for the myriads who toil.

We will suppose that John Smith and Joe Jones first
discovered it, then to whom does it belong? Well, we
will suppose that, being God-risen (certainly not man-
risen) from the depths of the sea, it belongs when discovered to certain amphibians that are found to infest it.
It cannot be denied that this title to it would be as good
as the title of any other of God's creatures. Do the jungles of Africa belong to the monkeys of God's creation,
or do they not? Does the land belong to the aborigines
who first inhabit it, or does it not? Yes, it belongs to its
first occupants, which were in all probability a low order
of vegetables, then later each tree owned its quota, and
since it had not the faculty of locomotion but was able
to draw its sustenance from the land and air immediately
around and from the rains that showered on it from the
clouds, it would, if it could have uttered sound and
expressed what we call thought, doubtless have said : " I
am content ; I have enough. All I have to request of
my fellow-creatures is that they will keep at a respectable distance so as not to tax the sustaining capacity of
my little plot of land through which my roots interlace
and ramify." Later on come the beavers and gnaw down
the trees in a certain area of country adjacent to the
water brooks, and use their trunks and branches for the
construction of dams, which they chink with mud. To

whom does the denuded land then belong? Certainly to the beaver ; and it then has no other or greater value than that represented by the beaver in gnawing down the trees. Later come some gigantic and powerful herbivora and begin to eat the grass and the bushes and to render the country unfit for the uses of the beaver, and, being more powerful, possess themselves of it. Later, through a multiplicity of epochs, came primordial man, and he took control of all simply because he could. Then the strongest races and tribes of men, to the extent that they desired, dispossessed the weaker and possessed themselves of the land, just because they could. Later the sword and cannon of the so-called civilian overcame the bow and arrow of the so-called savage, just because they were more powerful and could.

The sword and the cannon acquired as just and as equitable a title from the bow and arrow as the bow and arrow did from the teeth and claws of the beast, and thus force was of necessity law—might was right until some social system was established by which the wants and desires of men multiplied, and for the good of the whole individuals consented to be governed. Civilization and the migration of man from the lands and climes in which he originally had his being caused diversification of wants, and diversification caused division in production, and division in production caused trade and exchange, and trade and exchange caused profits, and profits caused accumulation, and so on to the end. But to revert : If the resurrected island of Atlantis belonged, not to the man or men who discovered it, but to the amphibians that were found on it, because they are of God's creation, how long would it be before by the rightful exercise of superior force some stronger animal, possibly and for the sake of argument we will say elephants, would drive off or kill out the amphibians, and if they desired to do so, graze exclusively on the succulent grass of the newly acquired pastures? How long thereafter, by superior force, would it be before man would drive off the elephants if he should choose to do so? Therefore the man who has the title by force has the rightful title when civilization, or call it what you may, was in such a state or condition as to have recognized no higher arbiter.

When the higher arbitrament was instituted succession to possession might proceed under it, but original titles are none the less good for all that. The title that comes straight down from the original patent or grant of the king, if the king had the title (even though by force whilst force was custom and law), is the best title to-day, and it is a just title.

To argue that man is not entitled to landed estates to-day that have become valuable by reason of the increased and increasing demands of modern civilization, because when they were worth nothing save the effort of the crow or eagle in flying over them, their remote ancestors became the possessors by the highest recognized right of the time and at the highest price (be that price force) that any one was willing to or could pay, is wholly untenable except on the hypothesis that no land should be owned save by God himself, whatever idea that expression may convey. Why should land not be owned? It is unquestionably, though God-given as the single-tax men put it, subject to improvement by labor and to deterioration by neglect, just the same as all other property, and more so than much other property. They admit that man is entitled to own and enjoy the products of his own labor, yet if a man should devote a lifetime of toil to the reclamation of a tract of land from a marsh near

5

the sea, or remove rocks from another on the slopes of a
hill, or carry water to another in the heart of the desert
—all absolutely worthless without that labor, and the
only value they subsequently possess is admittedly the
product of that labor,—yet because that labor-product
created land (which it did, because to the extent that it
could have been or was available before the application
of labor it was not land at all) and not bricks or buttresses or bridges, it should not be owned, or, which is
practically the same, it should be taxed to its rental
value so as to make it undesirable or useless property, is
a proposition that appears inconsistent, untenable, and
ridiculous. Again, if instead of applying his labor to the
reclamation of lands from the sea, the deserts, or the
hills, he had devoted his life to any ordinary avocation,
and as a result of his labor he had amassed wealth to the
amount, we will assume, of $10,000, and from motives of
safety or individual preference, or for any reason whatever, he had chosen to invest that wealth or labor-
product in land that some other man had reclaimed or
occupied, would not the tract purchased be as much the
fruit of his *toil* as the wealth in whatever pre-existing
form he had it was the fruit of his *toil*? Where the
demand for land is less than the available supply, it is
virtually open for occupancy and use by any one who
desires. One hundred and sixty acres of land are
available to any American citizen, and when population
was sparse many a desirable claim was located ; but as
said population became denser, the available or desirable
tracts were located until those that are left are either
sterile or unproductive to a degree that makes it more
desirable to buy, or, in other words, to exchange the
products of labor for a tract that some other man has
previously located than to take the available tract for

nothing; or, if the man desiring land has nothing to
represent labor-product to give in exchange, he prefers
to remain in some thickly populated city where he can
sell his labor by the day or beg an existence from the
populace, than to go and take up such land as remains
available, as much does to this day. All who own land
(save those who inherited it from their ancestors) in the
general sifting out of the thing will be found to have paid
or given labor-products for it to about the measure of its
value at the time; if not so, then some other man would
have given more and he would have possessed it. Even
the man who inherits succeeds to a title for which value
has been given by his sire or his grandsire, and if these
sires had a right to their own they should have the right
to dispose of their own. All land is practically in some
sort of use in all countries where life abounds. If a man
owns ten thousand acres in the State of Dakota, around
which he chooses to build a wire fence for the very purpose of keeping off cattle that would otherwise consume
his grass, this cannot be said to be actually out of use,
for the very apparent idleness to which he seems to con-
sign it is perhaps the very best use to which he can put
it, for the reason that the falling and decaying grass enriches the soil, thereby creating a greater yield when he
chooses to turn it over with a plow, if to use it thus is in
turn any greater use in fact than the previous apparent
idleness. But, says the single-tax man, he is holding
land for speculative increase which if thrown open to the
people would be used by being worked with a hoe instead of being used to grow grass to make the labor with
the hoe subsequently yield more. Yes, he is holding it,
though really perhaps in the best possible use; we will
say, for argument, that it is for speculative increase.

We will of course conclude that, when, by reason of

cheaper competitive lands being brought nearer to the
market by better facilities for transportation than previously existed, the value of his land is reduced one
half, he should rightfully call upon the state to make
good his losses. I have given, he might say, the
product of my labor to the extent of $10,000 for that
land, and to-day no man will give me the product of
labor to the extent of $5,000, and I want the difference
from the state. Equally reasonable would be this demand with that from the state to take away not only any
possible gain but his land itself by taxation tantamount
to confiscation. How untenable the proposition.

It is said that if blows are aimed at an inflated blad-
der they should not be too severe, or the lack of resistance will dislocate the shoulder. But, say the single-tax
men, the condition practically will be about the same as
at present, because the people will be on the land as
now and be entitled to its products to the extent that
they use it by their labor. Well, if practically the same,
then better leave it as it now is.

But how would the land be occupied? If open to all,
of course the tracts nearest to the markets and most conveniently located as regards facilities for transportation
would be entered upon first. There might be a grand
scramble for Central Park, New York, and for the highly
rich and verdant fields of the interior of the State of
New York, and for the alluvial plains of the Ohio and
Mississippi valleys, but soon they would be engaged, and
the unfortunate who failed to get his allotment there
would finally conclude that rather than take it where he
could get it he would accept a dollar per day cleaning
streets. Then again, who is to determine what consti-
tutes use, or what amount one man may rightfully use?
To this was answered, just whatever he will use. Some

man might claim that he was using one thousand acres
by permitting it to grow up in grass, and object to the
occupancy of any part of it by the man who wanted to
grow potatoes.

It would be necessary to have a general inspector
appointed, or, in other words, a "use or non-use arbi-
trator," whose edicts would have to be supreme, and at
times he would find it necessary to employ military force
to eject a non-user and inject a supposed user. But the
supposed non-user would say : " Hay is more useful this
year than potatoes, because there was a plethora of potatoes grown last year, which have been largely buried,
canned, and made into salads ; and a large part of the
hay crop of last year rotted in the stack, was put up
moist and heated in the barn, so that people need hay
for their horses, and it is better to use land for that
thing which the people want than for that thing of which
they possess a redundance already. Furthermore, I have
hay-seed, and I must have ground to sow it on. I
have mowers to cut, rakes to gather, and forks to stack ;
and with these implements and my labor I can handle
all the crop this ground will produce. Then I have four
boys, all of whom till this year have been going to
school ; now two have finished—that is, they have gone
to school as long as I can afford to send them—longer
than I ever went myself,—and this year, and from now
on, they must work and earn their salt, and we need all
this land, every foot of it, and next year we will use
more. And then there is Sallie, she is going to get married next Christmas, and the probability is that I will
have to take care of her husband, that he will live with
us, and, while I will do what is right by him, yet he has
got to pitch in the same as myself and the boys, so we
will want to use several acres more on that account.

Then just over there lives Bill Smith ; one of his best working chaps died last summer, so that he cannot use what he worked last year ; I should have a slice off of him."

Thus in practice there would unavoidably arise questions and contentions as to *use*, in the proper and rightful signification of the term, and non-use ; disputes as to who should occupy the most desirable and most accessible, and who the least desirable and most remote. Again, to tax land alone and to exempt all other property would work a monstrous injustice to a number of worthy citizens and insure an unwarranted benefit to twice or thrice as many more. To derive all revenue from land by collecting everything from it that is needed for governmental support simply and solely because land is open to the scrutiny of all eyes and cannot be secreted, or, in other words, just because from land the process of collection and assessment would be *simpler*, expecting that the landowner would be recompensed by an increased price for his products, is a proposition altogether different from that which proposes to tax land to, or near to, its rental value, for the very purpose of opening it out for *use by the public*. If simplicity in assessments and collections is the end to be attained, the desideratum sought, the panacea for human ills, then why not make it simple and tax every human head one hundred dollars per year, or one hundred cents, as the needs of government may require.

The head cannot be secreted in the sand, like that of an ostrich, and held there long enough to escape the visuals of the assessor.

Since taxation to full rental value is tantamount to confiscation, and since to dispossess a man of the products of his labor appears ridiculously inconsistent and absurd, we will treat for a time that view of the subject which aims at taxation on land on account of simplicity in assessment and collection and the non-secretiveness of its character, refraining from urging against this view of the case the conclusive and incontrovertible argument that *head tax is simpler and even less subject to secretiveness, because there can be no dispute as to values.*

The value of all property in the United States, as per census of 1880, was forty-four billion dollars, of which farm land represented about ten billion, or one fourth the total valuation. To this we will add one twelfth the whole for the valuation of city lots, exclusive the improvements, and call the value in 1880 of that class of property which alone the single-tax men propose to list, one third the whole, or, say, fourteen billion dollars.

In most sections of the country farms are taxed for State, county, school, and road purposes, on an average of one and one half per cent. City property, houses and personalty as well as lots, is taxed on the average about two per cent., which, to produce the same revenue on the valuation of the land and lots only, would have certainly to be doubled, so that to produce revenue exclusive of that required by the federal government an assessment would be required, doubtless quite equal to three per cent. on the average. The requirements of the federal government properly administered are about three hundred million, to derive which from a valuation of fourteen billion would require a levy of a little over two per cent, making a total of at least five per cent. on the valuation of 1880. Land pays well that yields five per cent., hence such a levy would be tantamount to confiscation, or the producing power of land would have to be materially increased. How could its net producing power be increased, or, in other words, how could the profits of labor on soil be greater, unless operatives were forced to work for a lower price, or unless its produce commanded a higher price? Why oblige the farm laborer to work for less or the consumers of farm products to pay more, just for the sake of simplicity in assessment and collection and to avoid secretiveness, when by applying a direct head tax both simplicity and non-secretiveness are more effectually secured without any such useless discrimination? Values of lands and city lots have not since 1880 averaged very far from about one third the property of the country, and it goes without saying that, if all revenue is taken from one third the valuation, the rate must be trebled. If the rate on land is trebled, the land is in consequence no richer, and will yield no greater crop with the same labor. Hence the result is inevitable that the cost of production must be diminished or the price of products advanced. There could be no wisdom, therefore, in changing existing conditions as to taxation on the grounds of simplicity—certainly not by the adoption of a simple plan which works an injury when there is a simpler one that works none. To tax land as proposed to any less amount than that which is tantamount to confiscation, effects no result save a certain degree of simplicity, which as shown has its penalties, tending in no degree to open land for general occupancy to all who would use. The single-tax men really propose and mean to confiscate landed property, if they mean to accomplish any result whatever, for the simple shifting of taxes off other things to land for the sake of simplicity is meaningless, objectless, and useless, and, working as it does a great discrimination, is objectionable, wrong, ridiculous, and absurd.

Governments are instituted and maintained for the

protection of life and property ; hence all of that thing
which is protected, to wit, property, should bear its
share of the burthen—not land alone or any other
thing alone.

Then, instead of calling themselves single- or land-
tax-only advocates, the proper term to have applied
is " *land confiscationists,*" for that in fact and in effect
is just what they desire, otherwise how could " equal
access to natural opportunity " be obtained ? The single-tax men look upon the appellation of land confiscationists as an opprobrium from which they shrink,
though they are obliged to admit that this and this alone·
in fact and truth they are, just as the Democrats called
themselves " tariff reformers," when " *free-traders,*" as
soon as it can safely be reached (be it said to their
credit), in fact and in truth *they* are. The land confiscationists send their orators abroad into the land to
proclaim the truth to the masses. The farmers are
appealed to in persuading tones to join the band and
free the land.

Aid us in confiscating your farms to the state (though
of course with these words slightly sugar-coated), and
we will exempt you from all other taxation ; you need
not pay one dollar for duties on imports, nor a farthing
for tax on beer ; you will therefore be enabled to buy
your clothing cheaper, have your horses shod cheaper,
drink your grog on a cold winter night cheaper, and so
to the end of the list, but you must sacrifice or confiscate
(sugar-coated) your farms.

"Well," said the sage old rusticuses, " that may be
very good for those who have no farm ; they can be
liberal, but we have been able to raise enough potatoes
to buy these things, and we can see no sense in giving
up our farms in order that we may get other things a little

cheaper. Even if the state would promise to give us
everything for nothing, we would rather keep the farms.
If you have got a scheme by which taxation can be taken
off the land entirely, we are ready to help you out ; but
to agree to aid you in making land sustain the whole
load, we believe we would rather pass." In Australia
the land-tax idea began to take root, but it was soon observed that, to the extent that such a system sought to
accomplish anything but simplicity in assessment and
collection and avoidance of secretiveness, it was illusory
and absurd—*a pseudo-bleptic phantomnation.*

There is no greater reason why land which is property should be owned by the state and open to occupancy
to all, when there is any person or being who is willing
to pay the product of labor for it, than there is for sub-
jecting all other property to the same identical conditions, which is communism, plain and simple, without the
conservative balance.

When governments hold unoccupied lands, as is the
case in Australia, where the sentiment took root, and in
America, some years ago, it is of course policy to invite in occupants ; but when these conditions as to land
exist, the pre-emption, settlement, and pioneer occupation are about the full measure of its value. When
population increases, and roads and churches and
school-houses and fences are built, then land has an
increased value, and should become possessed or owned
only at that increased value, and this was not the case
originally when pioneership paid for it amply and well.
The land confiscationists, when forced at times to
lick the sugar off their pills, admit that practically they
are what they are ; yet they claim that there is no injustice in it. Many kinds and classes of property they say
are ruthlessly destroyed in the prevailing rage for inno-

vation, and by the invention or substitution of something that suits the purposes of civilization better, and if it suited civilization better to confiscate the land, why not with equal reason and equal justice adopt that policy, as well as to have adopted the railway carriage in place of the old stage-coach ; that the introduction of the car practically confiscated the coach, and no one questioned the policy of the proceeding; that whatever a majority of the people wish must be law, if it be to live on nothing but moonshine, and if enough of them could continue to live to enforce such a law, it would be enforced.

It is of course undeniable that the majority should and must rule, but it will be a long time and a cold day before a majority is to be found who will pass a law to the effect that every individual should commit *hari-kari* or hang for a week by his toes. If a majority should say, " We will confiscate land," then so be it ; but he who waits to see it will live beyond a century. The argument that property is daily confiscated by the substitution of something better than the old, reacts upon itself, and is completely answered when we say, " Make available to man or cause to exist a substitute for land that is better than land, and the natural course of events and not confiscation schemes—the failure of the unfittest to survive—will work its abandonment." No legislator ever proclaimed that the stage-coach should become common property ; if so, he would have been unwise and revolutionary ; but it served its time in the march of life, and succumbed to a fitter machine when natural causes made it so, and likewise, and to the same extent and with equal justice, will land succumb when in the march of the world's affairs something fitter can survive.

To say that you shall not own land is one thing, and to produce a substitute that people would *rather* own is quite another; a blind man might almost see the utter folly, irrelevancy and absurdity of their position, so plain is it.

Aside from the access to land for the purposes of agriculture, there is the mineral and metallic feature to be considered. The living of all, in some shape, comes out of the ground. A man pays the product of his labor for a hundred acre tract, presumably for purposes of agriculture, and discovers thereon or thereunder a rich vein of coal. To whom does that coal belong? It is the gift of God not to one man in particular but to all men in general. It belongs rightfully and justly to him who owns the land, and by the same identical chain of titles from the beginning, and no man or set of men has a right, either inherent, expressed, or implied, to dispossess him of that coal without his consent any more than (if by a cataclysm of nature he should become dispossessed) he would have the right to force any man or set of men to *repossess* him against their consent. Man is entitled to the benefit of good-fortune to a reasonable extent, and should not be asked or expected to share same with the public (except after it has become abnormal, useless, and unweildy) any more than the public should be expected to share his misfortunes, his sickness, or disease until they become abnormal and too great for him to bear; then all now admit that the public should share his burthen—that is, provide him a bed in a hospital and a competent nurse, and bury him if he dies. Since it was long ago admitted and in practice that the public should share with the individual his extraordinary afflictions, to the extent that would not be hurtful to the public by placing a premium on idleness,

so likewise should it be admitted that the individual
should in turn share with the public his extraordinary
benefits, to an extent that will not be hurtful to himself
by depriving him of reasonable reward for his energy and
his strife. Whilst it is neither fair nor equitable nor just
to institute that condition in society which will interfere
with, hamper, or oppress any individual in the possession
and enjoyment of the fruits of his labor or the rewards
of his good-fortune, yet, as civilization progresses, the
current opinion of the world rather settles down to the
belief that monstrosities in individual accumulation are
like monstrosities in nature—that is, undesirable and of
no account ; that when a man, either by dint of hard
labor or good-fortune, has amassed an estate equal in its
productive capacity to the labor of several thousand of
his fellow-men, or, in other words, when he owns the
labor of several thousand of his fellow-men by securing
possession of a certain amount of the wealth that their
labor had produced, and which wealth he has acquired
by his tact, his shrewdness, his energy, his skill, or his
good luck—all recognizable and properly creditable to
his account in a well-conditioned state of society,—
nevertheless, when this accumulation had become monstrous, which by reason of its own accretion, aided
by an increment which the need of society contributes,
as it frequently does, that it is not, in fact, an injustice
to the individual, it works him no harm nor causes him
any discomfort to say to him that *you shall hereafter
contribute* to the support of government a larger proportionate share of your inordinate wealth than shall
be required of your brother who possesses it only
to a reasonable competency, but that this increased
proportionate contribution shall work you no injury nor
cause you any discomfort in truth and in fact.   A titled

aristocrat in England was said at one time to own and control about half the coal out-put of that country. His wealth was of course colossal but it represented the accumulation of much time and many favorable conditions, for the reason that the progress of civilization and the increase of population is slower in England than in America, where there now lives richer men whose estate represents the accretion of but one generation, because the progress of civilization in America and the increase of population—consequently the increase of demand and the gain from the strides of unearned increment—are faster. Unearned increment or the accretion of wealth in America is actually more rapid in many cases than disintegration by inherited division. For example : individuals of the third generation lived, in 1890, whose estates, though originally but a part of the grandsire's possessions, are now greater than the original in its entirety. This could not have been the case in England but for the prevalence of the idea of estate tail and primogeniture, an institution completely dissipated in the minds of those who have progressed sufficiently to recognize even remotely that there are no natural rights whatsoever inherent in one man and not as well in another. It usually happens that to make any great storehouse of nature available to the people industry and enterprise must both be expended and accumulated capital must be forthcoming or nothing can be accomplished.

If all men had access to land and its belongings these great resources of latent and undeveloped wealth would in the main be operated in a crude and primeval manner, without system and method, without concentrated brain force and energy—all essential to the best results in enterprise and business. If such property could not be owned and ten thousand men should elect on their individual

motion to enter in upon and mine coal as a profitable
occupation, they could not, other than by a combination
of interests directed to the construction of tramways,
hoists, and other necessary apparatus, possibly do other
or more than to operate in the most crude and ineffectual manner—such as digging in the pit and then on their
backs conveying the product to the entrance of the mine
or to the dump, resulting unavoidably in a smaller aggregate of production. When this had been accomplished,
such is the natural situation of mines relatively to the
world's consuming centres, that transportation would
have to be provided for. Since, though land be free,
man could, under single tax, own countless thousands
of railway carriages, and, even under the said system,
combine them into trusts so as to prevent opposition,
and, worse than all, *avoid taxation,*—colossal transportation companies would notwithstanding "uninterrupted
access" be organized to carry the coal to the nearest
point of consumption, and since only by their intermediation could the product be used at all, they
would exact for this service such a compensation as
would leave to the operator and his "uninterrupted
access to natural opportunity" an amount simply sufficient to maintain his bodily existence, and in no case
more in effect if indeed as much as if the transportation
companies had owned the mines as well as the railways
and improved their appointments (as can only be
done by concentrated capital) and paid the operators
their per diem. Greater would be the chance of increased compensation by rigid and inflexible labor organization than by "uninterrupted access to natural
opportunity," and, be that organization inflexible and
rigid, howsoever, in the end and on the average supply
and demand will settle the whole question, so that the

intermediation of labor combination, restrictive legislation, or any device whatsoever not bottomed on the eternal substratum—the natural ebb and flow of things—will
ultimately become absolutely ineffectual and abortive—
if not "then is an adder better than an eel because his
skin is painted." What signifies the price of a man's
labor ?—simply what it will buy, or, in other words, the
amount of the things produced by the labor of other men
for which it can be exchanged.   If, therefore, all men
should demand and all men should secure an advance in
their wages, would not the price of all commodities inevitably advance in proportion, so that the condition relatively would be exactly the same ? If two bushels of wheat
had heretofore been worth one pair of boots, what matters
it if things are so altered as that four bushels of wheat
are worth two pair of boots ?   If, however, the coal miner,
only, by combination secures an advance in his wages,
his labor is of course producing relatively more than
that of the bootmaker,—rather his product secures more
of the product of his fellows than heretofore,—so he is
happy ; but, whenever his condition has been bettered in
any noticeable particular, here come along ten thousand
men and begin to apply for jobs as miners, and ere long
they acquire proficiency ; hence increased competition
follows and the price goes down though maintained, it
may be, for a time by labor organization, but in the end
and on the average the level will be reached.   It may be
asked, then how do some men gain wealth in excess of
others at all ? To which we answer, in ten thousand
ways, but all depending upon the utilization of and consequent profit derived from the labor of his fellow-men,
or by the natural accretion of property of which he has
become possessed, by the natural demands of society—
all of which is right, just, and proper ; but for the good

of many and to the harm of none it should be determined not to permit it to go too far. Cause men to contribute to government in proportion to their ability, and ere long their accumulations (which beyond certain limits are not often the result of their own energy or ability anyhow, but of fortune or of the natural accretions of property inherently) will cease.

This it will be found, after schemes and plans without number have been proposed and concocted, after man's brain has been racked till confusion and chaos has characterized his being, is about all that can be done to better man's condition, and consistently with man's right to property and to a reasonable reward for his energy is, in fact, all that should be done ; in other words, *put a governor on the engine and then turn on the steam.*

Better this than to continuously try to regulate the speed by tampering with the throttle direct. Let the speed check itself, let the slothfulness accelerate it. Before the governor will work, the engine must have motion ; so before civilization can progress it must have motion, and as the force that creates motion in the engine is steam, so the force that creates it in civilization is individual energy and action, and not theories for the eradication of poverty, nor for the extirpation of disease (both equally impossible), nor for " uninterrupted access to natural opportunity," nor the lack of it, nor by schemes for discriminating paternalism in government, nor by anything of kindred import. Another and equally untenable proposition of the single tax, or land confiscationists, is that to impose a tax on the products of labor is to discourage and thwart the exercise of that labor ; that to tax a house—the product of a man's, or of many men's, toil—would discourage the building of houses, and not only so, but to tax the products of labor is inherently

6

and of itself unjust, and to tax anything save the " God-
given inheritance " on which we live, breathe, and have
our being is hostile to progress and inimical to the best
interests, aims, objects, hopes, and aspirations of men.
With reason equally cogent and uncontrovertible, we can
say that the air and water are the " God-given inheritance," and if the principle of taxation, which is simply
a human institution for providing means to protect
human property against human viciousness and unrestraint, is applicable only to the crude material substance
of nature, these too are not justifiably exempt, and
should by some human device be made returnable to the
assessor.   If it is right to tax only the " God-given inheritance," it is right to tax any one as well as any other
of these God-inherited things, and wrong to exempt one
and overburthen the other.   It could be reasonably
closely estimated how many respirations man makes in a
day—that is, how much air he vitiates—and, likewise, how
much water he drinks and how much he uses for his
bath, and on each thousand respirations of a man of or- .
dinary pectoral development a certain levy might be imposed, and, aside from the price of convenient and
expeditious delivery, a certain levy could be made on
each thousand gallons of aqua pure consumed ; these,
together with the other God-given inheritance—land,—
forming a grand triumvirate of natural objects that are
not man-produced or man-altered, hence the proper
subjects of taxation—the three forming a *tout ensemble*
too utterly just and equitable, too absolutely perfect
and indiscriminating, too entirely alleviatory of the
burthens that oppress mankind, to be considered possible of human contrivance or invention.   The scheme
itself must therefore be " God-given," as are the articles properly subject to taxation.   Why, in the name

of all that is just and reasonable, yes, "in the name of all the gods at once," should not property—all property —be the proper subject of taxation, since it is in the interest of property, in fact, solely for the protection of individual rights in and to property and life that taxation is to be or should be imposed on anything? The imposition of a tax under proper regulations does not interfere with the exercise of individual energy any more than a hat on the head interferes with individual thought. A man who had intended to construct a house, either for occupancy or investment, is seldom deterred therefrom because of taxation. He builds with a knowledge of the fact that certain taxes must and will be imposed, and figures that rents and income from the use of his house will be correspondingly high. It is a well-known fact that in communities where taxes are high rents are usually commensurable, and profits and returns correspondingly so ; and in .places where reverse conditions exist reverse results obtain : in a word, the ability to pay a tax is proportionate to the productive value of the property, and it matters not if temporarily a disproportion should exist, in the end it will be found that on the average the proper ratio remains. It is but a fair conclusion, deducible from commercial experience generally, that if taxes on houses were taken off, the rents, in the regular adjustment of things, would proportionately decline, just as the tax on spirituous or malt liquors adds that much to their price, and in the end is paid in full by the men who shall buy, so likewise is the tax on a house paid in the end by the man who shall use, bringing about a balance, compensating the owner, and not deterring him from constructing. Why do sane men urge such nonsense as a remedy for social wrong? *Why shoot quids at giants or storm citadels with sand?*

If houses are constructed or steamships built in excess
of demand for legitimate use, rents and traffic rates will
decline, taxation or no taxation ; and if demand exists
in excess of supply, rents and traffic rates will advance,
taxation or no taxation. Hence, to the winds with the
theory that taxation retards and thwarts individual enterprise, and that taxation on earth, air, and water alone
would expedite same—it is a barren ideality. Again, it
is a fair supposition that taxation in the aggregate and
on the average amounts to about twenty-five per cent.
of rent, or say a house yielding eight per cent. on cost
will pay about two per cent. in tax. It cannot be proven
that with no tax twenty-five per cent. more houses would
be built should the demand remain the same. It may
be urged that demand would increase, which proposition
is equally uncertain, because demand usually follows increase of population, not decrease of taxation, and will
more likely be doubled if population is doubled than if
taxation is halved. There is no more justice anyhow in
taxing property that is the result of the "God-given
inheritance" (which is valuable only as man's labor
makes it so) than to tax anything else he may own.
A man cannot eat the land nor sleep on it comfortably
in most localities without blankets or some other article
which is the product of his labor, and since by the same
rightful title that a tree holds certain soil by its roots he
becomes the owner of it, and then of products made out
of it by his labor, and to protect which products (all of
them) he institutes government, and to support that
government he imposes taxation, it is right that all of
that property should contribute. Of course by common
consent all men who constitute society could in the beginning mutually agree that some one commodity should
bear all taxation for purposes of simplicity, or that

some article of luxury should be chosen because it
would bear more lightly on the less fortunate of the
state, and this commodity would thereafter be held and
possessed with reference thereto, and the thing would be
just and equitable ; but after man's energies have been
expended, and the products of the labor of some have
been invested in houses and some in merchandise and
some in land, he who maintains that that land should be
confiscated opposes the first principle of common justice
itself. It is highly desirable and strictly proper to select
some article of luxury from which to derive most of the
tax, for from that source it is least burthensome on
society, and *what can possibly be more luxuriant than the
extraordinary accumulations, and the useless and burthensome
accretions, of individual wealth*—all wholly luxurious except to the extent that luxury is marred by anxiety and
care ? From this source all taxation should be taken
that is consistent with a proper regard by society for the
reasonable expectations and rewards of the individual,
and *not from land only*, not from water only, nor from any
other thing only, *except these extraordinary accumulations
only*.

To the land confiscationists, to the government absorp-
tionist, to the agrarians,—in fact, to all who are opposed
to acquiescing in the conditions of affairs as they are
just because they are so, and who do not admit that they
could be better just because they are not bettered,—
which class of the world's people (excluding the anarchists, who are nothing) are not only worthy of highest
respect and consideration, but are essentially its brain,
its bone, and its sinew, is proposed this affirmation and
disproof anxiously awaited, to wit :

*Any enactment or law that burthens all mankind the
same, the benefits of which are available to all mankind the*

same, will not materially alter the relative condition of all mankind.

A restraining enactment is like a load upon the shoulders of society. Some will sustain it easier, and make progress under it better than others, simply and solely because they are inherently stronger, because they are favored with more encouraging or, as the case may be, less discouraging circumstances or conditions. So, on the other hand, is abolition of a restraining law or the enactments of a supposed beneficial law like unto an assistant or an impetus to society ; consequently being applicable to all mankind both as to benefit or burthen as the case may be, and mankind still retaining their individual attributes, characteristics, and instincts as before, or being the same as before—the subjects of favorable or unfavorable conditions and opportunities, which will always be an incident to the world's affairs, just as daylight and darkness are incident to and consequent upon its rotation on its axis, it follows inevitably that their *relative* conditions cannot be materially altered. Give to all mankind equal and uninterrupted access to natural opportunity and—if there is anything valuable in it—some will make better use of it than others, until in the end the same relative condition will exist as before. If we would take a horizontal view of mankind in general, as he peregrinates the surface of this mundane sphere, prosecuting his little, but to him, great, business, he would perhaps resemble the great Egyptian pyramid in the valley of the Nile and its surroundings, the masses likened unto the sands that lie in myriads at its base, the higher classes in horizontal planes above and above to the acme of human preferment and earthly renown at the top. It is asked what could be the relative difference in their conditions if the whole thing was lifted up one thousand feet, or the whole settled down one hundred feet?

Laws under which all have the same opportunity and all sustain the same burthen certainly leave the previous *relative* condition unchanged. The only remedy therefore is to enact laws that *do not* offer to all the same opportunity and which place on some greater burthens than on others ; and to so adjust these laws as to leave to him by whom the greatest load is borne, ample opportunity for life, liberty, and action, and not to make the load so light on any as that they should have life, liberty, and action thrust upon them and be maintained without effort, is difficult, but by Phronocracy it is explained.

It can be accomplished by making all men contribute to government in proportion to their ability to contribute and by not permitting men who contribute nothing to participate in government at all. It will be, of course, urged against the proposition that it is *per se* and *ipso facto* socialistic, to which it is answered : yea, verily, but it is a very mild and harmless type of that disorder ; rather it is conservative socialism, which recognizes man's right to a reasonable, yes, liberal, reward for his energy and his action, and proposes, in addition, to recompense him for the sacrifice of his extraordinary accumulation, by guaranteeing increased security and protection for the reasonable and abundant remnant that he may yet retain, by denying to men who have no property all right of participation in the government that is instituted for the protection of property.

It is admitted also that in addition to this conservative socialism a certain additional socialistic spirit should prevail, but this may be to a certain extent curtailed.

For example, it is a self-evident proposition that all

streets in cities must be maintained at public expense
for the free and untaxed use of all ; that this is in the
nature of a thing necessary ; also that cities should, but
to the least possible extent, maintain almshouses for the
poor, since poverty cannot be absolutely abolished ; also
support hospitals for the sick, since disease is the twin
brother of poverty, though perhaps born first. Cities
should likewise support a cordon of police, and a trained
brigade for the extinguishment of fires, and appliances
for lighting their streets, for cleaning same, and for the
removal of garbage and filth—all admitted to be in keeping with the natural order of things ; also public docks
and wharves might at times be necessary, and if so should
be provided. So likewise should counties support public
roads, and, at times, public asylums. All these things,
however, are matters of exclusive local control, and are
not uniform or the same throughout the land.   ·

This may be objected to on the grounds of socialism,
as are also public parks and edifices ; but these objections appear technical and captious, and of course avail
but little. No man can deny the socialistic feature.
Yet certain things appear proper just because they are
necessary, certain things it appears to be the communities' right to do just because they are required ; and, all
consenting, or a very small minority objecting, they are
done. In fact, such socialism as is practised appears to
be a benefit to property ; a broad, smooth street and a
level country road increases the value of property, even
though everybody can use it on the socialistic principle.
The government absorptionists then conclude that if it
is good for a county to maintain a road, why should not
government maintain all roads ; to which it is replied
that if it is good to eat three meals per day, why
not three hundred ? Three hundred are not thought

wholesome for the body, and three are a benefit ; so likewise free streets and country roads are in practice and in conformity with the natural order of things good and wholesome, and the absorption of any more of the people's business by government is not good or wholesome. It is much more hurtful to place too much with government than to leave too little with it, and since the people are the creators of the government and the government when created is administered by people like themselves, why give to simple agents what can be as well, yea, to a better extent, performed by the principals ? The enlightened world has ceased to believe that governments of right should possess many if any prerogatives or powers other than such as are required to preserve domestic order, to maintain the public defence, regulate commerce between sections, and provide uniform standards of currency, weights, measures, and the like.

CHAPTER V.

> " This is the state of man : to-day he puts forth
> The tender leaves of hope, to-morrow blossoms,
> And bears his blushing honors thick upon him ;
> The third day, comes a frost, a killing frost ;
> And—when he thinks, good easy man, full surely
> His greatness is a ripening—nips his root,
> And then he falls, as I do."

TRULY it may be said, and in candor we may confess, that in treating so great a subject all men

> " Have ventured,
> Like little wanton boys that swim on bladders
> This many summers in a sea of glory,
> But far beyond their depth."

And that though striving to seek truth, banish falsehood, and to reconcile the apparent inconsistencies of society and to better regulate its operations, they have received no other or greater reward than to be left,

> " Weary and old with service, to the mercy
> Of a rude stream that must forever hide them."

However, it will never do for progressive man to content himself with the reflection that whatever is is best, for if so, what now is never would have been. Neither should we refrain from the careful consideration of a proposition because it at first appears unreasonable.

> " Our doubts are traitors, which make us lose
> The good we oft might win, by failing to attempt."

There is great room and great necessity for the betterment of social conditions throughout the world, and where there are both room and necessity, efforts will be continuous, and, as society advances, better and greater will be the result.

Anarchy will not do, and is offensive to order ; out-and-out agrarianism, communism, or socialism will not answer, for they are inimical to the natural right of man to the fruits of his own labor ; government absorption will not do, because of being in effect the same thing ; land confiscation will not do, because it is impracticable and non-efficacious. All other systems and plans that aim in any way at property rights should be abandoned, and those who look to legislation will soon discover that through it lies the only possible remedy ; yet legislation that is of such character and intent as to affect all men alike will leave the relative condition the same, and hence be ineffectual and abortive.

Legislation, therefore, that will apply to men differently is about the last resort. It is agreed that colossal accumulations do no man any good, and that in the interest of the popular weal great properties should be as popularly owned as possible consistent with a due regard for prudential considerations and efficient operation, just as it is thought well in the legislative assemblages of the world to get at popular representation as nearly as

possible consistent with the stability in government. As
it is discovered that each $1,000 of wealth in America
will earn about as much as one stout, healthy, and even
frugal laboring man can possibly save, it follows that, in
effect. for every $1,000 a man possesses, he owns one
man. It is evident that no man's wants can possibly be
more than one thousand times as great as those of the average man, and that if by reason of his self-importance
he should perchance conceive them so, the community
should think it but a wholesome reprimand to remind him
of his mistake. He cannot with one wife well sire more
than one and twenty children, and in practice scarcely
equal ten ; he cannot eat much more nor drink much
more, nor possibly live in a style or condition more than
a thousand times as comfortable or elegant as the average, because human ingenuity cannot contrive it ; he
cannot in fact properly use for either his wants, his pleas-
ures, or his luxury a thousand times as much of anything
as the average of his fellows ; why, therefore, should any
individual possess more wealth than a thousand times as
much as the average of his fellows ? It is beyond dispute that this maximum will provide for all possible
wants, either necessary or luxurious, and leave in the
balance a good compensation for greed besides. It is
therefore proposed that in proportion as a man's estate
is large, so in a like proportion should his *tax rate* be
large. It is assumed, and very justly, that all estates
will produce a revenue, and statistics and experience
make clear the fact that about 5 per cent. income maintains property at par in stable communities on the basis
of one hundred, and that such as comes under this is, in
the natural course of things, considered and counted less
valuable, and on this safe and reasonable assumption all
dealings with incomes can be abandoned, and, from mo-

tives of justice, simplicity, and accuracy, the rate can be imposed on the property direct. It the owner fails to collect his income it is no fault of the state, and the general average of assessments arrived at from current evidence of values will work no great injury. Then, as this rate is to be made cumulative in the ratio that the property is cumulative, it should so advance as that when a reasonable maximum has been acquired the rate will equal the current revenue, beyond which amount it can never go ; that is, beyond the amount on which outgo for government will equal the income from revenue, the estate cannot increase. Since it is thought fair and right and just that when any man owns one thousand times as much as the average man he should own no more (for more would be of no value), that amount was at first to be recommended as a maximum. Since the average wealth in America is about $1,000 per capita, that allotment would be 1,000,000. The rate, therefore, is to be made cumulative, so that when a 1,000,000 assessment to any individual is made, it would equal 5 per cent. interest, which rate would be five cents on every $1,000 cumulative.

The system is proposed to be applied by the *general government only*, as a means of deriving its own income, and to the extent that it is adequate, the only means the general government shall apply, leaving to the States and the cities their unquestioned rights to adopt their own means and methods for raising local revenue.

Since local excises in many places aggregate 2 per cent., and on the average is little less, it is found that when the government's cumulative rate would be applied, outgo would equal income on a basis of 5 per cent. before the estate reached an aggregate much exceeding half a million dollars. To provide, therefore, for extravagance and local excises, and in a spirit of utmost liberality, it is finally proposed that the annual rate on every individual estate shall be equal to the cumulative amount of 1 cent instead of 5 cents for every $1,000 in that estate ; or in other words, that every man's rate per thousand shall, for the purpose of the support of the general government, be one hundred-thousandth part of his estate, which would make outgo equal to income on a basis of 5 per cent. interest when the estate reached $5,000,000 instead of $1,000,000, or the labor of 5,000 men instead of 1,000 men, or to the richest 5,000 times the property of the average instead of 1,000 times, as had originally been thought proper. However, since for local purpose a rate equal to about 2 per cent. will have to be provided, in effect outgo would equal income on a basis of 1 cent for each $1,000 cumulative, and 5 per cent. interest when the estate aggregated about $2,500,000, which would be equivalent to the labor of 2,500 men, or to the highest above the average an estate 2,500 times as great instead of 1,000 times as great, as was at first proposed. This, in the estimation of any reasonable person, is more than is required for any man's comfort, or for his luxury. Furthermore, owing to the perfection of the system of assessment and the better administration of public affairs, as will hereafter be explained, all or nearly all secreted property can be discovered, so that the local rate can be materially reduced, averaging instead of 2 only about 1 per cent., which, on the basis of 1 cent for each $1,000 cumulative and 5 per cent. interest, the estate may reach about $4,000,000 before outgo would equal income, which gives to the favored individual the labor of 4,000 men and an estate 4,000 times as great as the average before he shall be called upon to halt. This by many is regarded as excessive, and an effort may be made to place the cumulative rate at 2 cents for every $1,000, or one fifty-thousandth part of the value of the estate ; in fact, widespread and forcible might be the public opinion in favor of the million-dollar limit, notwithstanding local assessment, which, reduced as it would be by good government and proper assessments to 1 per cent., would leave, notwithstanding the cumulative rate, a fortune to the favored individual of about $800,000—an amount by many deemed amply sufficient, representing as it would the labor of 800 men, or an amount 800 times as large as the average wealth per capita, and equal to the largest estate in America a hundred years ago. If from less than $1,000,000 to over $200,000,000 in one hundred years, what may it be in the next hundred years ? It is discovered, in figuring up the value of individual estates, that myriads are small and but few are large, hence the cumulative rate would average but little and would scarcely yield enough to produce the revenue required by the general government, which, properly administered, should be between $250,000,000 and $300,000,000 per annum, so that in addition to the cumulative or graduated tax a percentage of increase would doubtless be required to meet the requirements of the government, and a corresponding percentage of decrease could be made in case the revenue should become too great ; but in any event and under all conditions, the cumulative rate would be first applied and then either added to or taken from by percentages of horizontal increase or reduction as the case may be. The rate per thousand being just one hundred-thousandth part of the aggregate of the estate makes it very easy of calculation, and whilst it will be opposed by the rich as socialistic and unjust, it should be supported by

the middle classes on the ground of absolute justice.
One man can afford to pay a rate per thousand equal to
the one hundred-thousandth part of his estate just as
well as another man can ; in fact, the rich can better
afford it than the poor, and it is, in truth, no discrimination, and really not unjustly socialistic at all. The one
hundred-thousandth part of a big estate is of course
greater than the same part of a small estate, but the
large estate can better afford it, and hence conditions
are simply just and equitable. After much discussion
and endless research into details and statistics for information relative to the magnitude of individual estates
from which to ascertain the average, so as to form a
definite idea what the cumulative rate would be, it is
determined to recommend the one-cent-per-thousand
basis, and to empower the government to increase or
diminish by horizontal percentages as demand might
require, which will answer all purposes, especially in
view of the fact that, owing to the crude and incomplete
system of assessment and the opportunity under it for
large secretiveness of wealth (which can be almost entirely remedied, as will be explained later on), no definite
information can be obtained, and what is secured leads
to the belief that under a proper system it would be so
much changed as to afford no reliable basis of calculation. The advocates of all other systems of social
reform, such as the out-and-out agrarians, the government absorptionists, the land confiscators, and so forth,
have simply paraded their views before the public from
the hustings, through the prints, and by divers means
and methods, and have incited the people to anger
and rage by playing upon their prejudices and their
passions, but have dealt only in generalizations. In
other words, they say that the whole thing as it is is

radically wrong, and that their particular scheme would right it, and thus generalize and elocutionize and philosophize, but fail to specialize—fail to say just how the thing could be accomplished; in fact, this they cannot say, because their propositions are impracticable and consequently cannot be put into feasible and succinct shape. To put an impracticable thing into practical working shape is impossible—for example, it was asked of the socialists, shall we introduce a measure into the Federal Congress declaring that all property shall be confiscated and held in community; shall we elect congressmen, senators, and State legislators, favorable to this policy, and if we succeed in so doing can we even then enforce our decrees and our mandates?

Will present holders of property not use forcible measures to prevent, and combine for their own protection to preserve their rightful possessions, the homes of their wives and their children, the property for which they have expended their toil and their labor? In a word, is it at all reasonable to conclude that the present holders of estates will all disgorge voluntarily that which for generations has been owned, loved, and enjoyed? Rather is it not more reasonable to expect that force would be resorted to to prevent, and that force would have to be resorted to to carry out any such violent and unjust decree? In consequence of which facts, why tamper with legislation at all, but by one organized effort, as the anarchists would recommend,—and which in fact would in practice be necessary even though intermediary legislation was passed,—strike amid the thunder of a million guns, and with glistening bayonets and swords, together with a brand of fire, a rod and axe make wild sport of blazing homes, and in the wake of ghastly carnage and of blood cause massacre to seal right's eternal grave,

7

and "thick night to pall us in the dunnest smoke of
Hell ?"

In fact, there is nothing more feasible than reasonable
connected with the whole proposition. All property in
community practically means anarchy in its operating
effects, whilst milder to the ear and softer to the tongue,
yet they are twin demons littered the same night—anarchy the elder but not more powerful.

There appears to be no feasible plan of getting at
the thing anyway, probably because all minds able to
plan and devise are opposed to any such nonsense. It
takes brains to plan out anything, and in such assemblages brains will never commingle. It is clear that to
carry any such propositions force, and force alone, would
avail, and it would have to be most powerful and continuous ever to prevail. To talk about accomplishing
a thing of this nature by enactments of law seems ridiculous, and just what enactments would be proper to
meet the situation no advocate can say, so that there
is always a chaos of complaints, at times wild and
incendiary utterances from the stump, but no tangible
plan proposed. The people have been made to believe that monopolies are absorbing the earth and its
belongings unlawfully ; that large estates are the result
of the grossest subversion of existing law, the effect
of purchase and sale of judges on the bench, of
combinations and intrigue against the popular
weal, and all such platitudinous badinage and bom-
bast.

The facts are that there doubtless exists, not one dollar of property in the hands of any of the several
one-hundred millionaires that is not held within the
recognized pale of the law, otherwise ten thousand sharks
and legal vampires would be ready to pounce upon the
victim as a hungry wolf upon its inoffensive prey ; in

fact, all kinds of imaginary claims are trumped up against the rich for purposes simply of blackmail and slander in the hope of propitiation for suppression, which in many cases has been obtained.

All claims as to unlawful possessions are either the result of ignorance, falsification. or of a diseased imagination. Anything not held by sanction of the highest court is usually brought to the test of that tribunal before the owner can secure respite from ceaseless exaction and legal annoyance.

The fault is not in the courts nor in the administration of existing law. What is needed is new law to meet the case, presented and passed in some feasible shape. Property, or the results of the people's labor on earth, is of course becoming unreasonably centralized, in fact, as was once frankly admitted by one of the hundred millionaires, entirely uselessly so. This gentleman possesses brains and is philosophical in his reflections, his penetration is deep, his ratiocination able. He admitted that one million dollars was enough for any ·man to own ; that his accumulations above that amount were the natural and unavoidable results of the equally unavoidable developments of his properties—developments made necessary by the ever and rapid increase of the population of the locality and for the use and benefit of the people of the country.

He had by the exercise of wise perspicacity and the dint of circumstance and opportunity whilst engaged in the strife of life become connected with railway enterprises (he might, had circumstances operated differently, been in almost any other avocation), and had become rich by development and good management. He could not force the public to sell their stock cheap or to buy his stock high. All profit that he ever made in this manner was the result of a square bargain and sale be-

tween men. If he could by presenting to a man from
whom he desired to buy, a certain kind of argument
in consequence of which the latter became convinced
and concluded to sell, he had not wronged that man, any
more than the grocer who sells flour or the tailor who
sells cloth had wronged the man with whom they dealt :.
he could force none to sell, he could force none to
buy, and if as the results of any such deal he profited,
was he not entitled to the profit ?

Once possessed of railway property, the development
of the country made necessary great extensions, increasing demand caused increased earnings, and hence, as an
incident to this development, which he did not and
could not create, or in any sense alter or control, he became very rich.   Had the country retrogressed instead
of progressed, had population diminished instead of increased, for which condition he would have been as little
responsible and as powerless to change as he was the
former condition, he would not have become so rich—
possibly have died poor.   To the extent that favorable
conditions made him, so might the opposite have ruined
him.   It is found that great fortunes are accumulated
in those pursuits or enterprises that are, by reason of
favorable location or conditions, or in consequence of
the force of human preference and desire, in and of
themselves prosperous.   For example, America being a
large country, the whole land for three thousand miles
abounding in profusion with the means of subsistence
and the necessaries of life, the government throwing
aside all embargoes to traffic between the States, the
people being enterprising and the land being rich,
drained by vast rivers and favored with genial climes,
the inevitable consequence is that not only the native
population but millions from abroad seek those rich

fields and pastures green, and from ocean to ocean, with
no State restrictions, there is a natural desire and demand
for communication and transportation. Hence railway
property has increased beyond all conception, until even
in 1890 America, scarce aged beyond infancy in the
world's family of nations, contained more miles of railway than all the world combined, and why—simply and
solely because natural conditions have favored—in fact,
demanded it.   The shipping interests in England have
become greater than those of all the world combined, because her colonies are vast and separated by countless
miles of trackless sea ; trade and communication are not
only desired but demanded, and as ships alone can supply the condition, ships are constructed, and that, too,
by the very nation that requires them most, as railways
are constructed by the very people that require them
most. So that with America excelling all the world with
rail, and Great Britain the proud mistress of the deep
and dark-blue sea, the two nations, akin by blood and
similar in intuitions and desires, speaking the same
tongue, having the same aspirations, characteristics,
hopes, and aims, practically control the business—in a
word, the property—of the world, each developing in the
identical line best suited to its natural conditions ; and,
as in America from the rail, so in the British Empire
from the sail, are the greatest fortunes accumulated.
Those interests therefore have been the developing ones,
by reason of the natural order of things, in these countries, and the individuals who have prosecuted this business have participated in and received the benefits of the
development—in other words, have become rich, not entirely by reason of their own superior energy or sagacity,
which if displayed in other avocations void of such
opportunity might have achieved no marked success,

but by reason of the enterprise they have followed essentially and the general progress which by reason of natural courses has attended them.

It may be asked why all men, therefore, have not engaged in these favored industries ; to which it may be answered, why do not all men become members of Parliament or of Congress ? There is much in circumstance, in opportunity, in the unseen, unknown, and unknowable influences and energies of the Great Whole. It is undoubtedly true that natural conditions and circumstances do, in a large degree, control and determine the progress of the world's affairs, and regulate the status of men in the world.

Human preferences, likes, dislikes, and other motives and agencies, work no inconsiderable part, but it is equally certain that if a man's energies, it matters not how powerfully exerted, are expended in the prosecution of an enterprise that is not blessed with the prompting impetus of favorable conditions and of human preference, they will be abortive and unprofitable. This has been forcibly illustrated in the case of steamboat navigation on the great rivers of America, which, though admirably adapted to transportation, have succumbed to the more suitable method—rail ; and the men who were most persistent and most energetic in these river enterprises are the ones who have fared worst, because they have declined just as the rail has advanced, and both have been wholly beyond the control of their votaries, who, as individuals, are no more responsible for the ruin of the boats than for the success of the rails, but simply followed along with each like puppy-dogs' tails. Thus, as the philosophical hundred-million-dollar magnate admitted, his fortune is largely—almost entirely—the result of the necessary development of his property, consequent, not wholly upon his energy or sagacity, but upon the people's wants and accidental circumstances.

It was said to this magnate that if his property beyond a million was burthensome, he might possibly find people willing to relieve him of the excess. "Well," said he, "if conditions had been such that I never could have amassed the excess I would doubtless have been just as comfortable, just as well contented, and no doubt much happier and freer from annoyance and care, especially if I had been provided with increased security in its retention and control; but since conditions are such that John Smith and Joe Jones can and have also become hundred-millionaires, I prefer to stand as high up on the ladder as they, in fact this is about the only satisfaction I can obtain, other than what a few million would insure."

As with the socialists, so with the " government absorptionists " (about the same thing in a different garb), there has been no tangible plan or method proposed by which their ends could be attained, other than by the untimely and unjustifiable intervention of the *vis major*, an expedient alike hostile to both humanity and progress.

What, it was asked of the votaries of this faith, is the first step you propose to take and what the intermediary agencies incident to the accomplishment of your ultimate end? Do you propose that all enterprises and industries now owned by private individuals shall be turned over to the government and an adequate recompense given therefor? If so what is the individual going to do with the value received in exchange? Shall he bury it and start anew on a common level with all and devote his time and thought to the government shop, receiving therefor such articles of human production as he can eat and wear, and be allotted a house such as is sufficient alone to protect him from the cold, or shall he be forced

to yield all his treasure to the coffers of the state,—his
lots, his land, his houses, or his mines,—receiving no
compensation for the previous efforts of his industry and
toil, and be obliged to labor in the common throng on a
level with and in pursuits as arduous as he who yields
nothing to the state and whose past efforts have been un-
availing to himself and of no good to society ; and if
either of these, what shall be the first step taken to start
the ball in motion ?

Echo answers : We will " introduce a bill "—a thing
easy of accomplishment when nothing else can be done.
We will set forth in that bill the pronunciamento that
all must deliver up their property to the state and
receive therefor no compensation whatever ; on the promulgation of which proclamation we expect to receive
the plaudits of the world, sounded with such multi-
tudinous vociferations that the reverberating echoes
resounding from hilltop to hilltop will go thundering
down the peaceful stream of time, to be reflected back
with accelerated force and power, weighted with com-
mingling sounds of universal praise and timely tenders of
worldly wealth, until the only possible manner of avoiding the terrible catastrophe incident to a mad and frenzied rush will be to convince the masses that it is useless
for all to come at once, or in fact for any to come at all
until the bill becomes a law, which it is sure to do prior
to the time of the practical inauguration of the metemp-
sychosis.

Well, what is to be the wording of the bill, what its
provisions in fact ; is it to begin with a " whereas " and
end with a " what is it," and what is to be its middle ? Is
it to be rushed right through, or debated in " Committee
of the whole on the state of the Union," or what is to be
done with it ? Is it to contain the pronunciamento that

all men are born free, equal, and possessed of certain inalienable rights? Is it to conflict with the existing judicial opinion as to the federal constitution and render necessary the packing of the supreme bench? Thus to the end is nothing tangible proposed because there is nothing tangible to propose—nothing regarding which any document can be drafted. The only hope for the introduction into society of any such system is the arbitrament of force, the right of might, and this held together and controlled by a military despot in whom all power must be centred and who could carry out any decree it matters not how violent; the thing itself being in direct conflict with the end to be sought and desirable only on the theory that good could result from evil, that order could best be promoted by confusion, system by chaos—in a word, life from death, for any such condition would be social death and confusion worse confounded, sans top, sans bottom, sans everything save the rankest and most useless form of heterogeneity and confusion.

It is seen that any effort to alter social conditions must proceed regularly and be bottomed on reason, aided by feasibility, supported by men of force, method, and character; hence its progress must necessarily be slow and tedious. As a glacier will move quite a distance in a century, so will the conditions of society gradually become affected by moderate innovations. The system of the United States government was for a century considered experimental, and may in fact yet prove to be such, unless by the curtailment of the ballot better conditions are adopted. Men of no education and no property elect to office representatives of the same calibre, and hence public business becomes seriously affected by actual incompetency. As it requires some brains and education to write a resolution, so it requires some capacity to understand one when written, and as it requires prudence and sagacity to wield the affairs of state and men of property and credit to give it prestige and responsibility, so it must soon be necessary to prevent the alarming degeneracy that is admitted to be rapidly pervading the personnel of public assemblages ; and one of the greatest possible arguments for the curtailment of the ballot is the actual incompetency of many of the inmates of legislative assemblages because of the increasing prominence of the irresponsible and ignorant voter.

Under such conditions it is vain to expect any concession from the better classes to any modification of the social state.   Millionaires can protect their property simply by the inherent force of the property itself, by buying favorable and thwarting unfavorable measures proposed by vicious legislators ; and so when the " conservative compromise " is brought forth money may seek its downfall ; but such is the irresistible power of the reliable middle classes that this will be impossible, and as time progresses, and as they gain in representation, they may become sufficiently the master of the situation to control the destinies of the future state.   The single-tax men or land confiscationists are ahead of the others both in intelligence and in the reasonableness of their propositions.   They have elected no representatives to Congress solely in the interests of their cause, and but few to any legislative assembly who had not other aims and affiliations, neither have they proposed in Congress any definite measure for which they asked the support of their associates.

They do not assert their faith boldly as confiscators of land, as the Democrats will not boldly assert their free-trade predilections and preferences ; the former carry a mask called "single tax," and the latter "tariff reform," both misleading and disingenuous. The single-tax men, however, are in a position to draft a bill or to propose legislation containing a declaration that all existing methods of taxation should be abolished and a certain levy placed in lieu of all on land values, but what is the rate to be? Their proposition in effect is that land shall be taxed practically to "its full rental value," but this term in a bill drafted, introduced, and referred, before it reached the voting stages, and had been the victim of amendments, would look rather vague and indefinite. It really means that land should be confiscated, but the tax term is milder, it becomes the mouth better. It will not do to say the land should be taxed five per cent., or ten per cent., or any fixed per cent., because all land does not possess the same rental value, and whilst any certain levy would confiscate some, it would not answer the purpose, because it would not confiscate all. To have passed a bill containing no more definite provision than "to full rental value," or even a percentage of rental value, would have been the instrument and means of ceaseless bickering and dispute between assessor and occupant as to what was rental value, and would be indeed as utterly impracticable as is the whole scheme irrational. It sounds well enough to talk about man's equal right to natural opportunity and "a' that ' and "a' that"; that the earth belongs in usufruct to the people, and "a' that"; that man is entitled to what he produces—to the fruits of his own toil, and "a' that"; that labor is paid out of its own product, and "a' that" and "a' that," most of which are aphorisms as old as the adamantine hills, and, with slight modifications, as true as they are ancient; but how are they to be accomplished by land confiscation? That labor is paid out of its own products, it is useless to deny. Every one will admit—at least all should admit—that in the process that is carried out in the conversion of a piece of crude iron ore, worth comparatively nothing, through its many stages, till it assumes the form, the polish, and elasticity of a watch spring, in which state it is worth more than its weight in gold, the labor expended is paid, though of course indirectly, out of the thing that is produced. To deny this would be to argue as irrationally as to maintain that "land confiscation" is either just, reasonable, practical, or efficacious in accomplishing any good to the world. But as with all other propagandisms, though in this not as lamentably, even the advocates themselves fail to propose any definite measure. They do not say " Be it enacted thus and so," so that the people can get at just the thing they seek. Generalizations could have been prated about till the crack of doom, and had the American colonists of King George III. never got down to hard-pan and issued their pronunciamento in certain exact words and phrases meaning certain things, backed with an inflexible desire and an indomitable purpose to put the meaning of that thing through though they should drink their brother's blood, the grand confederacy of sovereign stars, than which none more glorious ever shone in the galaxy of nations that now stretch from ocean to ocean, and ere long may stretch from the isthmus to the pole, comprising the natural geographical limits of the greatest nation on earth, might never have been independent ; and so likewise will all generalizations which, though pleasing to the ear, always fail of any practical good. The land confiscationists, however, in adopting for their shibboleth " single tax," appeal forcibly to those who seek simplicity in all governmental affairs, which is in fact the tendency of all thought relative to government; yet it is not the shadow that weighs, it is the substance, and if the substance is too transparent to cast a shadow it amounts to nothing. If single tax could be fully applied, and result only in simplicity, the game is not worth the candle, for greater simplicity could be obtained by other less objectionable methods. The single-tax men, too, hoot at the idea that all they claim for it is simplicity, for they frankly admit that in the interest of simplicity alone it would be useless to advocate such a radical upturning of the world's social affairs; that what they desire is something to benefit the people and secure a more equitable distribution of the products of human labor, and they favor that thing which will accomplish that end, and it matters not how complicated (for people can understand anything that people can propose), and that they oppose anything that fails of this accomplishment, it matters not how simple. It takes a machine somewhat complicated to reap wheat and bind it into sheaves and to thresh out the grain after the sheaves are bound, but a machine that will do this work effectively, though complicated, is not to be compared with one that will not, though simple; hence it is the end, not the means, if the end is fair, just, and honorable by any means that are equally so.

Since nothing has been definitely brought forth by any of the reformers, the leaders of the most liberal and conservative of each should conclude to concentrate on the regulation of the extremes, thus letting the mean take care of itself. *Men may have an abundance, but not a redundance.*

Men who have nothing and know nothing shall have no voice in the affairs of government, but all shall have an opportunity.

They should, therefore, propose that the following amendment to the Constitution of the United States be adopted :

" *Congress shall have power to impose a rate of taxation on every one thousand dollars of individual property equal to the one hundred-thousandth part of the total value of the property, the same to be uniform and invariable throughout the United States ; and to prescribe as a condition for suffrage both an educational and a property qualification, the former to be the ability to speak, read, and write the English language, and the latter to be the ownership of real property or government bonds to an amount not less than five hundred dollars ; and to pass such laws as may be necessary to carry the provisions of this amendment into effect.*"

This is the key to the whole situation and the foundation for the whole structure ; it is the beginning, the middle, and the ending.

All advocates of reform have but to vote for, and support for the Federal Congress and for State Legislatures, men pledged to the support of this amendment. No other officials are necessary. The amendment could be adopted and become law if ratified by three fourths of the State Legislatures and by two thirds of their delegations in Congress—that is, in the way the Constitution itself provides, and when adopted it would be a part of the supreme law of the land, adopted in the only lawful way, and a party called the " Phronocratic or Conservative " should make it the keystone to its creed. The recommendation of the said amendment is thought proper in view of the fact that many cherish the belief that Congress has not the power, without an amendment, to impose such a tax or to pass laws in pursuance thereof ; that a simple act of Congress passed by the usual majority might be unconstitutional and void, but

that by an amendment the right would become fundamental and unquestioned, and that, pending its consideration and ratification by the States, its provisions could
be scrutinized with care and circumspection and subsequent enactments necessary to carry its provisions into
effect could be calmly considered and planned.

It is in no case to be applied to corporations, but
solely to the individual holdings in those corporations,
on the basis of the value of the stock and bonds held by
individuals therein. The reason for its non-application
to corporations is obvious, conclusive, and clear, to wit :
In placing a check on the concentration of wealth it is
not in any sense in keeping with the progress of the
times nor apace with the advancing tendencies of modern
civilization to hamper or oppress enterprise. Great un-
dertakings are not only desirable but necessary. Long
lines of railways have to be projected and built ; canal
and waterways, bridges and highways, tunnels and sub-
ways all have to be constructed, and it requires wealth
aggregating countless millions to accomplish these works.
Many individual properties cost over one hundred million dollars, and cannot be created without this expenditure, and civilization cannot go on without their
creation ; the wants and needs of the people demand
them, and go they must, and will. They cannot be
divided into separate properties of less value ; hence
means must be at hand by which they can not only be
constructed, but controlled and operated as an entirety,
as a whole ; and this means is *the corporation*, on the
multiplication or concentration of the capital in which
there need be no limit whatsoever. One corporation
might own the railways of the world, the magnitude and
extent of which in America alone in 1890 was such as to
maintain a bonded indebtedness of about five billion

dollars and a share capital of variable valuation of about
the same amount, both of which at a par valuation would
amount to ten billion of dollars, or in 1890 about one
sixth of the entire assessable property of the great Republic, representing in production the aggregated labor of
ten million men. As strange and as anomalous as at
first view it might appear, it is actually thought better
and more desirable—more in keeping with popular demand and efficient public service—that (under the proposed system of taxation) all this property should be
owned by a single rather than by many corporations ; but
in said corporation there would be many individual
owners. In concentration there is both efficiency and
power, and the baneful effects of monopolistic organization is greatly mitigated and assuaged if the said organization must of necessity be owned by many individuals
rather than by a few or by a single individual. In other
words, it is found to be absolutely necessary to the
progress of society that organizations of a monopolistic
nature must exist, otherwise enterprises of " great pith and
moment " would, in truth " with this regard, their currents
turn away and lose not only the name but the very fact
of action." It is, however, recommended that these
grand enterprises shall to the greatest extent possible *be
popularly owned ;* that they must be owned by as many
individuals as is consistent with proper and efficient
direction, management, and control, and not by as few
as possible to the utmost limit of the " freeze-out process "
of the avaricious managers.

It is undoubted that a board of directors chosen by a
hundred shareholders can be as efficient and reliable as
those chosen by a single holder of the bare majority, and
the officers and agents chosen by these boards would be
as assiduously devoted to the interests of these trusts as

those elected by and under the mandate of the one-man power ; in fact, better and more efficient could the management of such corporations become because of the fact that there would be no absolute guaranty of perpetual succession, such as under individual control of majorities is usually assured by superserviceableness and intrigue against the interest of minorities. It has been proposed to allow to no stockholder more than one vote. This would tend to lessen autocratic control, but would in no way reach the question of colossal individual accumulations, nor promote the principle of *popular ownership*, or that a *tax rate proportionate to property is the best tax rate on earth.* It is observed, too, that small holders of corporate interests are in the main more conservative than the large holders ; in fact, the possession of any property causes prudential care and conservative operation, which position may be exclusively demonstrated in the establishment of a property qualification, though small, for the exercise of suffrage. The very fact of owning something begets a disposition to protect that something, and the man who becomes eligible to citizenship by the possession of five hundred dollars will be as prudent and as painstaking, as desirous of securing reliable men and of strengthening the public faith, as is the owner of his millions. Where the treasure is there the heart is, and a poor man's five hundred dollars representing, as it in most cases would, a greater part of his worldly goods than the rich man's million does of his worldly goods, the former would be on the average more prudent and conservative and less disposed to enter into schemes of profligacy, extravagance, and waste than the latter.

There is a vast difference between him who possesses something, and hopes to retain and increase it, and him

8

who has nothing, and has no hope of ever gaining anything.   The former is prudent and the latter reckless, or
the one fit for citizenship and the other not.   As in the
affairs of government, so in those of the great corporations.   There would be a wholesome check placed upon
recklessness and extravagance, the vaulting ambition
would less often overleap itself, earnings would be more
properly applied toward the payment of dividends than
to extravagant salaries to ornamental presidents, who in
most cases are the protegés of the owners of the bare
majority and often share their receipts therewith.
Neither to so great an extent could needless branches
and appendages be constructed to fatten the purse of the
contractor, who is often a partner with the officers in
control.   Furthermore, and to greater advantage still,
popular ownership would beget popular contentment
and insure a management more in conformity with the
popular weal.   On the theory that it is more in the interest of localities that representatives in Congress
should be chosen from among their own people, and
in numbers representing about one for every thirty thousand votes, rather than to have one man run the entire
legislation of the country, so likewise would it be found
better that monopolistic enterprises should be more
popularly owned and governed and operated by officials chosen by the diversified interests.   In keeping
with this very principle one of the greatest American
magnates once sold a large part of his interest in one of
the greatest corporations, believing, yea, knowing, that a
more popular ownership would beget popular contentment, and popular contentment would avoid trouble
resulting from blackmailing legislation and other schemes
of popular revenge ; also that it would tend to increase
popular patronage, and consequently perhaps increase

the value of what he retained more than the sacrifices consequent upon disposition and sale : and thus, in fact, it is said to have resulted.

But whether or not it be to the interest of the great monied magnates to thus placate the public, is not the point for discussion, but whether or not it is in the interest of the public that great and necessarily monopolistic corporations should be as far as practicable more popularly owned, is the question, if indeed there can be any question about a matter so self-evident and reasonable. Most of the riches resulting from unearned increment are gained in enterprises of such magnitude as to be practically exempt from competition by reason of inaccessibility by any competitive establishments, and if these are once started, and bid fair to continue, such is the advantage to both of concentration and consolidation that they are merged into one ; the anaconda swallows the elephant, and then lies down to digest its meal, whilst the public continue of necessity to patronize the monster because they can do nothing else.

It, however, being evident that monopolistic enterprises are necessary—in fact, almost the unavoidable outcome of the world's affairs,—and that from enterprises of this character large unearned increment will unavoidably be acquired in any prosperous state or community ; now, therefore, the equally unavoidable conclusion, though held in the dark for thousands of years, must be reached, viz. : we will distribute that increment as widely as we can, or, in other words, we will cause him who has most of it to contribute to the State that supports it and guarantees his interest, to an extent proportionate to his ability ; the necessary result of which will be that when he acquires a certain limit, outgo will equal income, and he can acquire no more, giving

increased opportunity to his friends just behind and
their friends and their friends.

"*Extremes beget limitations*," hence the force of the
expression :

> " That I am wretched,
> Makes thee the happier :—Heavens deal so still !
> Let the superfluous, and lust-dieted man,
> That slaves your ordinance, that will not see
> Because he doth not feel, feel your power quickly ;
> *So distribution should undo excess,*
> *And each man have enough.*"

CHAPTER VI.

Practical application of the cumulative tax—Support government in
proportion to man's ability—And no property or no knowledge,
no vote—Takes burden off of the weak and puts it on the strong—
Equity and efficiency of assessment—Limits all individual estates
to about four million—Tax collectors in congressional districts :
their method of assessment—Necessity of not limiting corporations—" Watering " stock not specially objectionable, but division of ownership vital.

" LIFE is but a narrow veil between the cold and barren peaks of two eternities."

Why, therefore, should any man desire to own the
earth ? If he had it all he would yet be poor. Why
should he desire more than will insure comfort, luxury,
and even a fair compensation for cupidity and greed besides, for more than that but burthens him ?

Why should not the brain that is capable of wresting
from the world so much of its treasure, when a sufficiency has been obtained, be willing to devote its operations to research into the fathomless abyss of the great
unknown and as yet unknowable ?

Who knows or can demonstrate to the contrary
that, " As the cloud is consumed and vanisheth away,
so he that goeth down to the grave shall come up no
more."

Why, therefore, should there not exist less unremitting
strife and more humanity in the world ? In brief and
in fact, since an abundance is enough, why want more ?

To finite minds the end is but to die, yes,

> " But to die, and go we know not where,
> To lie in cold obstruction and to rot :
> This sensible warm motion to become
> A kneaded clod ; and the delighted spirit
> To bathe in fiery floods, or to reside
> In thrilling regions of thick-ribbed ice ;
> To be imprison'd in the viewless winds,
> And blown with restless violence about
> The pendent world."

O thou impenetrable and unknown ; thou inscrutable mystery that art veiled in night ; be thy ultimate the earth, or heaven, or hell—'t is all beyond our ken ! "Come, come, you spirits that tend on mortal thoughts," open this blinded eye, make keen and capable this narrow faculty of human comprehension, and proclaim what was, what is, and what is yet to be ; make intelligible and clear the object, the purpose, and the end of life, the omniscient motive and intent of this and that and these —of the Universe, the earth, the air, and the wild tempestuous seas ! But to the issue.

The very fact that individuals were required to contribute to government in proportion to their ability, and that those who contributed nothing could have no voice, would be of itself not only one of the greatest possible bulwarks to the continued ascendancy of republican institutions in America, but the monarchies of the world would stand aghast and trembling, so that, as soon as it was fully realized that thereby security could exist without a king, instead of saying " The king is dead, long live the king," it would be thought quite as safe to say, " The man we, who own the property of the state, have chosen to do our will, is dead, let the man we have chosen to succeed him take his place." Then empires would begin to tumble like meteors in the night, with scarce that faint effulgence which, against even the dark background of centuries of ignorance and vice, would be necessary to make their presence known.

The institution of this protective condition would likewise strengthen property rights, increase domestic security, and, by reason of lifting the burthen off of the shoulders of the weak and placing it upon the heads of the strong, the oppressed would be given greater opportunity ; in fact, as great as could be considered consistent with man's right to own property at all (which is admitted), and the strong would not be unjustly oppressed. The conditions now and heretofore existing in society are and have been just the reverse of this. The rich men, by reason of their faculty for secretiveness, and for the further reason that it is more difficult to count ten million grains than ten thousand grains, and by reason of their influence upon the assessor as to property not registered, usually pay a tax that is *proportionately as small as their estates are great*, and, the greater the estate the less proportionably it contributes, whilst the small home of the widow, the trust bonds of the infant, and the small accumulations of the aged and decrepit, are taxed full up and ofttimes excessively.

This all admit to be wrong, and even those who oppose the cumulative rate upon the flimsy pretext that even then some property would be secreted, will be obliged to admit that the said cumulative rate on what *is found and assessed* would, to a great degree, compensate the state for that which is secreted.

In other words, if, as in the present, a man with five million dollars could secrete two and a half million dollars and pay about one dollar per hundred on the balance, he would really be paying only about the half of one per cent. on the whole, but if, under the cumulative-rate tax (notwithstanding the greatly improved system of assess-

ment), he should yet secrete two and a half millions, his
rate would still be two and a half per cent.. or he would
be contributing just five times as much to the state as
under the present condition of affairs.

The increased facilities for assessments would render
secretiveness much more difficult, and there can be imposed for it very severe penalties, as will hereafter be
explained.

The first and most important consideration is : What
amount of money will the cumulative tax secure to the
treasury of the country ; however, this cuts no figure as
to the question of sufficiency or insufficiency, because
horizontal percentage of increase and reduction can be
fully arranged. There is no way of getting at the thing
with absolute accuracy, because the number of large
estates relatively to the small cannot be definitely ascertained. The question as to what will be done with the
excess of the estates of very rich individuals will also
appear as an objection, though not serious.

At one cent on each one thousand, or a rate equalling
the one hundred-thousandth part of the estate, and estimating five per cent. as the income that maintains estates
at par, it is clear that outgo would equal income, allowing
something for local assessment, when the fortune equals
about four million dollars ; in fact, the net income from
three millions would be about as much as from four. A
man could, of course, keep all he could pay taxes on, but
if he kept much more than three million dollars he would
soon be running in debt, and the state would gradually
absorb the excess, so that, without any mincing of words,
of sugar-coated terms, like the tariff-reform free-traders
or the single-tax land-confiscationists use, it is boldly admitted that all excess would be confiscated and the work
would be boldly carried out.

Of course the natural tendency of this would be to encourage the one-hundred-millionaires to disgorge, to give to their uncles, their cousins, and their aunts large amounts of property when it was evident that the cumulative system was in fact to be enforced, rather than permit the state to own it, on the theory that blood is thicker than water,—to give to their kin rather than to their country.   Of course the government has no power to say that this should not be done, especially if done before the system took effect ; even thereafter it would not be necessary to say that a man should not be a benefactor to his friends, especially to his relatives, rather than be a benefactor to the state.   A one-hundred-million-dollar man would have to divide among thirty or forty people before either would have an estate that would be *small* enough (how singular the term) to yield them any net profits, and a two-hundred-million-dollar man would have to divide among about one hundred before his estate would be *small* enough to be of much value to any, and since this would spread the thing out into lots of fifties and hundreds, it would effect of itself a tolerably good division and still force these fortunate relatives to contribute in the ratio of *their ability—(the essence of the whole scheme and the key to equitable distribution and the only key).*   So why not let the poor kin have it ?   Again, it would be urged that one-hundred-millionaires would temporarily transfer their property to their uncles, their cousins, their sisters, and their aunts just prior to and pending the date of assessment, with a tacit agreement that it should be re-transferred as soon as assessment-day is over ; or they would pay to different people, for example, their clerks and other flunkies, certain small salaries to consent to have the property assessed in their names, but with the understanding that the in-

come should be paid or given back to the original one-
hundred-millionaire. This could be obviated in several
ways ; but if it could not be obviated at all, what pleasure
or what object would any individual have in accumulat-
ing more property than he could ever possibly need if he
had to use such subterfuges to retain it, and subject
himself to the great probability of being detected, in
which case he might lose all, even the very liberal amount
that he could own and handle without any subterfuge,
and also to liability to arrest and imprisonment besides.
Of the most obdurate objector it could be asked : Would
not these penalties and the maintenance of the necessary
machinery by which to evade the law *at least deter*, if it
did not absolutely prevent, men from acquiring such useless property as to render evasion necessary, and to the
extent that it did deter them, would it not be the end in
part at least attained ? Such could be the methods of
assessment that, notwithstanding a very dubious desire
to do so, it would not be possible to succeed very well,
and, considering the penalties, the game would not be
worth the candle, and it would not in practice be attempted to any great or even to an appreciable extent.
The first step to be taken would be to propose the
amendment to the Federal Constitution, so as to remove
all doubt as to the power of the general government to
impose a cumulative rate of taxation, and as it would
require the sanction of three fourths of the State Legislatures and two thirds of their delegations in Congress,
its adoption would be necessarily slow, but its introduction would command immediate attention, and the
monster magnates would begin to think. A few might conclude that the thing was reasonably fair and just anyhow,
and that, since it was coupled with a proposition preventing the waifs and irresponsibles of the community from

having any voice in governments, giving the machine
over into the hands of those only who knew something
and owned something, thus adding to the security and
the uninterrupted enjoyment of the competency, yea, the
abundance, that remained, why not let the dance go on ?
Some might be satisfied in the reflection that they would
be as rich as any other man, and they would have enough,
and it would not be so bad after all. It is astonishing
how human character is affected by the removal of the
desire to excel.

To excel another man any man might desire a billion,
when if no man could excel him he would be content
with only a million, or rather with that amount which
would insure absolute protection against want and enable
him to enjoy such luxury as he desired in company with
his family. The difficulty would not exist in the opposition of the great millionaires, if so their numerical
strength would be comparatively so small that it could
not delay, much less thwart, the purposes of the cumulative principle. The number whose estates would be
materially affected, that is, the number of estates which,
under the cumulative rate, would be called upon to pay
more than their accustomed contributions, would be
small ; hence, aside from their general recognition of the
eternal fitness of the thing, the middle classes, or the
reputable citizens with moderate yet comfortable estates,
should be almost unanimously in its favor.

The proposition would have coupled and indissolubly
linked with it its proper counterpoise, its compensating
advantage, to wit : "qualification for suffrage." And
just here is where the shoe will pinch. So abominably
promiscuous has become the suffrage system of the
United States, and so corrupt and mischievous its practices, that almost the entire machinery of government

has been permitted to drift into the hands of professional
politicians and charlatans ; in fact, except on great oc-
casions, such as presidential elections and heated contests
for the larger offices, the commercial population takes
no interest in politics, knowing as they do that the
bosses of the lower wards and the henchmen under
them—both equally corrupt and void of any principle
save the most questionable and devious means of securing the success of their candidates—will control the
election, it matters not how unjustly, whether they vote
or not.

The proposition, therefore, would receive the bitter
opposition of both the professional politician and his
henchmen, both utterly unfitted to wield the destinies of
the state, yet both hitherto essential to the success of any
candidate or the establishment of any principle.

It is evident where the qualification condition would
disfranchise ten voters in the slums of Chicago and New
York and ten negroes in every State of the South (both
classes as utterly unfit for suffrage as the blackest cohorts
of the prince of darkness would be to a seat in Heaven
beside our Lord and Saviour), it would perhaps not disfranchise more than one or possibly two in the prosperous rural districts and smaller towns of the North, East,
and West, and perhaps a smaller proportion of the *white*
population of the South, and it is this portion of the
citizens, together with the conservative middle classes
of all the cities in the country, that must ultimately ex-
terminate the political bum, the parasite and boodler of
the great metropolitan centres, and the voodooistic African
barbarian of the sunlit South. The party shibboleth, as
stated, should be " cumulative taxation and voting qualification," " North American annexation," and " anti-
centralization," to secure which the adoption of the

amendment making sure the right of Congress to impose
it would be the first consideration.

To do this would be required only Congressmen and
State Legislatures, and for which positions the support of
all friends of reform should be pledged. The amendment should be called the "conservative amendment,"
because it looks for support to the conservative middle-
men of all parties—to those who think that the conservative mean is better than either extreme.

Of course prior to the passage of the amendment it
would be useless to propose incidental legislation, but
for the better understanding of the people a few of the
principal proposed enactments to follow its adoption
could be made known, though of course until the fact
was once established, it would not be possible to pre-
arrange all the minor details, any more than it would be
possible to say just what the exact height of a child
would be when grown to maturity, before the child was
born. Incidental legislation for the purpose of improv-
ing the system could be passed almost every year, just as
enactments are currently passed as to the application of
the tariff and decisions of the treasury called for even
pending the annual meetings of Congress. Coupled with
the general arguments offered in support of the amendment, it might be given out to the people that certain
primary acts would be passed covering the principal features of the practical operation and such alone as were
necessary to insure its unquestioned feasibility. Still, as
to the practical carrying out of the measure there can
not be the slightest doubt even in the minds of the most
violent of its opponents. In the first place there would
have to be created by the general government an official
to be known as the "collector of revenue." There would
perhaps have to be one of these for each congressional

district in the country, and the apportionment of districts could be arranged on the basis of the qualified voter. This collector, like the Congressmen, should be elected by the people, but should be removable by the President if in the latter's opinion he should be negligent, dishonest, or incompetent; but the successor should be likewise chosen by the people, so that whilst the President could destroy he could not create this official.

The same also should apply to postmasters; they should be elected by the people in the towns, cities, or localities in which they exercise their functions, and should likewise be removable by the President for cause to him deemed sufficient, in which case the people would choose his successor. This power of removal would be necessary in view of the fact that the business both of the collector and postmaster would be so closely connected with that of the general government that if from obstinacy, caused by hostility to an administration of the federal government opposed to his own politics, or from incompetency or from neglect, any such officer should mar the efficiency of the service, it would be but right that he should be removed, providing always that the people name his successor. This successor, being mindful of the causes that prompted the removal of his predecessor, would of course exert his efforts to remedy same, so that it would very rarely occur that either a collector or a postmaster would be removed, it mattered not how adverse his politics might be to that of the dominant administration, and one removal by the President would be all-sufficient to correct the evil in his elected successor. All minor officers of the civil service that cannot, in the nature of things, be elective, such as clerks in the departments at the capital and under the collector and postmaster in their respective districts and localities, should be thrown open to competitive examination. This system is opposed because it is said to be no test of a man's efficiency or competency to perform the duties of these offices that he should have his head crammed with miscellaneous information such as was necessarily the test that examiners would apply. It is agreed, however, that general information does no harm ; that a man who knows something is, other things being anything like equal, better in the performance of any duty than he who knows nothing. A letter carrier is none the less worthy or efficient because he might know the boundaries of every state or the identical confines of every nation of Europe, or the geographical location of every town or hamlet on either continent ; but it might be that he who knew not these things might be incompetent, it matters not what might be his " political 'fluence." The civil service under the Phronocratic proposition is to be as efficient as possible and wholly exempt from partisan control. The patronage of the President should be curtailed and all officials elected by the people within the limit of reason or possibility; and in view of the fact that the ballot may be curtailed and purified, that none save those who know something and own something can participate in elections, the better classes will assume control and in their hands can more safely be placed these increased elective opportunities. When the President has chosen the heads of departments, or in other words his cabinet of counsellors and advisers, appointed foreign diplomats and the governors of the territories, he has done quite enough of this class of labor for the pay he is receiving, and it is thought best to relieve him of that annoyance.

Aside from the collections that would have to be provided for in each district, the President would have to appoint one whose residence would be in New York City, whose duty it should be to assess all non-resident property located wheresoever—that is, the property of any foreigner located in the United States.

The salary of the collector of taxes should be at all times the same as that of a Congressman, and that of all postmasters should be determined by the number of stamps cancelled at their offices, and where a reasonable percentage of this amount would not afford adequate compensation, the rate could be named by the Post-master-General. Every individual would have to be required to pay his government or cumulative tax *in the district in which he resided*, and to the collector of same. It would be the duty of the collector of every district to report property found in his own, to the collector of the district in which the owner resided ; for example, if a farm should be owned by John Smith in the sixth district of Illinois, and John himself should live in the fourth district of Ohio, or in a town in that district the collector of the sixth Illinois would be required to report to the collector of the fourth Ohio, the fact that he had discovered in his district 10,000 dollars worth, or whatever the amount might be, of property belonging to John Smith, resident of his, the fourth Ohio district, on receipt of which information, the collector of the fourth Ohio would proceed to add 10,000 dollars to John Smith's list of property and apply his cumulative tax thereto. So in all the districts, as to all the others, and as to foreigners, each collector would report to the one appointed by the president who resided in New York. It is useless for objectors to say that this could not be done because these objections are seen at a glance to be prompted by the wish, not by the thought, and even if a few thousand should be missed, what matters it when millions are missed as it is, and must of necessity be under any system, because human affairs are not more perfect than human beings themselves, and they are not strong when too severely tempted. It is not a good argument against a thing to say : Oh, it is not absolutely perfect, what human thing is perfect ?

It cannot be denied that this system of ascertaining and reporting individual property would be by far the best contrivance that has ever been invented, surpassing infinitely the cumbersome system of internal revenue, where an army of storekeepers, gaugers, marshals, deputy marshals, and others has to be maintained at an expense to the government in many cases more than the revenue derived therefrom, for the purpose of supervising and controlling the distillation of whiskey and most malt liquors. Furthermore, since States and localities have their respective local assessors and collect their revenue from the property (not from the trader and manufacturer) of the country, the central government always cumulative, and the local usually direct, the two would be a great aid to each other and would usually reach very correct results. All corporations would be required to have some distinct central office, and this corporation (which as such would be exempt from government tax) would be required to report to the collector in the district in which its central office was situate, once each month if need be, the names of each individual and the amounts of stocks and bonds held by said individual during that month or other period to be named in that corporation. All companies should be obliged to have a register open to the inspection of the collector or his subordinates, containing a complete and accurate list, not only of the total capitalization of the company, but the monthly average of shares held by each

9

individual, also the same as to bonds ; and each individual would be obliged to register both with the
company and with the collector the exact number
of bonds and shares of stock, and the amount of each
that he held. Bonds payable to bearer should be none
the less subject to registration, and any shares or bonds
held that were not thus registered, should have no
binding force against the corporation, and should be
subject to confiscation by the government, simply on
proof of non-registry for two consecutive offences. To
registration objection would be urged on the ground of
detail, labor, espionage, and the like, but it would certainly be sufficiently practicable to cause great good ;
and even if it should merit these objections, would not
the benefit outweigh the burden ?   Why should property
be owned that cannot be listed ?   List it and tax it and
that *cumulatively too !*   Stock- and bondholders would be
thus obliged, or incur great risk, to register their holdings both with the company on its books and with the
collector in the district of its central office on his books,
and in the event of failure upon the part of the company
to keep this registry open when desired to the inspection
of the collector, its charter could be at once annulled
and its property offered for sale, the proceeds of
which sale would be divided among the stock- and
bondholders (the latter holding precedence to the par
value of their bonds) on the basis of the *last complete
registry* shown by the books of the collector.   The individual for failure to register with the collector after
two months from the date in which he acquired his
holdings, could not only be subject to entire confiscation, but to criminal penalty as well, the latter to
be determined by trial before the United States judge
in the district in which the offender resided.   These

penalties could be made to fit the conditions as experience would suggest.

The confiscation, however, could be summarily declared by the collector and the possessor, could only be reinstated by appeal to the federal courts, which should, in determining his case, take into consideration only the question whether or not the failure to register was the result of ignorance, error, or neglect, or of wilful intent to secrete his property; if the latter, there would be no remedy, and the former excuse could not be urged but once. If any individual had made temporary transfer to any other individual for the purpose of evading the cumulative rate, on conviction before the United States judge he could be made liable to imprisonment of his person, and forfeiture of his estate as occasion might require.

Stock in corporations is usually transferred only on the books of the company, but it is sometimes, for speculative purposes, not entered thereon because of inconvenience. The plan required for the application of the government's cumulative rate would force this registry, not alone of stock but bonds, which would have a most salutary effect in curtailing wild and ruinous speculation, and in elevating the character and tone of all stock exchanges; furthermore, it would act as a protection for the conservative investor against the reckless speculation of the ordinary stock gambler; it would prevent large and rapid exchanges for purely speculative purposes, hence give steadiness and tone to the markets of the country. The system of enforced registration has been in effect in England for many years, and there works well and practically. In fact there is nothing impracticable about it, though those opposed to the system will try to make the people believe that changes and transfers are so rapid that they could not be registered to the extent required by the provisions of these laws, to which it may be replied, " Then let them be a little slower," and we will all try to live. Forcing a man to register what he owns is no great hardship, and it is a simple duty that he owes to the state and to the mercantile community. The adoption of the system would aid materially the ascertainment of a man's commercial standing, hence determine to a large extent his credit in his business. In making up individual returns, they should be permitted to deduct from their total any indebtedness they might owe, provided the party to whom it was owing added the same to his returns. Since corporations in their individual capacity would pay no tax to the government collector, but would simply be obligated to show up the exact holdings of individuals, if any individual should seek to reduce his returns by reason of a debt due to a corporation, the latter would be obliged to produce evidence of the indebtedness if required by the assessor, and show that it gave to the individual ample and sufficient value for the said obligation, and the individual would be obliged to show proper and regular disposition of that value to the satisfaction of the collector before it would be deductable from his full list of property. What corporations would owe or what they would own matters not, because they would not be assessed, and what they owed or what they owned would determine the value of the stock on which the individual would pay tax, and the value of their bonds would not be difficult of determination. The corporation should, when required, show to the collector a list of its bills payable and to whom due, and if any individual owned such note and failed to report it, it should be liable to confiscation. Notes

or obligations between corporations themselves would
be of no consequence whatever, because the government would have to do only with individuals, and
the holdings of corporations, or the debts of corporations, *i. e.*, the floating debts, would affect the value
either by increase or decrease of the stock held by
individuals. This individual restriction will not hamper
enterprise, but simply give more people an opportunity
to avail themselves of the profits of enterprises essentially monopolistic in their nature, and afford the means
whereby individuals could support the government in
proportion to their ability. If the conservative people
consider the thing right in principle, details as to listing
and espionage will be easily arranged.

The necessity of non-limitation of corporate concentration is seen in many enterprises. For example, the
bridge across the East River between New York and
Brooklyn, the magnificent structure completed in 1890
across the Firth of Forth in Scotland, the Saint Gothard
Tunnel under the snow-crowned Alps, and many other
instances are at hand, and as civilization progresses these
will be extended both in number and magnitude.

It may be possible some day to bridge the Atlantic
Ocean, and if so why not do it ? There was a time when
it was thought impossible to cable it, but that time has
long since passed. It is by no means impossible that
some day a single corporation may exist with a capital
of ten billions of dollars ; in fact, if the railways of
America had been, in 1890, owned by one company
(and with cumulative taxation why not ?), they would
have represented about ten billion, and would perhaps
be operated more cheaply and expeditiously than now.

There is no denying the fact that increased capital
increases facility, and that increased facility increases

cheapness as well as expedition, hence it is actually better to operate large enterprises under one head than under several heads. This is forcibly shown in the case of the American Standard Oil monopoly. This institution, by dint of good management and opportune conditions, secured such concentration of capital as to enable it to practically command the railway rates of freight on its products, and when these became inadequate it constructed its own pipeways, thus possessing itself with facilities for transportation and distribution in excess of all competition, which resulted in colossal fortunes to the few individuals, and that, too, in the face of an actual reduction to the consumer of the price of the commodity ; so that in this case, as in many others if managed in the same way, increased facilities, consequent solely and alone on concentrated wealth, not only result in colossal fortunes to their projectors but at the same time reduce the price to the consumer. It cannot be successfully urged that this institution is a great detriment to society, and if that condition had existed by which its members, who were made one-hundred-millionaires, had been obliged to contribute to government in proportion to their ability they would not have been very seriously oppressed and many more individuals would have participated in the profits. It may be urged that great enterprises would never be constructed but for the enterprise of a few very rich men, that the public purse will never open to any great project, and that if the purse of great individual capitalists was closed or emptied by government there would be no great enterprises. It is a sufficient answer to this to say that if the public don't care sufficiently for an enterprise to contribute toward or to invest in a company that seeks to put it forward, then the public will not grieve much by reason of its non-ex-

istence, and to permit these things to be, just to make
the rich richer when the public is indifferent, is a policy
that may soon be abandoned, be it said to the good sense
and humanitarianism of the conservatives of the earth.
Things are not as they used to be. Once kings held in
their hands the lives of their subjects, now the subjects
hold in their hands the destinies if not the lives of the
kings. "A man can fish with a worm that has fed of a
king and then eat of the fish that has fed of that worm."
The proposition that great enterprises will not go on is
by no means proven ; it is a simple dogmatic assertion,
and like all assertions unsupported by evidence, affects
only the character of those who utter them. It is found
that popular investment in corporations is largely, if not
wholly, withheld by reason of the very fact that some of
the individuals are rich enough to obtain complete control, which usually results in the destruction of the small
investor. With one man who owns fifty-one per cent.,
the hundred men who hold together forty-nine have practically no voice. They can not elect a single director nor
have any voice in the management whatever, yet it would
not do to urge that majorities should not control, because
that would in fact check enterprise and prevent concentration on anything or in any direction ; in other words,
discontented minorities would be forever interfering
with the business of the organizations, creating discord
and confusion which must inevitably so hamper the
progress of the enterprise as to render its business unprofitable, it matters not how favorable its opportunities ;
or, in other words, that a house divided against itself
must fall. It is therefore futile to assume that majorities
should not control. By-laws have been adopted by some
corporations requiring a two-third vote to accomplish the
election of a director or to determine any policy, but this

and similar concessions to the minority invoke a great·
injustice to the majority, and its plans are often frustrated by captious interference. There must be a head,
and this head when once chosen must control and direct
till the end of his term. But where majorities are held
by one or two men there is never any or at least little
opportunity for an alteration of the policy or management of the organization in the interests of or in conformity with the views of the remaining stockholders,
whereas if majorities were held by many men the control
never would become autocratic, but when the officials
are once chosen and the policy fixed its administration
can be quite as efficient as when wholly in the hands of
the one-man owner. Why could not a certain individual
of unquestioned fitness and capacity manage the affairs
of a railway, a bank, or other corporation if chosen by
ten or even a hundred men to constitute the majority as
well as if elected by only one, and in corporations,
monopolistic in their nature, the result of the combined
opinions of many stockholders is usually more in keeping with the best interests of the corporation, and always
more representative of the rights of the community
(which should not be wholly ignored) than are those
subject to the autocratic domination of the one-man
power in the selection of managing officials. When the
officers are once chosen, even though at the behest of
several rather than of one, they are none the less able to
handle the business of which they are the recognized
head with equal decision, individuality, and firmness ;
and if at the end of a term the management had been
successful there would be no question as to succession
for an indefinite period, and if not, then necessarily and
properly a new management should prevail. Thus,
therefore, under the present system, when a few very

rich men can combine, or one can, at his option or fanciful caprice, " freeze out " the minority, there is not only no inducement for the public to take stock, but an absolutely unquestioned and sensible reason why they should not. Later, when it may come to pass that no great corporation can ever be controlled by a single man, or, if involving a vast sum of money, even by a few men, the populace will spring to the front with avidity and in great numbers and participate in the construction of great and needed improvements. Nearly all great enterprises in America, by reason of the rapidly increasing population, gain an immense amount from the increments of society. Properties costing originally one or ten million dollars soon pay interest on from four to forty millions, caused solely by the increase of public patronage and the monopolistic character of the improvement. In other words, the conditions are such that a rival establishment can not be constructed until the necessity has grown so great as to make the value of the original many times its cost. This is notably the case with the elevated railways in New York City—in fact, with railway properties almost throughout the entire American Republic.

The actual cash outlay required to construct the first-named improvement was perhaps not more than $10,000,-000. In 1890 it was carrying 600,000 passengers daily, producing a gross earning capacity of about $30,000 per day, and paid good interest on four times its cost. Thus, therefore, there is an unearned increment of $30,000,000, and that, too, in face of the fact that prices for transportation have been reduced to the minimum— less than originally authorized by law. In a word, there appears to be no possible way of reducing the income ; a lower price would cause increased travel at little increased expense to the company, but to great increased inconvenience to the public, so that it is really a question whether or not, in making prices low so as to serve a great many, the company is really serving any as they should be served, and this very principle prevails in many other places.

It is a question whether or not many kinds of service are not too cheap. Many people would gladly pay increased prices for increased privacy and comfort, and in the case of the particular enterprise to which allusion is made—the Manhattan Elevated of New York—it became not a question of price but one of actual ability to accommodate the public at any reasonable price. The city has grown so enormously, and its geographical position and topographical features are such, that there cannot exist for some time any successful rival—in fact, such is its patronage that the company itself would gladly build more lines, but they are thought to be an infringement upon the street space and an injury to abutting property. And the same conditions prevail in many localities and in many enterprises.

The unearned increment will frequently add vast sums to original investors before competition can be engaged in, and all this attributable to the increase of population and consequent demand, and these conditions may yet continue, and in proportion as " freeze out " is reduced, popular participation will be increased. If populated in proportion to its area and resources as densely as are most of the countries of continental Europe, excluding Russia, America would contain several hundred million ; and if as dense as Asia, or of some of the most thickly populated of European states—for example, Belgium, which contains over six hundred to the square mile,— it would aggregate more than the estimated population

in 1890 of the entire known world. The space within
its present limits, before the acquisition of British North
America, Mexico, and Central America, rather before the
complete establishment of "from the Isthmus to the Arctic" policy *(which must come)*, contains more arable land
by twenty per cent. than the whole Empire of China,
which supports over half a billion people.

The acquisition of the British possessions on the
north, and of everything on the south to the Isthmus of
Panama, would add no great per centum to the existing
population, but would increase materially the territorial
area, and consequently the ability to sustain more
people ; and whilst the population, unaided by any such
impetus, has increased about three per cent. per annum,
or one third itself every decade, completely doubling
itself every generation, with the fresh stimulus of more
rich land, under a more stable government, and under
that progressive state of society whereby a few could
not own the many, and those alone who were worthy
could participate in government, the population would
be largely augmented in numbers, and inconceivably so
in character, until it would appear as though Europe
would be obliged to adopt the same institutions or lose
her prestige on the face of the earth. And thus the unearned increments would grow as to railways, highways,
canals, and waterways, as to land,—in fact, as to everything that could not be multiplied and increased so as
to remove the monopolistic features, but these increments would be more equitably divided. At present
and for some time past great objection has been made,
and the public have been told that great wrong has
been inflicted upon society, by reason of an increased
capitalization of certain, in fact, of nearly all, corporations, a process commonly called " watering the

stock." The wrong inflicted by this is more imaginary
than real.

If a corporation has a net earning capacity of five
per cent. on ten million dollars, its shares in the older
and more thickly settled parts of the country will sell at
par on the basis of one hundred, and, if its prospects are
good, at a higher rate. If subsequently, by reason of
this very increase of population and demand, and at the
lawful rate for traffic, its net earnings should be doubled,
as is the case in many instances, then, as a matter of
course, it would pay ten instead of five per cent. on its
then capitalization, and if five per cent. previously
maintained it at par, then ten would just as reasonably
cause it to be worth two for one. What matters it
whether the capitalization is ten million and worth two
for one, or twenty million and worth only par. Unearned increment has doubled its net earning capacity,
and it is the merest child's play—the rankest ignorance
—to say that the simple doubling of the shares works
any injury. People need not buy them, but they do buy
them, and at times are glad to get them—especially will
this be so when that condition is instituted wherein no
one man, or even a few men, can autocratically get half
and control all. There is no serious objection then against
" watering the stock," and there should never have been
any. The wrong is not there, it is deeper down than
that, but the superficial observer cannot see it, and that
is the trouble.

Just so blatherskites prate about unlawful holdings,
and so forth, all of which is nonsense or ignorance, or
both. From such shallow-pated reformers as these the
millionaire fears no result, and they will never accomplish
any. A certificate of stock is nothing but an evidence
of ownership, and if any man owns two shares worth

together two hundred dollars, he is no richer than if he owned only one share worth two hundred dollars. Likewise is there great injustice sought to be practised against corporations by obliging the organization as such to pay tax on its property and then force the individuals also to pay tax on their shares. This is radically unjust. One or the other should pay—not both. The cumulative rate takes the individual, only leaving the corporation alone, because corporations must have no limit—if so, civilized progress must stop. The vital objection to all previous propositions for political, commercial, and social reformation is that enterprise would be stifled. *Not so under Phronocracy ; but great properties would simply be more popularly owned. Likewise* under other systems would effect follow cause in almost *exact proportion.* Give to the populace *all* the needs of life free and without labor, and there will soon be nothing to give ; give *half* free and do not increase prices on the other, and labor competition will inevitably reduce labor's pay. Phronocracy has a tendency in the same general direction, but it *cannot be proportionate.* One hundred men may be relieved of taxation to the extent of one dollar each ; but one man might be burdened to the extent of one hundred dollars. In no way is it possible for the latter to secure increased revenue *proportionate to his increased tax ;* but he can, nevertheless, *own and enjoy what is reasonable and just.*

CHAPTER VII.

Probable result of the practical application of the cumulative tax— Distributes corporate and other ownership to a maximum limit of about four million to one individual—More practical and simple than income tax—Requirements of the federal government fully met—More equitable distribution assured—Average levy on all property only fifty cents per hundred—Evasion impossible— Least burdensome and most certain and just of all taxation— Greater distribution useless and hurtful—The only true " protective system."

HAVING outlined some of the principal steps that are proposed to be taken looking to the adoption of the amendment, and before entering upon an explanation as to how the thing can be accomplished, it is well to consider slightly more in detail the supposed result of the system.

It has been partially explained how it is proposed to make the assessments and collections, and the penalties to be inflicted for violation of the laws incident thereto.

There would be, in fact, but few cases of violation on record, because on the average estate the government's levy would not be large ; it would only seriously affect the many times a millionaire, and these are going to be comparatively few, but their present estates are colossal.

For example, the rate being based on each one thousand dollars, and equalling one cent for each, or the one hundred-thousandth part of the estate, would apply itself as follows :

Total Value of Estates.	Rate of Taxation Cumulative.
1,000 dollars.	.01 per mille.
10,000 "	.10 " "
100,000 "	1.00 " "
1,000,000 "	10.00 " "
5,000,000 "	50.00 " "
10,000,000 "	100.00 " "
100,000,000 "	1,000.00 " "

It will be observed, therefore, that allowing nothing for local taxation, and estimating five per cent. as the rate of income that maintains investments at par, when the estate reaches five millions outgo will equal income, and that thereafter a continual loss will result to the capitalist until, when the one-hundred-million estate is subjected to its operations, the whole would be absorbed at once. The continual loss on estates above five million would, of course, soon consume the excess, so that unless distributed to the uncles, the cousins, and the aunts, it would be taken possession of by the government. All forfeitures to the government—that is, property of which it would become possessed (which would not be great nor frequent)—could be every six months put up and sold, and the proceeds turned into the treasury as a part of the government's fund. The property would, of course, usually be bought by those who were not *too rich* to own and pay taxes on it. For example, if the government became possessor of a block of one million of the stock of a certain railroad company, it would simply offer it for sale and put the proceeds into the treasury.

The individual from whom it came would simply lose it by reason of violation of the law. The means for ascertaining individual holdings would therefore not be seriously complicated, and, as has been said, since the cumulative rate would not be severe on the majority,— on none, in fact, till they became millionaires or over,

—the disposition to secrete would be by no means great nor general In the case of stocks and bonds, however, there would be some question (especially in the case of securities not listed on the stock exchanges) as to their proper assessible value.

There was a proposition to assess all at one hundred cents on the dollar, which, it was urged, would prevent the old objectionable practice of "watering stocks," and cause all companies to issue only that amount of securities that could be maintained at par. This looked simple and just to that uninitiated and superficial observer who had heretofore imagined that there was a great wrong inflicted by increasing the corporate capitalizations. This would prevent that, it is said, and would be simple and reasonable, working no injury to the individual holder, for the corporation would always reduce its capitalization to the maximum, which would be worth par. It is a satisfactory argument against this to say : what would prevent the corporation from so reducing its capitalization as that, though assessed at par, it would really be worth three or four for one ? It would therefore be found better to assess all at as near its current selling value as could be ascertained.

In the case of the largest corporation (which would be the most important and contain the greatest number of shareholders) the monthly average would afford a very good criterion, and in most cases there would be very little difficulty. The collectors and individuals could usually arrive at a very fair conclusion, both for the government and the individual. In case, however, all efforts at determining the value should fail—that is, in case they could not agree, the government should have a right to demand of the company, say, one per cent. of its securities, and the company would of course obtain these by calling them in from the individual holder. These securities the collectors could offer for sale on the open markets after proper advertising, paying, as a matter of course, the proceeds thereof back to the corporation; but the price they brought should be the rate at which all individuals in that corporation should be assessed during that annual payment. The government would take no note of incomes. If the holder of property received none, that would be his own misfortune and not the government's charge, and if he received forty per cent. on a property that could only properly be assessed at par, that would be the individual's and not the government's gain. All it would want would be its revenue on the cumulative basis. If property did not pay, such as vacant city lots and the like, that would not be the government's business, and the individual could sell them and invest in something else. Taxation on incomes has been tried (not cumulatively, however), and it does not work.

It is difficult to ascertain at all times and from all property just what the income is; but it is not difficult to ascertain that a man has property, and whether it brings in an income or not alters not its liability to the cumulative tax. If it continuously paid no revenue, in the natural course of things the value would decline, unless it was caused to advance by increasing demand, as city lots or suburban farms or any other class of property. The cumulative feature would be the essence of the whole thing any way, and it would be imposed on property direct, because property should pay its tax. With greater complication and less certainty of result it might be placed upon incomes; but it matters not how the cumulative rate is applied, it would work the same result under all possible conditions; why, therefore, should the gov-

10

ernment bother about incomes, which are an incident to
property and dependent much upon its management and
control, when it could effect the same, in fact a better,
result from the property direct on the assumption (which
is just) that if it does not yield income, it should.   The
point now is also raised that, since corporations would
not be called upon to account to the government nor be
in any way subjected to the cumulative tax, all business would drift into corporations, and there would be
no tax collected.

Corporations could only be organized by five or more,
and in some States by not less than eleven men or more,
and of course be they five, eleven, or eleven hundred,
they would be obliged to account to the collector as
individuals.

There would be no difficulty in regulating the system ;
it is not of course as simple as simply taxing the land
only, but its votaries will likely be men who are not seeking simple things.   On the ground of simplicity and
perhaps of convenience a simple gown might be worn
made of sufficiently thick material to protect us from
the wind, but society likes a little more complication.
The advocates of a more equitable distribution of the
property of the earth and of stability in government, by
the exclusion from participation in it of the rabble of the
earth, are not seeking simply a simple method of collecting taxes, though all things considered the plan would
prove in fact to be the very simplest ever devised.

All that there would be in it different from what every
county assessor in the land is doing every day would be
simply to get the whole of a man's estate together and
have the tax paid to one collector so that the cumulative
rate could take effect.

The requirements of the general government, relieved

from extravagance, are now about $300,000,000 an-
nually ; but notwithstanding the increase in population, the decrease in the public indebtedness, and the
curtailment of the useless, unwarranted, and unreasona
ble pension lists, and, above all, by reason of the curtailment of the ballot and the betterment of the management
of public affairs consequent thereon, the annual expenditure can be very much curtailed. Almost wasteful extravagance and prodigal expenditure can be nevertheless
indulged in as to the improvement of inland waterways
(which the general government controls), the erection of
coast defences and similar public improvement, also the
construction of a navy, which may soon be more necessary than heretofore, by reason of the eventual acquisition
of almost all the Greater Antilles and many islands in the
Pacific Ocean ; yet even with all this, $300,000,000
per year should be ample, and may exceed the average.

It is clear that $300,000,000 could be obtained on the
basis of $61,000,000,000 of property (which is less than the
census return of 1890) by the imposition of the exceedingly small levy of but five dollars on the thousand, or
fifty cents on the hundred of property valuation.

It may be, however, that the cumulative rate of itself
would not equal that figure. It would require an estate
of just half a million dollars to create a rate of five
dollars per thousand, and it is evident that the average
estates of the people generally would not reach that
figure, notwithstanding the vast excess of a comparatively few. The vast majority of the public who would
be owners at all would hold property in amounts less
than $100,000, so that whilst the rich would be obliged
to pay from twenty to forty dollars per thousand, so
many people would pay less than one dollar per thousand, that the average might not be five dollars, thereby

rendering it necessary for the government to impose in addition to the cumulative rate a special uniform levy.

The cumulative rate would be figured first by simply dividing the property by 100,000, or by counting one cent for every thousand of the aggregate, then to this would be added any special rate that might be fixed. Of course the direct levy might never be needed, and it would be variable as the wants of the government would require, but the cumulative rate would be identically and essentially the same, and would have always to be counted first. For example, if an estate aggregated $100,000, that individual's cumulative rate would be only one dollar per thousand, whereas if an estate aggregated $1,000,000, his cumulative rate would be ten dollars per thousand as against the other man's one dollar per thousand.

When any estate reached five million dollars, then the rate cumulative would be fifty dollars per thousand, or just five per cent. interest, which would make this an unprofitable estate, at least less so than if it had been three or four instead of five million dollars. There would be no evading the cumulative rate except to secrete the property, and this would be desired only by the rich, and they would fear the severe but just and proper penalty. It would work like unto a governor on an engine; it would start her when she was slow by opening the throttle, and stop her when she was fast by closing it. There is no property whatever that should be made exempt from the cumulative tax, not even government bonds, but the government might, if it chose, relieve its bonds from any special levy that it found necessary to impose on other property; but it should be made an express condition that all property should be subject to this cumulative tax, without any power anywhere to remove it other than by a total abolition of the fundamental law that created it. This would, of course, be necessary, for otherwise some large capitalists would evade the cumulative rate by buying up that class of property that was exempt ; hence none should be exempt. Municipalities might exempt their bonds from city tax, but there should exist nowhere any power, except by the abrogation of the amendment itself, to relieve any property from the cumulative tax.

The very origin and essence of the system of regulating the extremes of society pre-supposes its application to everything, otherwise its utility would be nil. Of the many who have written on the subject of political economy, all have given ideas more or less valuable, as to the best manner of securing wealth, both individual and national, but none as yet have invented a feasible system for *equitable distribution.*

To give to one man, or to permit such conditions to exist in society as will enable one man, which is the same thing in effect, to amass a fortune ridiculous and monstrous in its magnitude, is not an equitable distribution even to that man as an individual. It is not the result of his own genius, it is not required as a reward for his genius if it is the result thereof, and hence is useless and unnecessary ; and, to permit it to exist whilst our eyes are confronted with an astonishing mass of human wretchedness and woe, it is not surprising that some have thought, as did Hobbes, that "hostility is the natural bent of man, both to things around him and to his own kind."

And that others, as did Rousseau, "that the savage life is far preferable to the most enlightened civilization"; that it would be better that all should breathe the foul air in the gloom of a cave, than that a few should luxuriate in splendor in the palaces of kings and others in their very shadow die of wretchedness, squalor, and starvation. Cicero, in substance, compared the world to a theatre which is common to the public, and yet the place that any man has taken is for the time his own. Assuming, however, that what a man has is his own, it is proper that he should control and enjoy that (his own) to within a reasonable limit ; but since everybody admits that all men must, as in a civilized state all men do, sacrifice a modicum of their individual liberty for the well-being of society, why should they not likewise sacrifice their unnecessary accumulations for the same beneficent purpose ; and since one man is not better able to sacrifice liberty than another, but is able to sacrifice property better than another, why should he not thus sacrifice ?

The man or party that seeks to completely eradicate poverty will find his task abortive and impracticable, if, in fact, it is not wrong. " The poor ye have always with you," means more than it says. The poor ye *must* have always with you is, or to the extent that any man has ever been able to prove to the contrary, as natural a condition as to breathe air or to drink water. Its rigors, its wretchedness, and its horrors can be and should be mitigated, but there is no possible scheme consistent with man's right to the fruit of his labor, by which it can be *absolutely removed.* " Things without remedy should be without regard." " Why, therefore, should we fools of nature thus shake our disposition with thoughts beyond the reaches of our souls ?" Yet it is perhaps as well that all vanities should have their votaries, all fads and phantomnations their followers. Discussion does no harm, for it only kills the phantomnation quicker than 't would die of inanition.

" The world is still deceived with ornament ;
In law, what plea so tainted and corrupt,
But, being seasoned with a gracious voice,
Obscures the show of evil? In religion,
What damned error, but some sober brow
Will bless it, and approve it with a text,
Hiding its grossness with fair ornament?
There is no vice so simple, but assumes
Some mark of virtue on his outward parts.
How many cowards, whose hearts are all as false
As stairs of sand, wear yet upon their chins
The beards of Hercules, and frowning Mars ;
Who, inward search'd, have livers white as milk ?
And these assume but valours excrement
To render them redoubted.   Look on beauty
And you shall see 't is purchased by the weight ;
Which therein works a miracle in nature,
Making them lightest that wear most of it.
Thus ornament is but a guilded shore
To a most dangerous sea ; the beauteous scarf
Veiling an Indian beauty : in a word,
The seeming truth which cunning times put on
To entrap the wisest."

Between the point of greatest poverty and that of
greatest wealth there is a wide gulf, a great chasm, but
it can and may be partially removed. No individual
should soar too high, and none, if he but exert himself to
an extent slightly beyond that required to breathe, can
sink too low, unless by a combination of extraordinarily
adverse conditions he is forced there, and if so, and his
case is worthy, he is now provided for in an asylum or a
house for the helpless and infirm.

But to further inquire into the practical results of the
application of the cumulative tax. Foreign investment
in America has been very great, and in many cases very
remunerative. It will be urged as an objection to the

system that British gold would be withdrawn, and properties would be thrown upon the market, and widespread
confusion and dismay would prevail in all branches of
business.

The Briton, as an individual, would stand the same
before the law as an American as an individual. The
foreign holders of property of all kinds would simply
be reported to the collector in New York, who would be
the only one of the whole list appointed by the President, and the rate for their holdings would be made up
in the same manner. Not only would it not in any sense
deter foreign investment, but it would actually encourage
the same for the reason that the administration of affairs
would be more perfect, greater security and protection
would be assured, and the whole thing be made more
satisfactory. America can get along without such foreign investors as this system would hinder, but it would
hinder none.

Even England herself would doubtless begin to devise
ways and means looking to the adoption of the same
system, but such are the characteristics of her people,
such the reverence for their ancient and honorable institutions, that even though most of her prominent men
should acknowledge its justice and its benefits to the
state, yet it would take possibly centuries to introduce it
though it should have worked well in America. There
would be no difficulty experienced in making the assessments, and a list of those who paid taxes would be
recorded on the books of the collector, together with
their address, which list would be accessible to everybody—to the commercial agency man in completing his
books, to the merchant and tradesman in general in the
extension of credits ; to all it would be of incalculable
value, and all free to the public. It would be about the

best possible criterion as to a man's actual wealth, for the reason that errors would always be on the safe side. When the rate increases as the property increases, there is a double force applied against the tax-paying citizen, who under no circulations could afford to unduly misrepresent his holdings. *Furthermore, everything that he owned would be found listed in the place where he lived*— a valuable aid to business men.

In making up a list the collector, through his subordinates, would canvass the district, and using the same means as are now employed in regular assessments, first put down all country real estate, then city property, then securities which, if in corporations existing in his districts, would be reported by the companies, or if remote, then by the collector of the district in which they were located, together with any other kind or class of property in said district. The individual would present his list, and when compared with that aggregated by the collector through his various avenues of information, if all things tallied, the collector would simply divide the whole by one hundred thousand, and say to the individual : "Your cumulative rate for this half year is thus and so, plus any special levy of, blank, dollars per thousand, making a total of, blank, dollars per thousand, which you will pay over to the cashier."

This would be simplicity simplified, and more and better justice would be done and excesses absolutely destroyed. The greatest confusion would exist in the first application of the system in the city of New York, where the question of excess would be most frequent. Here, however, there would be a number of collectors, as many as the city had representatives in Congress ; and since many corporations, though organized under the laws of other States, for convenience and profit maintained offices in New York, they would be obliged to make returns in that city, and ere long things would work smoothly.

The corporation should designate some place as its principal office, and whether its principal mercantile business was transacted there or not, there would be the place where it would make its report to its resident collector, who, in turn, would be obliged to make a report to the collector in other districts, stating the names, residence, and amount of any stock- or bondholder of this company, whose office was in his district.

It is no argument against the system to say that, notwithstanding its completeness, some property would be secreted, more than it would be an argument against the internal revenue system on spirituous and malt liquors to say that at times some illicit distillations are discovered ; but, on the contrary, the increasing feature of the cumulative rate would compensate the government for any evasion that might occur, and the individual, though perhaps in a few cases successful in evading, would nevertheless be subjected to the increasing rate, which has never hitherto been made available as an offset against withholding property from assessment.

To all those who say in effect, " Oh, they will evade the rate." ; " It can be evaded," etc., etc., it may be answered that if but poorly enforced it would be better than if not done at all, and even then would be the most just and equitable and least burthensome tax on earth ; but it would be a strange admission upon the part of an American citizen, and a sad commentary on our institutions, to say that the whole force and power of his government on the side of law, and for its rigorous and impartial enforcement in strict conformity with both its spirit and letter, would not be equal to the force and power of a few rich individuals in their personal efforts to defy it. Such forbodings give no concern, as of right they should not, for if so then all law is useless, a condition Americans are not prepared to admit. As stated, it cannot be definitely ascertained just the exact number of estates, nor the amounts held by each individual, nor can an approximation be made that any one could guarantee to be in any degree accurate, so that the people who are asked to support the amendment can only be assured that the cumulative rate would not likely average more than five dollars on each thousand (possibly not that), and that the government might be required to make a special levy to make good a deficiency. It is almost certain, however, that fully half of the property of the United States is now owned by people possessing estates that will average two million dollars, ranging, say, from one million to two hundred millions, and since under the cumulative system, after providing for local taxation, an estate of over three or four million would yield no revenue on a five per cent. basis, and that three million would yield about the same as four, it is a fair presumption that this maximum would be the limit of any individual's wealth. Therefore, if, as this estimate indicates, one half the whole property of the country is now owned by fifteen thousand (15,000) individuals, averaging two million each, and if, as a result of the cumulative system, no individual could own more than four million dollars and retain for himself much net revenue, and if, furthermore, as appears most probable, the hundred millionaires would distribute their property to their friends in lots of certainly not more than three millions each, rather than have their excess forfeited to the State, then the said half of all the property in the country would be divided into lots certainly

not exceeding one million on the average, instead of two-
million average as before. The whole assessment in 1890
being nearly sixty-five billion, the half would, in round
numbers, be at least thirty billion, which amount in one-
million-dollar estates would make the number owning
half, only thirty thousand. It is not unreasonable to say
that half the property of the country might still be owned
by persons holding estates averaging one million, on
which basis thirty thousand people would own half the
property of the country, instead of fifteen thousand as
now, and they could better afford to pay their allotment
of tax than the vast popular throng, as numerous as they
would be, could afford to pay theirs. A million-dollar
estate would yield at five per cent. the net annual income
of fifty thousand dollars, equal to the salary of the President of the United States; it would pay in taxation a
cumulative rate of ten dollars per thousand, to which
add about one per cent. or ten dollars per thousand more
for local levy (to which minimum it can be reduced by
good administration and the avoidance of secretiveness),
and the total would be, say, two per cent., or twenty
thousand dollars per year, which would leave the owner
a net revenue of thirty thousand per year, enough for
any ordinary man.

To him who had an estate of three million dollars, the
net result would be but very little greater. The three-
million man would have an income, at five per cent., of
one hundred and fifty thousand per year, and his rate
would, all told, be about four per cent. (three cumulative
and one local), making an outgo of about one hundred
and twenty thousand, leaving the net result the same, or
very little different. If the estate should yield six per
cent., the net income would be sixty thousand dollars
per year. But to illustrate the respective burden on the

people of the cumulative system, as compared with the present methods, we assume :

A man whose estate is such as to leave him after paying all taxes from ten to seventy-five thousand dollars per year, has enough. If his gross income is fifty thousand, he could better afford to pay twenty-five thousand in taxes than the man whose gross income is but one thousand could afford to pay one hundred in taxes, or, in other words, the one could pay fifty per cent. better and easier than the other could pay ten per cent., just because he is that much better able to pay than the last-named man.

Therefore, if out of the entire property of the country half would still be owned by thirty thousand men, or about one four-hundredths part of the present voting population, nearly all the burden would be placed on these few individuals who could easily pay it, and yet have much and to spare, and scarcely any would be placed on the mass of the population, because the rate of the thirty thousand, or one-million-dollar estates, would be ten dollars for the general government, and that of the remaining taxpayers, whose estates would scarcely average ten thousand dollars, would be but ten cents per thousand. The number of individuals who would pay the other half cannot be exactly ascertained, but under the equitable method of distribution which the system would guarantee it is certainly a safe estimate to say that there would be one hundred times as many men owning estates of one thousand and upward, averaging, say, ten thousand dollars, as there would be owning estates averaging one million dollars. This would make a total tax-paying population of thirty thousand individuals on the side of one-million-dollar average who would pay nearly all the tax (because of their higher rate), and

three million on the side of the ten-thousand average
who would pay very little on account of their lower rate,
or a total of three million and thirty thousand tax-paying
individuals, which would leave about two thirds the entire adult male population of the country without property, and, consequently, not contributors nor voters at
all.   Thus we have one four-hundredth part paying
nearly all, and about one third part paying scarcely any
tax, placing no burden whatever upon the non-taxpayer,
or on the man who works for hire at a certain per diem,
whilst under the protective tariff system these conditions
are just about reversed.

The popular throng who labor by the day must have
clothing, blankets, knives, forks, spoons, and house-
hold furniture, every one of which are necessaries of
life, and pay tax from forty to one hundred per cent.
ad valorem, so that estimating only the consumption of
the necessaries of life, *that two thirds* of the population
which under the cumulative plan are entirely exempt
pay under the the protective plan nearly all of the total
tax ; or, in other words, under the cumulative plan they
pay nothing, and under the protective plan they pay
annually about three hundred million dollars, and yet
that monstrosity is called "protection to labor."   A
grander misnomer than its title was never invented in
human nomenclature, and a more pernicious and dam-
nable heresy was never practised by a nation.   The
leaders of the Democratic party in America really believe this very assertion to be true, but they are afraid to
say so, afraid to say anything for many years, except
that protection is a good thing, but the country needed
less of that good thing—a position both timorous and
ridiculous and utterly indefensible.

They are afraid even to say in their platforms that

the Constitution of the United States does not authorize, nor ever intended, that any tax of any kind should ever be levied by Congress save solely and exclusively for revenue. To admit that that instrument authorizes taxes for other purposes would be to say that the government might collect money from the people for the purpose of distributing it again among the States for the education of some of the voting apes of Mississippi and South Carolina, a proposition to which effect actually was introduced in Congress, and it is said that the proposer actually was not tried at once for lunacy—a remnant of history still more surprising.

If, therefore, to the non-property-holding class, of fully two thirds the voting population, there is a saving of three hundred millions or thereabouts per annum, which amounts to almost forty dollars per head, and that nearly all that entire amount can, by the cumulative tax, be collected from about thirty thousand million-aires and the small remainder from three million men who would contribute only from one to about one hundred dollars per year, each in proportion to his ability, there remains no question as to the lightness of the burden as compared with the so-called "protective," or other revenue systems.

30,000 estates averaging $1,000,000 equals $30,000,000,000
    rate $10.00 per thousand, equals........... 300,000,000
3,000,000 estates averaging $10,000 equals 30,000,000,000
    rate 10 cents per thousand, equals 3,000,000
         Total amount collected..... $303,000,000

It certainly cannot be denied that the proper source from which to obtain all revenue is that which is least burdensome to the people and most certain to the government, and that the cumulative plan is the least burdensome has certainly been shown, if in fact the proposition needs any argument or elucidation. Even the rankest protectionists are obliged to admit that any scheme that obtains revenue for the government from the excessive accumulations of property is the best scheme, but they claim that its operation would be more unjust to the few who are rich than the protective policy has been to the many who are poor. This is about as forcible as the arguments of protectionists in general usually are, and it is simply answered by the statement, " Well, let it be so "; the masses in whose interest we are trying to legislate will, we hope, not severely complain at this so-called discrimination *against* the rich, who have been discriminated "*for*" since the date of man's first reign on earth, and turn about is fair play. It will at first startle the one- and two-hundred millionaires when they are brought into the full realization of the fact that they can no longer safely hold more than four or five millions of property. " My ! " some will say, " it costs us from one to two hundred thousand dollars per year to live." " Well," it is answered, " if you continue at that rate it won't be many years before four or five millions will appear to you as large a sum as it now appears small. Still you can consume a million a year in living expenses if you desire. So much the better for the butcher, the baker, and the candlestick-maker." If there never had been a man worth over three or four million dollars and never had existed such monstrous individual estates, nevertheless the cumulative plan would still be justifiable and the best possible system of taxation, even though it accomplished nothing more than collecting revenue for the support of government from the man who is best able to pay it, rather than from him who is least able to pay, as is the practical effect of

all other systems ; but accomplishing both and in a
manner (through the corporation) that still gives to
civilization full opportunity to progress, there is no
question as to its justness. The reasoning class has
reached the conclusion that there can be no equal distribution of property ; that such, figure it as you may,
is not the natural condition of things and cannot be
caused to exist by legislation, *but present conditions can be
improved.*

The property of America, in 1890, being about $1.000
per head, if distributed would have given each man,
woman, and child that amount of money, which would
doubtless have resulted in one grand drunken revel for
about ten days upon the part of about two thirds the
population, at the end of which time the other third
would have possessed it all, and ere long individuals of
that third by energy, tact, shrewdness, and good luck—
the latter no inconsiderable factor in the game—would
have grown richer and richer and the other poorer and
poorer till practically the same condition would exist as
that which the division sought to remedy.   Not only by
reason of the full appreciation of the truth of the statement, that in practice an equal division could not be, is
the idea abandoned, but also from a more or at least
equally cogent one, to wit : that if it could *it should not
be*, because there must exist gradations in society.   Men
are not all alike : some will work harder and save more,
and these are entitled to what they possess to a reasonable degree ; others will do less work and save less, and
those must bide the results to a reasonable degree.   That
reasonable degree with the former is a just compensation,
which three or four million is considered to be : with the
latter, the pangs of poverty, till, by reason of his utter
dependence, the state sends him to the poorhouse, *and*

11

*how can it be avoided whilst the earth turns as it now turns,
or rather while we are what we are ?*

Even if men were absolutely equal, there are ten
thousand occurrences in life that will put some behind
in the race with their fellows ; for example, he might break
a leg or lose both eyes, and leaving the nine thousand
nine hundred and ninety-eight to be imagined, we proceed to say what has never yet been thoroughly appreciated.

*By reason of these inequalities (whether they be natural
or forced by circumstances, they exist) laws should be made
which bear unequally—though not unjustly,—and such a
law is " cumulative taxation," or rather " the conservative amendment,"* and the method of its adoption is
clear, plain, and simple, and is in strict accordance
with the terms set forth in the American Federal Constitution.

Applying itself as it would most severely on the accumulations of capital, and least severely, in fact almost
inappreciably, to the possessors of average estates, and
wholly exempting those having no estates at all, it
would certainly be the least burdensome of any system
yet devised. Those favoring a taxation for protection
could in this plan find such as would be genuine and
real, but protecting the masses and not the classes, the
poor and not the rich.

It may be urged as an objection that corporations could
diminish their dividends, hence depreciate their stock, by
paying unreasonably high salaries to parties in interest.
To this it may be replied that they could not afford to
pay to many over $5,000 per year, which would be a
fair distribution; but those who, in any avocation, receive
over $5,000 can be subjected to taxation the same as
if they acquired their income from property ; that is, a

man getting $50,000 per year could be obliged to pay $10,000, which would be the cumulative levy on one million, on which $50,000 is the income. Those receiving salaries high enough to be worthy of notice could easily be ascertained by the assessor, hence this objection is not vital. If 60,000 instead of 30,000 people should own half the property of the country, their estates would average half a million dollars each, and their cumulative rate would be $5 per thousand, which would produce a revenue of $150,000,000 or half the amount required for the support of the government, the other half coming from perhaps 4,000,000 people in small amounts, leaving all others free. Why should such a system be opposed on account of "inquisitorial scrutiny." Let estates be scrutinized and taxed, otherwise let them be *not* lawfully possessed.

CHAPTER VIII.

How it may be accomplished—Hundred millionaires fatal to small investors—But great corporations, if owned by many, cause no harm—Great concentration of wealth necessary to promote enterprise—Power of Congress to impose the cumulative tax—No great difference between existing parties affecting fundamental principles involved—North Western Granger States and the solid South should join hands—Will settle the negro question in the South —Cumulative tax will lighten the burden on the South and West, and qualified suffrage will increase their proportionate vote and power—Will decrease country vote less than city vote— Granger States begin to see the folly of protection and value of Cumulative Taxation and Qualified Suffrage—Over four million farm owners in 1890, three fourths of whom will support the proposition—This added to conservative city vote is sufficient for success—States that first may support it—Others that may follow.

As has been said, the principal opposition to the creed represented by " Phronocracy" will not be found to exist among the hundred millionaires, who, even if so, are comparatively few, and the force of their money will aid but little the prolongation of existing conditions for the reason that measures of a direct and tangible bearing would be before the people, and they will be urged and supported by citizens above the slums of political prostitution and vice—such as are approachable only by appeals to their inherent manhood and honesty, and whose devotion to the cause will be so sincere that it cannot be shaken by the tempting entreaties of glittering gold. Of course there will be very many who will say, "Oh, yes, it is a good thing, *but it can't be done.*" Then nothing can be done, for nothing else should be done. Society needs a regulator and that is all it needs. *But it can be done.* All property is sufficiently known to properly distribute dividends, why not to *properly apply taxation?* The question is *should it be done?* If conservative citizens say aye—'t is done.

Really, the apparent difficulty of bringing it actually to be is about the only argument against it that cannot be answered without the least possible difficulty. No man can urge for an instant that a more general distribution of wealth would not be of benefit to society, if for no other reason than that it would rob individuals who had amassed their fortunes by the increments of society of a vast and dangerous power for evil against society. A few men possessing all the world's wealth with the means at hand to use it, as is always the case in any law-abiding community, could be as productive of commercial harm as the anarchists, who could with torch and axe make wild sport of society's richest thrones.

No one doubts that if the anarchist had all power he could, for a time at least, that is, as long as his power lasted, create havoc in any systems of social order ; so likewise is it within the power of a man, who has by the increments of society grown inordinately rich, to create anarchistic havoc in the commercial world. He can not only corrupt legislation and judges, but such is the force of his momentum and wealth that he can crush out honest opposition, and if by force he can crush out opposition he could undoubtedly cause to exist in the field of his conquests, or among the people of whom he was in this respect supreme lord, a condition more oppressive to their interests, more in conflict with their inalienable rights to the pursuit of happiness, than that which ever could exist in a state of healthy competition, or in enterprises naturally competitive. All business is being rapidly concentrated into large trusts and syndicates and from causes perfectly in consonance with existing conditions.

Increased wealth, as has been stated, renders possible the acquirement of increased facility, and increased facility greatly cheapens production, and increased cheapness in production results inevitably in one of two things (usually one of them); viz., that the price of the commodity is cheaper (seldom the case), or that the profits to the producers are larger (nearly always the case). These combinations are not made for the love of the people nor in order that the increased facility and cheapness in production that they guarantee will lessen the people's price, but always either to advance that price or make available the increased profit that will result in the maintenance of same, which can be done when, by reason of combination, the small competitor has been shut out. The greatest political heads of the day recognize this evil and seek to avert it by prohibitive legislation. Bills are introduced into the United States Senate looking to the abrogation of trusts or declaring their formation illegal, thus acknowledging a wrong state or condition of affairs somewhere ; but these acts fail to act. To say virtually that men cannot enter into partnerships (which virtually trusts are, and can casually be formed in the face of all law, on this pretext) is in fact an interference with personal rights, which, if thoroughly tested, it is very questionable if Congress or any other legislative body can do. Furthermore, notwithstanding the universally recognized evil consequent upon this concentration or centralization, there is yet a view that can be taken of it, which not only does not present the appearance of evil, but of actual benefit and good, to wit : where concentration aids excellence and efficiency in output, and yet maintains the price or lessens it, as has been done in a way that cannot otherwise be secured. No man can deny that the large wagon factories of America (some of which have grown so enormous that they can produce several hundred complete vehicles in a day) can produce and sell a better wagon for the same money than could possibly hitherto have been bought from the country cross-road wagon-maker and black-smith,—all consequent upon wealth, and the increased facility that it insures. This of course effectually ruins the cross-road wagon-maker save for little odd jobs of repair. Then, again, there are many enterprises that cannot be carried out save by great concentrated capital. For example, if in America no bridge-building establishment had acquired the ability and facility to construct a bridge like that spanning the Firth of Forth in Scotland either as to magnitude or in a reasonable time, what reason would there be in saying that four or five of the largest establishments could not at once combine together and be thus enabled to accomplish the same both in the magnitude of the trusses and other parts required and within a reasonable time ? In this would simply have resulted in a short time the establishment of a single bridge-building company, into which any one might have grown in a long time, and why seek to delay progress in that way ? Why say men shall not go into partnership when by so doing they may not only increase facility, but accomplish works perhaps otherwise impossible, or at least otherwise long delayed. The plan to pursue is (after everything has been tried) that of permitting corporate enterprise to grow and expand to any limit, but to see that one individual can not get it all. Well, we will look for a time into the manner of its doing ; that is, how the scheme could be made law,—how the amend-ment authorizing it could be carried.

Whilst it is thought proper to support an amendment to the Constitution distinctly authorizing such a tax to be levied, and voting qualification to be made, this step is taken directly in the face of much good advice as to the lack of necessity for anything, other or more than a majority in both houses of Congress and the President's consent ; still, to avoid the possibility of subse-quent litigation, and in view of the fact that the effect of its adoption would be so universal and widespread, it is thought best to begin the foundation of the edifice on the rocks beneath, and then its stability would be as-sured.

Many hold that Congress has the right to collect revenue for its support and from any source whatever, and that a levy per thousand of the one hundred thou-sandth part of every man's estate does not lack uni-formity; that it applies to all alike and, if not lacking in uniformity, there can be no possible ground for urging against it the objection of unconstitutionality.

Others claim, too, and forcibly, that it is time to look into the passage of an amendment granting explicit power when the right of levy and collection has been questioned and the case taken to the Supreme Court, and that pending any decision of that august body the working effects of the system might to a certain degree be tested, and if impracticable or baneful it could be abolished, and if not unconstitutional no amendment would be necessary, and that the entire test both as to its practical application and constitutionality could be made in half the time required to adopt the amendment, if, in fact, the sanction of the requisite number of State legislators and delegates of States in Congress ever can be secured.

These views are weighty and of much effect ; however, conservatism is the thing, and it is thought best to put forward the proposition for an amendment first, for in this way the popular pulse can be felt and its temper sounded ; it can be explained and discussed, and the people can become familiar with its provisions and revolve in their minds questions as to its probable effect.

There exists in the American Union, when all territories of the right political complexion—that is, all in which the population (whether sparse or great) are supposed to favor protection and the duty on wool and some other articles—had been admitted, and all, whether their populations are great or sparse, of the wrong political complexion—that is, such as are supposed to favor free wool and a little less duty on the other articles,—had been refused admittance, *just forty-four sovereign States.* The great Republican organization has stood for wool duty · and high rates on other articles, and the great Democratic organization (whose leaders are for free trade in principle and also in practice at the soonest possible day, and believe in a direct aim at the game, but are afraid to say so) has stood for free wool and a little less duty on other articles, and this, in fact, has been about the only difference between the parties, and words and phrases have been marshalled in every way to convince the country that much or a little less protection is just the thing, according as the orator is a Republican or a Democrat.

The whole tariff bill, or all the tariff bills that have been prepared, and all the speeches pro and con on each side might have been tossed up in the air, and a sword in the hands of an expert prestidigitator thrust through any one of the flying documents, and that one might have been passed with about the same average harm (not good, for they were all protective) to the country as that proposed by the able chairman of the Ways and Means Committee of the then dominant party in Congress.

However, there were, say, in 1890, forty-four sovereign States in the American Union, and others to follow when their politics, not their populations, are right. To pass an amendment to the Federal Constitution, it would require the sanction of the legislatures of thirty-three of these sovereign States, or, say, of all but of eleven, and of two thirds of their delegations in Congress, or thirty delegations.

This appears to be quite a formidable array, and rather tends to encourage the adoption of the plan that aims at the passage of a bill in Congress in the usual way, and leaving the matter, if contested, to the determination, as to constitutionality, to the Federal Supreme Court, meanwhile giving opportunity for a practical test as to the desirableness and efficacy of the measure.

There is an old adage that "politics makes strange bedfellows," and so it may appear in this desired reformation.

Hitherto the so-called Granger States have steadfastly supported the protectionist party, more by reason of prejudice and of recollection of the bloody days of the early sixties than from motives of self-interest or principle, and these, together with the manufacturing States of New England and the East, have been the unfaltering supporters of the Republican organization.

The Democratic or the would-be-if-it-dared to-be free-trade party has for years possessed no possible chance for political ascendancy save from the solid South (made so partly by reason of recollections of the war, but mainly so by the universal hostility of the whites to the domination of the blacks—the former owning practically all the property and the latter owning nothing), together with the city of New York, which frequently controlled the electoral votes of the State of New York and one or two States adjoining. It has been a constant source of vexation to the great Granger States of the North and West that the solid South, against which they cherished the lingering animosities incident to the war, should be able, with the foreign population of the city of New York, to occasionally control presidential elections. The senile and relentless press of the North, ever seeking to perpetuate these lingering animosities and to fan into flame the smouldering embers of sectional hate, is constantly heralding to the people the false assertion that the South is solid because it wishes to secure possession of the Federal Government, and when so possessed it would strike every vestige of war legislation from the statute book, re-enslave the negro, or compensate the former master to the extent of untold millions, also pay Confederate war claims, and pension Confederate soldiers ; in a word, bankrupt the nation, if such a thing was possible, to reinstate that condition of affairs which they had suppressed by the loss of blood and treasure in the ghastly throes of civil war. Not once is it admitted that the South, though of course keenly mindful of the loss of property and life, has accepted the inevitable and by every word and act has signified its inflexible purpose to stand by the nation in its entirety, and whilst they have no tears to shed except over the graves of departed comrades, and no apologies to offer for having engaged in what they considered an honorable and justifiable endeavor to procure their rights under the terms of the then existing Constitution, these States are now a part and parcel of a great nation and seek not to mar its glory by internecine strife or revolutionary legislation ; but they *can not* and *will*

not submit to negro domination ; they will not consent to
be governed by their former slaves. The general government may usurp all constitutional authority and trans-
cend the rightful limitation of its delegated power by
passing laws providing for supervisors of elections,
force bills, backed by bayonets at the polls,—and yet,
and notwithstanding all these and more, for the protection of their lives, their wives, their children, and their
property, they will never fail to exercise the most strenuous lawful effort and persistent ceaseless vigil against all
federal interference of any kind whatsoever in any form
suggested, before they will ever yield control to the
negroes, whose enfranchisement in their candid opinion
was a travesty on free institutions, a blight on the
national escutcheon, and a grim blot which, like the
blood-stained hands of guilty Macbeth, all ocean's
waters can never wash out. In this sentiment many
northern people concur and hope to see the condition
altered. Hence the Granger States and the South, which
by motives of natural interest should have been together,
have been kept widely apart.

Each section is to a great extent agricultural, and naturally each should have been, as the South always was,
hostile to legislation which protected the manufacturers
of the East and enabled them to monopolize the markets,
whilst their own products for sale were placed in direct
competition with those of the civilized world, a condition
to which they would not object, provided they were
likewise permitted to *buy* in the competitive markets
of the civilized world, which they are not. In these
respects, which are the only living issues in politics, the
South and the Granger States are about equally conditioned and why should they not act in concord and harmony ? *Because* and only because of war prejudices. It

requires some stronger incentive than that which has hitherto existed to overcome it, and in the proposition of the proposed amendment that incentive is found. That proposition covers essentially, what?

1st. Free trade as soon as it can be "conservatively" applied, looking only to the avoidance of revolutionary changes. To this the sentiment of the people of most of the Southern States have always been friendly, and to it all candid and unprejudiced minds admit that the Granger States should be friendly.

2d. It proposes that excessive individual accumulation shall be curtailed and that the revenue for the support of the government shall, in the main, come from that source.

To this proposition the South is disposed to be friendly, recognizing, as it does, first, that the plan is just, practical, and secure, and, secondly,—and by greater reason,—self-interest consequent upon the fact that most of the excessive individual accumulations are in New England and the East where protection has worked its natural results, and that naturally the burden would fall heaviest there. In this there would likewise be great relief for the Granger States of the West, and great sympathy should exist for the system occasioned by the same identical reasons that operate so extensively in the South.

3d. For the greater reason. The proposition involves the curtailment of suffrage by establishing conditions, to the effect that a man shall both know something and own something before he shall vote. This would strike the entire South like a fall of bliss from heaven, because it would inevitably disfranchise about ninety-nine per cent. of the negro vote of their section and leave uninterrupted control to the whites or property-holding element of the population. The paupers of the South are blacks, and whilst the representation of this section of the Union has been increased by some fifty votes in Congress and in the electoral college by the enfranchisement of the slaves, and notwithstanding the fact that their votes are in one way or another suppressed (as a matter of personal interest and self-preservation) so that they count but little in the control of affairs, nevertheless the South is not only willing but anxious to accept some proposition that will. deprive the negro of the right of suffrage,—to which he was never entitled and of which he was never worthy,—especially if that proposition looks to the disfranchisement of an equally irresponsible and unworthy class of foreign paupers and ignoramuses in the North, which would leave the relative condition as to representation in the respective sections practically unchanged. The North has for years been troubled about the negro question. Orators harangue the multitudes about suppression and violence in the South ; they say : " We freed the slave and amnested him, and thought by so doing that our political party would reap the benefit of his suffrage, as we should do ; but lo and behold, we are disappointed, we are betrayed. We have given to the South many additional votes in our national legislature and our electoral college, and these votes are counted against, not for, our candidates, thereby, instead of assuring us in political ascendancy indefinitely, it has been made possible for the South, aided by the foreign population of the city of New York, to control the national government, which was not contemplated by our leaders at the time of the adoption of the Fifteenth Amendment, and had we but vaguely imagined that such a result was possible, we would never have declared that amendment passed, but would

have vigorously opposed it. We would never have
strained our minds and our conscience to declare that
the requisite number of States had adopted it, when there
existed quite a question whether or not some that were
included to make up the complement were actually
members of the Union at the time they were counted.
We did all these things as matters of war necessity, and
to insure party ascendancy, and now our wayward birds
have come home to roost and we know not how to house
them ; or, rather, by reason of the ignorance and utter
bestiality of the negro, he can be led with a halter, terri-
fied by a threat, or controlled by false glamour and
counted against his benefactors.   What can we do ?

"The only means out of our dilemma is to send soldiers or supervisors of election to preserve the peace at
the polls, and this is offensive to our Northern brethren.
We cannot make a law authorizing said governmental
interference applicable to one State and not to another—
if to any it must be to all ; and then there might
appear to be nothing but profound peace at the polls.
The white people of the South may tell the ignorant
negro that he must stay at home on a certain day, and
the negro will seldom know until some weeks afterwards,
if ever, that on the said day there had been an election,
and thus by similar devices his vote can be suppressed
and the objects of it frustrated."

Consequently, many of the Northern States, for the
purpose of settling the negro question only (it appearing
to be of impossible practical settlement otherwise), are
disposed to favor their disfranchisement ; but this could
not be done except by the establishment of some uniform
law or condition that would apply to all, regardless of
race, color, or previous condition of servitude.   In the
North it is more than ordinarily desirable to prevent the

utilization of increased Southern representation, on account of the negro, against the aims, objects, and purposes of the party that freed him, but how can it be done unless he is disfranchised, and how could he be disfranchised unless by some general plan applicable to all the States? *And his vote in the North has been useful.*

The Granger population of all the States have also been very restive under the increasing power, representation, and control of the urban population, which in many of the States is increasing by reason of the discriminating influences of the protective system in favor of factories and against the farms, until it has drawn from the country into the cities much of the previous population. It is plain to all that the curtailment of suffrage as proposed would doubtless disfranchise many men in an overcrowded city, where it would one man in the rural districts, and especially is this true in the Granger States of the North and West, where the rural population is made up principally of owners of small tracts of land sufficient for purposes of eligibility. Even in New York, a State where many of the people reside in cities of a population of 100,000 and over, the farmers (being protectionists by recollection of war traditions and prejudice) could almost always secure a majority in their State Legislature, and of their delegation in Congress, and their United States Senators, but seldom the governors of their State, because in State elections the slums of the city counted as effectually as the counties in the country, and in many cases more numerously.

It is plain that if in the entire State of New York there are one million votes, and that if half were urban and half rural, any law that disfranchised even five urban where it effected one rural, the ruralists would certainly control in everything. For example, if out of 500,000 city votes four fifths were disfranchised (and there are almost this ratio of irresponsibles to honest men), there would remain but 100,000 urban votes ; and if in the rural districts there were disfranchised even half, or even as many as two to five city votes, instead of one to five as appears most reasonable, then there would yet remain 250,000 rural votes, or a large and substantial majority. The city of New York need have no fear in this result from increased "hay-seed" legislation, for the reason that a property-holding "hay-seed" legislator will, when legislating with a property-holding city legislator, enact laws more in conformity with the interests of both than can ever be secured by ignorance, irresponsibility, hoodlumism, and venality ; and the same will be equally true of all cities in every State.

Such figures as these even in their local application, to say nothing of the disposition among the ruralists in the North to settle the negro question forever, may cause New York to tremble in the balance on the question. The entire North, being especially vexed and annoyed at the realization of the fact that the increased vote in the South consequent upon negro suffrage (which fails to "suff") and the loafer and boodler vote of the foreigners in New York City could control presidential elections, or even approach the control of same, and as both these classes are vicious, uneducated, irresponsible and corrupt—the easy prey of their more intelligent managers and bosses,—will begin to think it a good thing on general principles to deprive all of them of their voice.

Especially will this desire be manifested in the Granger States. It would enable the Granger population of these States (in fact of all States, save a few) to control not only the affairs of their own commonwealths as

12

against the irresponsible loafers of the cities, but likewise to insure the electoral and congressional representation safe to their unquestioned majority.

Not only so, but the Granger will begin to see that the
policy of protection to factories has not benefited the
farms ; that the farms have paid most of the taxes and
received none of the benefits ; or, in a word, they have
been the contributors, not the recipients, and in consequence their farms are heavily mortgaged and their corn
is perishing with rot.   Here comes at last a proposition
that will necessarily tax the rich urban millionaire, who
has for about a generation continuously, and at long
intervals before, been receiving all the benefits for which
they (the Grangers) were taxed, and make him pay more
than he had hitherto paid, if, in fact, not one full
moiety of all and half, at least, of the other.   It also
contained a condition that would put into the hands of
the ruralists increased proportionate political power by
the decreased proportionate voting privileges that would
be possible of retention by the cities under the operation
of the law.   Here is both *increased representation and decreased taxation*—both an inevitable result.   Furthermore, it would settle the negro question of the South—
a canker in the flesh of all Northern men and a scar left
from a previous wound in the flesh of all Southerners,
but with them no longer an eating sore.   The latter are
willing to obliterate their scar and relieve the North of
the festering sore, if the North will consent to purge the
nation of its most baleful curse, to wit : *ignorant suffrage
and individual monopoly.*   The Southern States have
nothing to lose, because the disfranchisement would
affect but little the white population of their section,
and since the foreign pauper of the thickly populated
centres of the North would likewise be excluded from

the ballot in about the same numbers as the negroes of
the South, representation in Congress and in the electoral college would not relatively be materially changed:
The South might lose effectually the co-operation of
New York, which has hitherto been retained by the foreign ignoramus in the lower wards, unless, as in the
Northwestern Granger States, the New York farmer
acted on principle, supporting that which caused him
gain rather than, on prejudice, supporting that which
caused him loss. This is a problem which an actual
test alone could determine ; but the Granger States (now
becoming exempt from prejudice against the South) can
make common cause therewith (which both should have
done before), and, had some interest or object arisen
that appealed to judgment with sufficient force to overcome prejudice, would have done so before, and the
result may be astounding. Even those who reasonably
doubt the possibility of ever passing an amendment will
begin to think that the legislation may be secured in
that way. Here comes the solid South—solid for a progressive idea, for something apace with the advancing
thoughts of men. It cannot be urged that the object of
the solidity is the payment of Confederate war claims or
similar monstrosities, any more than it could be said
that the great empire of Western agricultural States
that form the advancing procession have become converted to the idea of re-enslavement and similar heresies.
Long and tedious, however, will be the advance—all
waiting for a considerable part of their own number to
start. Candidates for Congress and for State Legislatures who may espouse the cause at first, can have no
hope of greater success than simply the promulgation of
the creed among the people. Many will, of course, be
beaten and few elected, but in time the light will begin

to dawn.   The need for the reform that is proposed
is becoming greater and greater, the gulf between Dives
and Lazarus is widening, and the corruption in political
practices is more infamous and glaring.   Schemes and
acts looking toward ballot reform are passed but to no
avail, as all partake of the character of that policy which
seeks to purify from the surface a thing that is rotten at
the core.   But after many vicissitudes and varying success, with no deviation whatever from principle, the thing
will begin to spread.   The sheep will begin to jump, and
over will go the entire flock.

It is, then, apparent to all that the difficulties in the
way of the successful eventuations of the proposition are
more to be apprehended by reason of the inability of all
parties to thoroughly understand, than from their refusal
to extend support and sympathy when all is once made
clear.   In other words, there never should exist much
doubt that at least a majority of the voters of the country
would favor the proposition, for, aside from the comparative universality of the sentiments of the Southern
States and people, and the overthrow of anti-bellum
prejudices in the rural or Granger States in the great
Northwest, and the union of these two great producing
sections for the first time since the war for the enactment
of legislation directed to their own and not to the New
England manufacturer's good, the actual figures bearing
upon the subject indicate, if in fact they do not absolutely prove, that the scheme can be carried.   At least
none can deny that the showing is much more favorable
and formidable than would have been at any time supposed.   For instance, there were in 1888 about eleven
million voters in the entire United States, and in 1890,
say, in round numbers, twelve million voters.   There were
in 1890 over four million *farm owners*—not simply ten-

ants and laborers, but *farm owners*—in America. Each one of these, if a male and of age, has one vote, and each one would yet retain his vote under the qualification system, because he owns property. It therefore stands to reason that a large majority of this four million farm owners would vote for a scheme (when they had sifted it in all its bearings) that would *undoubtedly reduce to them the burden of taxation and assure to them increased representation.*

Consequently, if three out of four of these farm owners voted for their own interests, which (now that the era of prejudice has passed) it is but reasonable that they should and would do, eventually three million votes, out of a total of eleven million, could be counted in its favor from this source, and the same proportion of subsequent increases. There would remain eight million votes composed of the reputable classes of all towns and cities, and the disreputable classes of the same. If out of the said eight million there could be relied on as supporters only one fourth the whole number, which is an exceedingly small percentage, this would make two million votes which, added to the three million from the rural sections of the country and from the South and West in general, would make a total of five million voters, or nearly one half the entire voting population.

If from the eight million one third could be secured (a proportion not unreasonable), then these added to the three would make over five million six hundred thousand, or more than half the aggregate vote of the country in 1888. It is clear, therefore, if the matter was taken vigorously in hand, before the evils of Plutocracy have concentrated all wealth into the hands of the few, and curtailed the number of farm owners in the country, which is being rapidly done by the foreclosure of mortgages placed upon rural estates as a natural result of prohibiting tariffs—of the system which forced the farmer to sell in the lowest and buy in the highest markets,—that success would be more than possible even on the first probable affiliation of the people and before the benefits of the system could be fully explained. It would bring together the South and the West, and to this cogent force add the better elements of all towns and cities, and result in the practical disfranchisement of the negro, who is objectionable as a voter to both sections, and also of the loafer, the boodler, and the penitentiary bird, whose participation in the affairs of government is as ridiculous as it is wrong. The Northwestern farmers can, however, never accept the name of "Democracy," be that what it may in principle, for the name to them is odious, and in truth too much "Democracy" is odious to any man. "Phronocracy" will suit them better, and after the provisions of the amendment shall have been discussed until it has become thoroughly familiar to all who care to learn, and after several Congressmen and State legislators have been elected and the Granger States have chosen anti-protectionist senators, it can be formally introduced so as to bring the question up in every district at the succeeding election ; meanwhile candidates for State Legislatures could be supported so as to make it possible to seal the measure by the ratification of the States. First would come the northern States of the South and that part of it that was more thickly populated by the negroes would soon follow, and ere long the senators of some and a number of the congressional delegates of every Southern State would favor the proposition.

There are Virginia, West Virginia, Maryland, Delaware, North Carolina, Kentucky, Tennessee, Alabama, Mississippi, Georgia, Florida, Louisiana, Texas, Arkansas, Missouri, rather a good and grand array of probable enthusiastic supporters, numbering sixteen, which ere long could be relied upon in case the amendment was found necessary. Then would come the Grangers of the Northwest which would likewise be sending to Congress occasional members and electing State legislators favorable to the cause. There are Minnesota, Kansas, Nebraska, Oregon, Iowa, North Dakota, South Dakota, Montana, Washington, Idaho, Wyoming, and California, making twelve (12) additional, or twenty-eight in all, or, when a majority of their delegates were secured, six more than half the total number, with New York, New Jersey, Pennsylvania, Maine, New Hampshire, Vermont, Connecticut, Massachusetts, Ohio, Indiana, Illinois, Michigan, Nevada, Colorado, Wisconsin, and Rhode Island, or sixteen, from which to obtain the requisite number even for the adoption of the amendment if that should be required. The States of Wisconsin and Michigan would soon tremble in the balance, but owing to the relatively greater factory population than exists in the other States of the Northwest they would not as soon be secured, but ere long several of their congressional delegates would be obtained, making in all thirty States, or when solid the number required in the lower house, but several less than the number of State Legislatures. In fact it appears that the full complement of State delegations in Congress could be secured before even a majority of the States could send senators to the upper house favorable to the measure ; this, of course, by reason of the necessary delay required to alter the political complexion of that body. Hence a bill could not receive a majority in the Senate though the House might be able to ratify the amendment.

In States in which the large cities are located and throughout entire New England the necessary majority probably could not be secured. The opposition in Ohio, Indiana, Illinois, and to a great extent in New York and Massachusetts, would come from the dishonest politicians and boodlers who reside there in sufficient numbers to prevent the success of the measure. In New York and Massachusetts, of course, the one-hundred millionaires, or the millionaires from five and upwards, and their functionaries and attachés, would make some impression ; but of this class there are few in Ohio, Indiana, and Illinois, yet in these last named States there exists quite a number of small cities and large towns generally distributed over the whole area, so that there could be no distinct Granger or rural districts as is the case in some of the States of the great Northwest. Little Rhode Island has once enjoyed property qualification and was none the worse therefor, and would doubtless gladly reinstate that part of the proposition, but such is the force of her factories and her mills and the violence of their opposition to the abolition of protection that she would not likely be recorded in the column. Connecticut could not likely secure her Legislature nor a majority of her Congressmen, though the total vote of the State might indicate a considerable element in favor of the proposition. Pennsylvania would perhaps never yield, but Maine would likely surrender. This would make thirty-one States represented in Congress, or, when solid, one more than the necessary two thirds, but by actual estimation of the State Legislatures there would be greater difficulty in securing the necessary three fourths, though when fairly considered, all in all, no man can doubt but that there is *more than a possibility* of securing the adoption of the measure ; in fact, a better preliminary show-

ing than has ever existed for any measure of innovation
and reform, and all that would be required would be to
thoroughly inform the great class of conservative citizens
whose interests undoubtedly lie in the direction of its
adoption.

CHAPTER IX.

SUFFRAGE—a voice, a vote,—what is it, what does it
signify? What is its origin, and why its exercise?

In the beginning, when man's existence was doubtless
confined principally to the tropics, when his needs and
wants were simple, owing to the crude and circumscribed
limit and scope of his intellectual faculties and the
climatic conditions of the country in which he lived,
there was but little required of him save to pick berries
and gather fruit.

Each day provided for itself, and did so reliably and
safely. Hence he could sit calmly under the shades of
the palms, breathe the perfumes of flowers, listen to the
trickling brooks, and the songs of the birds ; in a word,
revel in nature's own, the outcome of its existing energies. Then truly could he "consider the lilies of the
field, how they grow" ; he could see that "they toiled
not neither did they spin" ; and whether more beauti-
fully than one of these "Solomon in all his glory was

ne'er arrayed," it mattered not to this contented individual. He knew not, or at least he had not the faculty
to imagine, how it could be otherwise ; that " sufficient
unto the day was the evil thereof," and that he need
" take no heed of the morrow," or rather he need not
fear want or seek to provide against it. Even that
species of the man animal that lived among the white
bear and the seal could, almost without effort, or rather
about as easily as the tropical man could pick the berries
and the fruit, possess himself of the flesh and fur of the
said native animals in amounts sufficient to supply his
simple wants, for he differed but little in intellectual
scope from them.

So that from nature's abundant storehouse ample
could be obtained at all times, and provision against
want was unnecessary. Why this condition has not
existed always, or rather why to-day it is or why it ever
should have been different, we have not the power or the
province of determining. The fact is that the condition
is different, and we are likewise powerless to cause that
to be which is not, and must take it as it is. Many human beings live on the surface of the earth between
parallels of latitude thirty and sixty, and in this region
of country the natural conditions are such that man has
many and wonderfully diversified wants.

He must obtain shelter in winter or he will die. The
fact is that man is possessed of a faculty that enables
him to provide against and protect himself from the
rigors of a land and clime different from that in which
he originated and to which he was doubtless best adapted,
and other animals are not ; nor do other animals make
such provision, nor do they exist in said unnatural
regions, except through and by the aid of man.

If man should suddenly be bereft of these faculties he

would shortly cease to exist, as would an exotic flower or a plant perish and decay ; so likewise would the animals that are not endemic, when shorn of his care, succumb to the elements not their own, and the greater these variations, rather the less copious that nature is in her supplies, the greater and more diversified is the hideous monster called "want," or perhaps the thing called "poverty," which is the inability to quiet the pangs of wants.

The hungry babe will cry, and if there be no milk it will die.

Who can say that, looking at nature practically and square in the face, it is the duty of each man to exert himself to supply milk for every man's babe ? The mare that suckles her own colt has about performed her duty to the genus *equus ;* it is to be hoped that she may always have grass, but a condition can be imagined under which she could not, and for no fault of the others of her kind.

Well, want begets a disposition to supply, and the labor thus expended is worth what it has accomplished, that is, the property it has acquired,—and the possession of this property becomes a right inherent in the individual, because he has paid value for it, *i. e.*, he had captured it, and some other man has not ; hence it is his and not the other man's.

The accumulation of property begets a desire for its retention and protection ; hence communities are formed, and in the natural run of things, though perhaps not more or less naturally than that the birds of passage or the wild geese have their leaders, leaders spring up among men, and hence chieftains and kings. The ascendancy of the king begets in the masses an idea of power and right akin to that which they acknowledged to the ruler of the sea, the thunderbolts, and the winds ; hence the idea of divine right, and, as a necessary con- comitant thereof, hereditary succession. It was and is (be it modified, howsoever), wherever it exists, a relic of barbarism,—nothing more,—and, like many other relics of the same, is by no means in keeping with that condi- tion of civilization in which men can calculate eclipses and measure the distance to the stars.

Fortunately the *world moves*, and more than a century has passed since a nation, then comparatively small but now the brightest of all the powers of earth, said, " *There is no divine right to rule*," and that "*all just power comes from the consent of the governed.*"

From this grand principle came suffrage,—the voice, —the expression of the governed as to who shall govern, and what may be his powers. It is possible, however, that the greatest blessings of human life may be in- dulged in too freely. It is likewise certain that he who is not adapted to a crown (even though he obtained it by divine inheritance) should never wear it, any more than he whose neck and shoulders are not fitted to the yoke (even though it be placed there by superior force) should ever bear it. A man to exercise the right to say who shall be the governor and what shall be his powers, should possess, at least, the ability to know what a gov- ernor is and what it is that is being governed ; otherwise the participation in the privilege is a mockery, and the right to do so had as well be extended to a brute. Why not as well, yes rather, extend the suffrage privileges to an honest dog than to a vicious man, if neither knew what suffrage was ; why not rather extend it to a horse, and, with equal reason, to anything ? A man should not participate in citizenship unless he is, to a certain extent at least, capable of bearing the privileges and in-

curring the penalties of citizenship, any more than a
man should be engaged as porter in a hotel who could
not carry a trunk, or as a blacksmith who could not
wield a forge. He should not be, and is not, permitted
to enter the army unless he is equal to a certain standard
of excellence, so that he can withstand and endure the
requirements of the situation. A blind man should not
be engaged as a pilot on a ship or a deaf man as a critic
of music, a lame man as a sprint-runner or a consumptive
as a pugilist ; in a word, things should be adapted to
each other—" the punishment should fit the crime," to
accomplish which is indeed " an object all sublime," but
it may be " achieved in time." Since governments are instituted and are maintained for the protection of property, no man should participate in government who has
no property. Hence the requirements should be that,
for the exercise of this the greatest and most important
function of human life, there should be *a standard of
excellence* or of fitness prescribed, just as there is for the
smallest and least important function of human life. It
is but natural, but proper, and right. Scoff at the idea as
demagogues and blatherskites may, there is not in public life in America in 1890 a single honorable, reliable,
and worthy man who does not say deep down in his
heart that *"universal suffrage is a farce."* He dare not
utter this opinion, because if so his political life would
end, but it may be different later. Many good men
always have been deterred from uttering their inherent
political opinions just because an uneducated, vicious,
and corrupt voting population, who could neither appreciate nor understand, yet who could cherish prejudice
and seek revenge, could determine their political life or
death, and with which class reason was of no avail ; and
at length and now money and corruption only, and uni-

versally, control. Not alone have public affairs reached
such a state that good citizens do not participate in
elections, and the successful candidates are too often
either of the vicious class, or in sympathy therewith, or
those who purchased their places with money, but
scarcely a measure of public import can be legislated
upon save by the same dastardly and infamous means of
prostitution and plunder. Not only this, but the ignorant and vicious are being elected to places of public
trust, ward "workers" to municipal councils, and boodlers to State Legislatures, until in fact actual incompetency
exists in these assemblages, and the wheels of government are becoming paralyzed. No politician who does
not covet political death dares do other or more than to
talk about ballot reform in general, but about nothing in
particular ; all recognize the great necessity, but no
leader will speak. Demagogues will reiterate the expression, when discussing purification by qualification,
that was made by an ancient public man to the rabble :
" Was it the man or the ass that voted ?"

This appealed well to the vulgar, but was of no use to
the wise.

By all means let the ass do the voting, if he knows
more than the man, and if the ass both owns and knows
more than the man, by all means let him vote. The
platform of the " Conservative Phronocrats" is that a
man should both know something and own something :
the first, because if he knows nothing he is less competent than an ass ; and if he possesses nothing he is usually
more vicious and dangerous to society, more fruitful of
harm and bad government, than an ass. This qualification is not only made part and parcel of the creed by
reason of the inherent justice of the thing, and by
the increasing necessity consequent upon the rapid in-

crease of population, but *as a compromise for the sacrifice of property* under the cumulative tax. Those who are extremists either way will not be part and parcel of this organization, yet those who lean toward the continuance of universal suffrage can yield their preference, and those who are inclined to think that cumulative taxation is wrong, yet since a competency could yet remain, they could yield their preference and agree to adopt the plan that strikes out both extremes—each a concession to the other. Many people will be brought over to cumulative taxation because it carries with it a curtailment and purification of the ballot, which they consider more desirable than one-hundred millionaires ; and others, because they think the abolition of one-hundred millionaires more desirable than a continuance of loafer, boodler, and ignorant suffrage. It looks like a fair thing on the very face of the papers. If individual property is to be curtailed, why should not suffrage, which regulates government over that property, be also curtailed ? Rather, if a man is to be compelled to yield a part of his property to the State, why should the State not give him in return a government in which property alone participates, thus guaranteeing greater stability and security for the retention and enjoyment of what remains ? Aside from the glaring and universally admitted necessity for ballot reform, and the almost equal unanimity of opinion that the only genuine and true reform is purgation by qualification, there appears to be ample justification for it in the compromise. Individuals who possess hundreds of millions of dollars can now protect their estates by buying up town councils, State Legislatures, aye, and be it said to the shame of America, even judges of the courts, and when dispossessed of this cogent weapon of defence it appears to be not an unreasonable concession that property and education only should vote, especially since by this policy politics will be purged of its rottenness and filth, and good or at least better men—more worthy citizens—will become politicians and the standard of the clan will be higher. Some objectors urge that by curtailment corruption could not be diminished, but that the price per vote would simply be increased ; yet even such objectors are obliged to admit that, if accomplished, the ratio of purchasable to non-purchasable voters would be diminished ; that those who could not be purchased before would be none the more liable to become vendors in consequence, and many of the class who have been vendors would have nothing to vend. If out of one thousand men under the universal system, five hundred could be purchased and five hundred were unpurchasable, it is certainly an unavoidable conclusion that under the qualification system the reduction would come from the purchasable and not from the unpurchasable class, and if the latter should be reduced to one hundred, leaving six hundred electors, it is not a reasonable conclusion that three hundred could now be bought, even at an enhanced price, as easily as the five hundred could before ; if, in fact, three hundred could be bought at all. Thus increased excellence causes increased pride —rather more individuality. Not only would the standing and character of the elector be very much elevated and purified, but, better and more, the *elected* as well. It has actually come to pass that a man of any respectability can not serve in a municipal council, scarcely any in the State Legislature, and the Federal Congress itself is not exempt from the iniquitous scourge of hoodlumism and venality. Something must be done or republicism must end—surrendering either to plutocracy with despotic power to enforce

13

its decrees, or to anarchy with its thirsty dagger drawn.

The proposition is to knock out both the one-hundred millionaire, and the loafer, each equally useless and as objectionable as they are dissimilar. In vain it may be urged that the one-hundred millionaire is a necessary ornament to society and must be retained, likewise vainly that the ward loafer is entitled to participation in the affairs of State and must also remain ; but not vainly is it said that enterprises should be prosecuted by the people who are worthy, and we will give them increased representation therein, and that the government is like-wise the proper function of the worthy, and since it cannot be worthily administered otherwise, we will give the unworthy decreased representation therein. In other words, *public enterprises are becoming too exclusive and government is not enough so, or too inclusive.*

Thus it is that the policy should prevail of increasing the number of individuals who can participate in business ; that is, afford greater opportunity to all men to enjoy the fruits and profit of enterprises by nature monopolistic and consequently exempt, by the force of the situation, from that competition which is essential to the life of communities as well as to trade, and of decreasing the number of individuals who can participate in government—both reforms very necessary and becoming more so daily. The same principle and policy that should prevail in increasing popular representation in private enterprises, out of which the living of all must come, should cause the decrease of popular representation in government, out of which the living of none should come, thus increasing opportunity in business and decreasing it in government, causing property to be more equitably distributed without elevating the worthless and the trifling and without thwarting enterprise, and at the same time guaranteeing increased security to property and elevating the character of government.

The proposed compromise on the curtailment of unreasonable accumulations on one end, and the purification of the ballot on the other, may lead to an animated discussion on the rights of women to suffrage.

By that class of the female sisterhood called "women's-rights advocates," many arguments and appeals have been made to representative assemblages for the extension of the ballot to their sex, and, notwithstanding the fact that the desire for the exercise of the franchise appears not to be very great, very general, or widespread, nevertheless some States have adopted it as applicable to schools and municipal affairs ; but nowhere is the sentiment growing.

Presidential conventions are not exempt from resolutions introduced for the purpose of keeping alive the agitation, but no party of any strength has adopted the measure as a cardinal creed or political plank in its presidential platform. It is persistently maintained, and not without reason, that since suffrage is exercised by the most lowly, degraded, and vicious of men, it would be but proper in the interest of the State, to say nothing as to the rights of the women, that she, who is admittedly more prudent and conservative, usually more painstaking and sagacious,—that she whose intuition was better than man's judgment,—should be permitted to vote as a balance-wheel on society, as a check on man's recklessness ; and that since all are ready to admit that in the social sphere women exercise a wholesome and beneficent influence upon men, cause them to restrain the violence of their passions, to elevate their hopes and moderate their desires, so in the sphere of politics and government would the same salutary influence be exercised and tend to purge the public of much of its iniquity and sin. Women are admitted to be the supporters of religious institutions, without the influence of whom they would doubtless degenerate and decay, and while man may in the progressiveness of his thought, in the boundless scope of his imagination and fancy, and in the ability he has acquired through scientific inventions, to sweep with a four-foot lens and incidental appliances the broad expanse of limitless space, tend towards the acceptance of views heterodox and materialistic, and, in consequence thereof, upset the foundation on which the moral edifice is constructed, yet women as a class will cling to the rock of faith with unflinching energy and never-ending devotion, thus causing to be perpetuated an institution, be it construed in any way whatsoever, is yet an agency of greater good than evil, and tends to elevate the moral instincts of mankind ; and as with this, so in government, it is claimed, would their intervention be salutary and always found upon the side of the moral and the good. When it is proposed to curtail suffrage among men to within the limit of those who know something and possess something, or, in other words, to within the ranks of men and not brutes (than which latter, an absolutely ignorant and degraded man or woman is little better), it will be urged with renewed and increased gusto that women who know something, and possess something, should, under this state of society, by all means vote.

The discussion has resolved itself into a kind of chaos of opinions. It does appear as though, if a woman is possessed of property, and pays taxes, and likewise is possessed of education and brains, she should par-

ticipate in that institution (government) which guarantees peaceable enjoyment of that property, so that it
begins to be discussed philosophically. Interrogatories
are propounded for the purpose of eliciting opinions as
to who woman is anyhow, what is she, what is her mission on earth, and what are her rights in the world ? Is
she or is she not responsible for the loss of Eden ? Is she
entitled to every opportunity open to man, and if so should
she or should she not be subjected to the same exactions
that are placed upon man ? If entitled to the same opportunity, then it appears reasonable that she should be
subjected to the same penalty. If she is to participate
in citizenship, those eligible for suffrage should be eligible to any official position that is open to man ; and if
eligible to enjoy the honors and emoluments of office,
then she should be called upon to bear the same responsibility as man in the nation's defence. She must hold
herself in readiness to climb the ropes and nail the
banner to the mast, to command a squadron on the deep
blue sea, to take in hand ten thousand men and march
up the hills then down again. She must be eligible to
appointments when young to the military and naval
academies of all nations, must serve as municipal police
as well as in State military organizations ; she must pre-
pare herself generally to win her glory on the tented
field as well as on the hustings, or the forum ; for whilst
" peace hath its victories not less renowned than war,"
yet citizenship has its penalties as well as its rewards,
and no woman could reasonably expect to participate
with men co-equally in the vote without being equally
ready to respond to the call of the draft. In a word,
participation in suffrage really and justly means participation in government in all that the term implies, and in
all its incidental belongings. Now, it is asked, are

women physically capable, or, if so, are they in their
proper sphere when called upon to assume and exercise
all the functions of government that men must occupy,
and if in their proper sphere is it for the good of the
women themselves, to say nothing of the good to the
State that is unquestionably vouchsafed in the proper
tutelage to the rising generations (which should not be
neglected, and which, if women were subjected to duties
co-equally with men, undoubtedly would be), that they
should be granted these privileges? Extend to individual women all the credit you will, and to women as a
class all the liberality and opportunity you may, and it
cannot be denied, or even for a single moment questioned,
that as a class they are inferior both intellectually and
physically to men as a class. Had such not been the case
from the very beginning, woman would now be in the
ascendancy and not man ; they would be considering
what rights they would extend to the men, and not what
the men might extend to them.

It has been urged that they stand to-day secondary to
man only because men have kept them down. Be it so.
Men have kept them down because men are stronger,
otherwise they could not have succeeded. In any
civilized state, or as civilization has progressed, it has
been the disposition of men to extend to women, if not
increased opportunities (which for their own good would
be questionable), certainly increased courtesies and ex-
emption from toil. As the woman advances in physical
and intellectual culture and strength, so commensurately
are these adorable qualities imparted to her offspring ;
as she is forced into the caverns of ignorance and gloom,
so has mankind failed to develop.

There appear to be certain avocations in life to which
even men in their varying attributes and propensities are

best adapted and out of which they are usually ill at ease
and worthless, so to a greater degree do there appear
to be two certain distinct spheres in life, one to which
woman is best adapted and out of which she is lost, and
the other in which the man is the most suitable occupant
and out of which he is lost.

There is undoubtedly a vast difference between mankind and womankind.

> " What a strange thing is man, but
> What a stranger thing is woman.
> What a whirlwind is her head, and
> What a whirlpool, full of depth and danger,
> Is all the rest about her.
> What she has said or done is nought to
> What she 'll say or do.
> The oldest thing on record, and yet new."

Her ideas are different and apparently her conclusions
are reached by the very opposite course of reasoning to
that which man would employ. Her ratiocination is
mysterious, her deductions seldom profound. Yet frailty,
though the name of many, is not the name of all. Her
tongue is often nimble and her thoughts oft keen, and
when good she is oft the best, when honorable she is oft
the truest, when handsome is oft the most attractive, but
when bad is oft the very worst thing in the world.

Differing, as they do, mentally and physically from
men, why should they not occupy that radically different
sphere ? Why should they

> " Offer war, where they should kneel for peace ;
> Or seek for rule, supremacy, and sway,
> When they are bound to serve, love, and obey.
> Why are their bodies soft, weak, and smooth,
> Unapt to toil and trouble in the world ;
> But that their soft conditions and their hearts
> Should well agree with their external parts ? "

It is urged that the conservative, phronocratic compromise would exclude many men from voting who
might be forced to serve in war. Why not extend to
woman the right of voting and exempt them from the
throes of war ? The answer is simple. The men who
would be excluded from voting are not fit to vote ; they
might be fit for war, and if so, so be it , but women are
fit neither for voting nor for war, not because of the
meagreness of their intellectual endowments (for a few
possess much), but simply because they are women, and
all deductions of logic, all the force of argument, yea
more, could be adduced and no better reason could be
given, and it is quite enough. They are entitled to the
higher right not to vote and *not* to serve in the nation's
defence. The desire to exercise the privilege is usually
pressed either by husbandless women or childless wives ;
both living in an unnatural state, hence seek unnatural
exercises, and cherish unnatural aspirations. It is found,
too, that where female suffrage has been permitted, such
as in the election of school trustees and, in some of the
Western States, of municipal assemblages, the conditions
as to government are not materially changed, nor is the
right exercised by a great percentum of the women. All
tests that can be applied lead the public mind to conclude that in at least three fourths of the cases the wife
would vote as did the husband, so that in effect it would
amount to an increase in numbers with the same identical results—an increased cumbersomeness without any
increased efficiency. With women who are not married
the practice would become a burlesque in which those
most capable and worthy would seldom participate.

It is argued that in the marital state women are called
upon to yield too much to their husbands ; that their
individuality is absorbed ; that they are nothing, no

matter how capable, save what the husband is, no
matter how worthless. To which it is replied : Would
not a total extirpation or even a decided alteration
of this condition be incompatible with the maintenance,
in its so-called divine integrity, of that psychical and
material dual-unity that the relationship now recognizes?
Is civilization in such a state that said dual-unity should
be discouraged, much less annulled? There is as yet,
perhaps, no decided proposed improvement that can be
logically supported. Female suffrage would in effect
alter nothing, and the evil or oppression supposed to
hamper female development would not be remedied
by it.

Women suffer from the contending forces of nature
and of their fellow-creatures just as men suffer, and, if
not protected by men, either by marriage or some other
social contrivance, would, in common strife with men, be
destroyed by men, simply because men are stronger.
Such strife can never exist. If the condition and estate
of men as a class can be improved by curtailing the re-
sultant monstrosities of society, women as a class will
receive their share of that relief. Later men may know
better how to improve woman's condition relative to
themselves than they now know, and then something
more efficacious than the ballot will be accorded them.

Many plans and schemes have been suggested as to a
modification of the relationship existing between the
sexes. Some hold marriage to be a failure ; others that
the bond should be absolutely indissoluble. Some claim
that there should be no marital tie whatever, but that
woman should be permitted to exercise what was considered her natural right of selection, regarding which her
instincts are claimed to be keener than man's judgment.
It is held also by some that by reason of the position

women are obliged to occupy in society ; that is, cut off
from many of the pursuits of occupation and remuneration
that are always open to man, they are necessarily forced
into a condition of dependence which causes many, to
whom the opportunity is presented, to make uncongenial
matrimonial alliances solely as a means of protection from
actual want ; that others are driven into the slums of de-
gradation, licentiousness, and vice from similar motives ;
in a word, that the dint of necessity, resulting mainly
from circumscribed opportunity, causes many an unhappy
marriage and makes many a woman wanton.

> " To lapse in fulness
> Is sorer than to lie for need ; and falsehood
> Is worse in kings than beggars."

So, likewise, is virtue more likely " never to be moved
though lewdness court it in the shape of heaven," when
comfort, contentment, and solace are secure, than when
the gnarling wolf is grinning at the door.

It is actually maintained that nine tenths of the inmates
of brothels, bagnios, and the like are driven there by necessity. Women of likely state who can not secure a
competency, in many cases not even the actual comforts
in life's honorable pursuits, are forced to yield even to
mild temptation, and then down, down into the seething
depths of hell is their inevitable destiny—their funeral
knell.

Beyond doubt, the monster want often prompts deeds
of daring, of diabolism, and disorder ; but want can
never be entirely relieved.

Forest fires will sweep the boundless plains, bringing
ruin to the wild flowers, the herbs, and the grasses.

Resistless winds will rift the mountain oaks, and the
energies of nature will make the continents tremble ; and

so in any social state will uncontrollable agencies cause differences in social conditions which legislation can never equalize and ofttimes never alter. Female suffrage will never alleviate female woes to a greater extent than unlimited male franchise has equalized man's estate.

Suffrage is a duty that responsible members of society always owe to that state of society which, for protection against viciousness and unrestraint, they have instituted, to guarantee its perpetuation and utility, and not a privilege that should be indiscriminately extended to the irresponsible vagabonds of the community as a reward for their mere existence as men. Why, therefore, should women seek to perform this *duty* when their thoughts can be devoted to things far more ennobling ; and why, with far greater wrong, should the irresponsible negro, the scullion, and the knave be permitted to perform it, when by their votes are constantly being committed many crimes so heinous to the State, that "the bandy wind that kisses all it meets is hush'd within the hollow mine of earth, and will not hear them"?

The government of the United States is a republic. Few, if any, of its citizens espouse the principles of monarchy ; hence *all are republicans.* However, under any *unregulated* system of society extreme conditions of wealth and poverty must occur. The Republican party in America to-day undoubtedly tends towards plutocracy and centralization, to a greater extent than does the Democratic party. This is clearly manifest in the advocacy by that party of protection to the classes, by systems of tariffs, subsidies, bounties, and the like. The tendency of the day is towards the increase of plutocracy on the one hand, till, to maintain its existence, it must eventually advocate a stronger centralized government, with a tendency towards monarchy ; and, on the other, an increase of democracy, until it verges on to socialism. In France, one hundred years ago, there existed the plutocrats, or Royalists, and, *per contra*, the Jacobins, or anarchists, the two representing the extremes of social conditions. Between these extremes there sprang into being the Girondists, who advocated republican institutions, to be operated and controlled by citizens less plutocratic than the Royalists, and less anarchistic than the Jacobins. Had the principles of the Girondists been extensively promulgated before the curse of plutocratic royalty had become so deep-seated in the hearts and minds of the masses, the rule of Jacobinism would no doubt have been averted, and the horrors of "the reign of terror" would have been anticipated and prevented by the more conservative Girondism that stood as a compromise between both. But, *a foe of reformation is a friend of revolution*. Hence Jacobin tyranny existed till its leaders were satiated with blood, and till the gaping wounds of a stricken people yearned for order and stability even by the creation of the dynasty of Bonaparte.

In America the time has not yet arrived for a bloody conflict between our plutocratic Royalists and our democratic Jacobins; but the time is at hand to avert its possible occurrence by a timely compromise, set forth in *Phronocratic Girondism ;* otherwise a temporary "reign of terror" may be precipitated, to be in the end supplanted by a system akin to a Napoleonic empire. The arbitrament of force usually results in the establishment of extreme conditions; and the sentiment of the body-politic in America to-day, however repulsive to thoughtful minds the suggestion may appear, is not wholly for relief from tariffs and similar systems of governmental paternalism and discriminating legislation, but for the *dethronement of plutocracy, to prevent the enthronement of its king.*

Questions of domesticity, such as marriage, divorce, religion, and the like, are not yet matters of special moment. All things considered, there is to-day no better regulation than one man one wife, each reliable and continent. Likewise as to religion. It is undeniable that in orthodox Christianity there are many apparent inconsistencies that are utterly in conflict with the reason of the philosopher or the discoveries of the scientist ; but the people at large are neither philosophic nor scientific, and require some restraining or consoling influence to check vicious tendencies, which the philosopher can dispense with. Likewise to the average mind, when beset with vexation, with tribulation, and with sorrow, much solace is · certainly vouchsafed in lifting the voice to the Almighty and invoking His blessing in the name of the Son.

More individuals in the world, as it is, are guided by sound than by sense, more by fiction than by fact, more by prejudice and passion than by prudence and penetration ; hence for the masses, as they now exist, faith is better than philosophy. We are guided by glamour rather than by research.

> " O place, O form,
>   How often dost thou with thy case,
>   Thy habit, wrench awe from fools, and tie
>   The wiser souls to thy false seeming."

The present is the time to dethrone oppression resulting from things temporal, and immediately confronting us ; but religion is likely to stand until men who *do not* believe can say something more definite than *that they do not know.* Regulate government, religion will regulate itself.

CHAPTER X.

MANY efforts have been made to secure what is called ballot reform, and all have been of no practical effect. In the large cities, from crowded tenements, notwithstanding registration, frauds are committed ; in fact, in a confused mass of human animals crowded into dens and dungeons, with really no habitation of a permanent and substantial character, it is impossible to arrive at any real and tangible system of ballot reform.

The only way to reform this class, who have no interest in any man or principle, but little comprehension of what they are doing when they vote, and absolutely no responsibility,—many actually preferring to lodge a few nights in jail than otherwise,—is to deprive them of the ballot. This class, together with the ignorant and degraded negro of the South, make popular suffrage a mockery, and really cause the laws and institutions that support it to be the proper subjects of ridicule. All reasonable men admit it, but the demagogues encourage the boodlers with high-sounding platitudes about manhood suffrage and the like. Still, popular opinion is waxing strong, and as the population becomes dense the necessity for curtailment becomes greater, and the entire North is still restive under the pressure of the suppressed negro vote of the South. The South will not submit to negro domination, and the North cannot force them to do so by any feasible plan. It is either to disfranchise the negro, or have his vote counted in Congress and in the electoral college, just as the white vote is counted. Schemes for deportation to Africa have been devised, but since the negro, unfortunately, is a citizen under the law, he cannot be forced to leave the civilized white and enter into the jungles of Africa with the barbarous anthropophagi of that benighted country. In fact, when in the state of slavery prior to the war there was scarce a negro who would have exchanged that condition of slavery for such liberty as he might have secured in Africa. There he would have been the slave of some barbarous chief, in whose custody his life would be imperilled and be subjected to the discomforts of uncivilized conditions, whilst as the slave of his Southern master he was usually well fed and clothed, and in the majority of cases protected. Deportation has resulted in nothing, and disfranchisement can be brought about only by some general law applicable to all citizens—let it oppress whomsoever it may. This sentiment—the willingness, yea, the eagerness of the South to accept it,—and the cry of ballot reform in the North, are what must eventually bring it about.

The only legal voters, as a matter of course, would be the taxpayers recorded on the books of the collector, and their names would have to be registered six months before the election ; or, rather, the taxpaying voter must have recorded his name and property a half year before he became a qualified elector.

The collectors for each congressional district would
be obliged to keep an alphabetically arranged list of
these names, which would be by no means difficult, and
these would be required to be printed in pamphlets and
sent to the clerks and judges of elections at every polling
precinct.

The voter on election day, when seeking to record his
vote, would give his name and address to the clerk of
his poll, which latter would refer at once to his alpha-
betical list of voters supplied in the pamphlet from the
collector, and if the said name and address was found
therein duly recorded the would-be voter would then be
required to write his signature in the poll-book in legible
English, and, if requested, to read a section of the Federal Constitution, after which he could cast his ballot.
In national and in some State elections, where the candidates were not numerous, a recording-box could be
used in place of a ballot-box.   One of these could be
labelled with the name of each candidate ; that is, for
President, Congressman, Collector, Postmaster, and so
forth.   The voter, after having registered his name,
could then, instead of depositing his ballot, simply touch
the handle of the box labelled with the name of the man
for whom he wished to vote, and the vote would be
recorded openly.   The aggregate of these would have
to agree with the number of signatures recorded, or
fraud would be *prima facie.*   To prevent dishonest
clerks and judges from forging the signatures on the
poll-books of men recorded in the collector's list who
had not appeared at the polls to vote, the officers of
each precinct could be required to give to the postmasters
in that precinct or town at the close of the polls a list of
the men who voted.   These lists the postmaster should
print and hold in readiness for any man who should

desire to receive one on application at his office for six months succeeding the election. Thus, if any man who had not presented himself at the polls should find his name recorded he would at once discover the fraud and forgery ; hence this would be dangerous business. Never could more votes be recorded than those on the collector's list, and these would have to agree as to exact names and address.

It is by such means that fraud can be absolutely prevented, and that, too, without the necessity of the expensive and non-effectual registration system now in force in large cities.

1st. The collection list would make known, six months in advance, who were the voters and where they resided.

2d. A printed copy of this list in the hands of the judges and clerks of election would be a complete registration.

3d. The signature of each voter who appeared at the polls to the book in his own handwriting, when compared with the name on the printed copy of the collector's record, would be a complete guaranty that that particular individual was a lawful voter and that he could read and write English.

4th. The total number of recorded votes could not be in excess of the collector's list.

5th. If there remained say one thousand uncast votes, that is, if one thousand or any other number of men recorded on the collector's list failed to appear, it would be, in the first place, difficult for the clerks or judges or any one else to forge their names and then count the votes, for the penalty for such fraud would be very severe ; but an additional safeguard, and an effectual one, would be the requirement that the names of all

14

men who were recorded on the poll-book should be
reported to the postmaster and by him printed on lists
and held ready for delivery to any man who should
apply for six months after the election.   Thus, if John
Smith or Joe Jones, living at No. 10 Mulberry Lane,
should find their names on the postmaster's list when
they were not near the polls on election day, it might, in
fact would, almost certainly send the clerks and judges
of that poll to the State prison.   The fact is, the system
would be so simple and complete that frauds would
not be attempted, and the question of ballot reform
would be forever and effectually settled.   In all elections, that is, State and municipal as well as national,
the collector's list would be the only authorized and
legal list of voters ; but the localities would sometimes
differ in their method of counting the votes as cast.
The registry box and no ballot is to be preferred, but to
have one of these for every candidate for every little
office would sometimes be considered too expensive.

Every candidate could, however, provide one for himself.   The State should incur the expense of printing
tickets at all elections for State and local offices, and
the Federal Government, through the collector's office,
could provide all boxes and other appliances for national
elections.   Boxes could be provided for all recognized
candidates of any party organization, and, as stated,
independent candidates could either provide boxes for
themselves or trust to the will of their supporter to drop
ballots into the box, in which case the ballots and records
of the boxes must, when aggregated, equal the number
of signatures on the books.

Usually there would be but few independent candidates.   Nearly every man who ran for office would be
the prearranged nominee of a very considerable party.

The voters would be of a higher character, and would usually have their minds made up in advance, so that any claptrap hoodlum who sought to create a sensation would usually count only his labor for his pains, and such would be few.

The qualification for suffrage as set forth in the amendment is the ability to read and write the English language and be the lawful owner of property in value not less than $500. This property should be either real estate to said value, which really signifies practically that the voter must own real estate (for almost any piece of real estate in America is worth that amount of money), or it must be government bonds, or both, aggregating said amount. Real estate can be seen and has a value known in effect to all, and government bonds likewise have a value that is known to all ; hence it would be impossible for the collector to admit to his list as a voter (who might be one of his chums) any man on the presentation of a security that was practically worthless. Since the rate of taxation on $500 would be so very insignificant the collector or any candidate for office might issue to his friends valueless stock certificates or worthless bonds, and pay the tax thereon just for the purpose of securing the vote of the individual, but this could not so well be done (in fact it would be too expensive) as the real estate or government bonds—both of which would always have a value readily ascertainable. The only way to purify the electoral system is to purify it, and though some educated individuals would not have the $500, and though some men owning many times $500 could not write their names, yet this would be their misfortune, as the community has already suffered too long the prostitution of its public affairs, to listen longer to such puerile complaints as would be made by these individuals. It is

"Get there, Ely, or stay out, and you need not whine about it either." The rigidity of the law would work much good with the people. Citizenship would have character and value and be prized. There would be a reward held out first for merit then for energy. The masses would be encouraged to learn something and to save something. Not only would the requirement as to the possession either of government bonds or real estate be made unconditional for the reasons named above, but because it would increase the firmness and stability of the Federal Government. Residents of States who would acquire their right to citizenship by the ownership of the securities of the government of the nation would not want to see that nation dismembered. Owners of real estate are likewise conservative. The amount would not be large, but it would be sufficient, and if not so could be increased.

The widow's mite is more than Crœsus' wealth in insuring conservatism of purpose. It is not a question of how much a man might own, but the very fact that he owns anything is a perfect guaranty and sufficient evidence of a trustworthy and frugal man to entitle him to its privileges. The bonds of the government for this purpose should bear say two per cent. interest only, and then of course be subjected to the cumulative rate. They would not be intended as an investment for profit, but for citizenship; hence no capitalist would seek their possession in large amounts. They should be on sale at every post-office in the country in amounts of ten dollars and upwards, so that any frugal man could gradually accumulate his competency for citizenship by small monthly purchases. Thus would the government be made a kind of savings-bank for the people, and it would be found that many voters would acquire their eligibility with these bonds.

On the basis of the voting population of 1890, it is estimated that not more than 15,000 thereof own fully half the property, and if the qualification system was in force it might possibly be that, of the ten million voters, one third, or about three million, would acquire eligibility. There might after the system became operative be only about one fourth of the adult males of the country who would be entitled to suffrage, and this, too, after years had passed, during which in anticipation of its inevitable adoption preparation could have been and doubtless would be to a certain extent made. On this basis not more than three out of twelve million would have voted in 1890. One half of this three million at least would acquire their eligibility by investments in bonds, so that on the basis of the vote of 1890 there would have been issued by the government for citizenship purposes the considerable sum of at least seven hundred million dollars of bonds. In 1920, on the basis of past increase, population will be doubled, and by reason of the equalizing effects of the cumulative tax, half the property, instead of being owned by about one four-hundredth of the voters who are supposed to own it in 1890, will doubtless be owned by a much larger proportion. In other words, there would be in any event about six million votes in all in 1920, out of a total population of say 120,000,000 and a male population of 20,000,000. Each year would add to the list of voters proportionately to the non-voters, but there never will, if in fact there ever should, come a time when all men would own property even in small amounts. In 1920 there should be 3,000,000 voters acquiring eligibility from the possession of the two per cent. bonds, and if so the government would be in debt to its citizens—distributed in all parts of the Union—to the extent of one billion five hundred million dollars. This maximum would

accumulate slowly and it would be about the only debt
the government should owe, and that to its own citizens,
which would cause national pride in America to be
almost if not quite as prominent a characteristic of the
people as it has always been in France. The accumulation of money in the treasury by reason of the sale of
these bonds might render it unnecessary some years for
the government to impose all the cumulative tax, and it
could be horizontally cut down for certain periods.
Frequently the amount in the treasury might be sufficient for the government's needs; but, of course, as
bonds began to mature the tax would have to be applied
to such an extent as was necessary to meet the current
expense as well as to provide for maturities. This would
be a matter of easy regulation by the Secretary of the
Treasury, and Congress would simply, upon the Treas-
urer's report, instruct the collectors to increase or reduce
the cumulative tax a certain specific percentum. It
might never occur that the cumulative levy would have
to be reduced, but if so it would be simple and unaltered
in its relative bearing on the large and small estates.
The property valuation of the country will continue
well apace with the increase in population at the
ratio of about 1,000 per head, so that in 1920 the
valuation will be, if things continue, about one hundred
and twenty billion, and what is more and better, it may
be owned by over six million men, and each year the
number of individual owners may be increasing instead ·
of diminishing, as is the case before the cumulative
balance wheel to society is applied. The annual expense
of the Federal Government should not be proportionately
increased, but should remain not much greater than
three hundred million, which amount would doubtless be
fully secured by the cumulative levy.

It may be argued by the capitalists that $500 in real estate or government bonds is not enough, or that designing politicians could make votes at their pleasure, or that a candidate for office could transfer temporarily a small piece of land or $500 in bonds to non-voting individuals with the understanding that it be returned after election. This objection is acknowledged, but the candidate would have to be out of pocket for six months. Every dollar thus transferred would be unlawful, and to secure many votes the candidate's purse would have to be long, and then, if after election the collector would find that many voters were making re-transfers, his suspicions and that of the public would be aroused, and the candidate might soon wear stripes as the fruit of his generosity. Furthermore, $500, whilst but little to millionaires, is considerable to the average candidate. If a man deserved election to Congress he would have to secure over ten thousand votes. If he should think himself short one thousand votes, he would require $500,000 for six months, with much trouble as to its return and heavy penalty for the wrong, altogether rendering it extremely improbable that he would pursue this course. If he should, however, desire so to do, he would find it just that much more difficult of accomplishment than under any previous system. When, as seems to be the probable condition even under cumulative tax laws, one four-hundredth of the voters may own one half the property, and one third the remaining male people the other half, there will not be, on a basis of $1,000 wealth per capita, too many $500 bills remaining to make suffrage too common, and at any rate it would be less common and of purer character than under any other system. Furthermore, the amendment can provide that it may be increased to $5,000 by simple act of Congress, or the cumulative levy could be decreased to half cent per thousand, making ten million the maximum instead of five.   It is thought wise and prudent not to go too far too soon.   Later the former could be increased, if the increase should be found desirable, but as a beginning $500 is ample and will work wondrous results.   It is just about as low as anybody thought it could be, and yet enough to elevate the tone of suffrage, increase the character of representation and the stability of governmental institutions and the natural rights of property to an amazing extent, and ten millions is thought to be too high a limit for one individual's estate.

The native-American agitation called the " Know-Nothing " party had for its objects the Americanization of the nation and the elevation of the character of suffrage.   It was held that no man should hold office or vote until he had been in the country full one-and-twenty years.   This party failed to acquire any ascendancy, though to a certain extent its purposes were sound.

It was, in fact, to such an extent anathematized and scorned that those who, in 1890, had ever had any sympathy with or attachment to the organization were almost proscribed from participation in all public affairs.   There is no good reason why a foreigner could not become a good citizen.   America is so far removed from the national contentions and strife that characterize all Europe that it is in no sense complicated thereby.   It is far better that a reputable, educated, naturalized foreigner who owns property should vote, than that a disreputable, ignorant, and indigent native should exercise that privilege ; for one is responsible and the other is not ; one, though he has been but five years in the country, yet has sworn to support its laws and aid in its defence, and as a better guaranty of his ability and sincerity he has become possessed of some of its property, perhaps some of its bonds, and having learned to speak, read, and write English, is capable of becoming informed as to its governmental and commercial policy. Of the participation of this man in suffrage there need never be any fear, and there is no good sense in naming twenty-one years as the minimum of residence if proper qualification could be attained in five.

Many native-born Americans are not fit to vote in forty years, but yet some foreigners might be qualified in one year. However, five years is thought to be a reasonable period of residence to enable a foreigner to determine whether or not he desires to become a citizen, and this period should not be altered. Any foreigner, after that time, who takes the oath of allegiance, and can speak, read, and write the English language and has acquired property, should vote.

This will make a better citizen and more worthy voter than simply twenty-one years of residence, if he remains yet comparatively a pauper and an ignoramus.

To the presidency alone is a foreign-born man not eligible, and this is perhaps proper from a standpoint of national pride, a feeling peculiar to all people. The foreign element of the States who own property are numbered among its best and most substantial citizens, and are always law-abiding and conservative. The wild-eyed anarchist, who would pillage, kill, and burn, never owns property, and when he becomes an owner he is never an anarchist. It is held that the inability to obtain work causes men to become furious against the possessors of property to a greater extent than the promptings of envy or a disposition to force a divide. It does appear rather severe that a man who is willing and anxious to do so cannot toil. Yet this is undeniably the case in very many instances ; but it is simply a relative condition as compared with the state of his fellows, and unavoidable from the very nature of society ; in other words, it is his own misfortune, resulting principally from his own inaction or imprudence ; but it may have been brought about by accident. Lightning may have prostrated him in the street, causing him to be unable to labor ; hence, naturally, if he ever had one, he would, unless very worthy, be apt to lose his job. A poor devil sometimes can't get work—that is, cannot toil, so likewise does a lawyer sometimes sit in his office for long and weary days and receive no clientage, so also a doctor may for many days have no patients, and both of these men are idle ; that is, they can't get work, they can't toil. So, likewise, is a merchant or manufacturer at times bereft of business, he has no orders and cannot run his mill ; so not only is his time going to waste, but his capital, accumulated under the natural operations of trade and by his frugality and energy, is slipping from under his feet. The conditions of these three citizens in three different avocations are precisely alike—*they cannot toil*. The latter class, however, by dint of their inherent excellence have made more hay while the sun was shining than they used during that period ; hence, though they cannot perhaps for a long period *toil*, have conserved the results of previous toil, and can live until the unfortunate situation has passed. The laboring man, or rather the profligate laboring man, who has not conserved the result of his energies, must suffer actual want, just as should the other three under similar circumstances and conditions. Much, but not all, poverty is the result of human worthlessness and improvidence.

That which comes from accident and disease is the result of misfortune. It would be especially desirable upon the part of society to lift the pangs of want from the shoulders of the latter, and even to a certain extent from the heads of the former, and it is now done to the greatest extent possible, in the maintenance of houses for the poor, and hospitals for the sick and the maimed. To extend it farther would be to place a premium on idleness and malingery.

Therefore, if by reason of improvidence or accident a man is dragged down, his condition is simply a relative one when compared with his fellows. He is not, therefore, entitled to their support except in cases of direst extremity. To deprive a man of citizenship because he has by dint of misfortune been deprived of property, is claimed to be a double calamity ; but it is decided to be more unjust to deprive another man of most of his wealth and then subject that which remains to the vote of the anarchist. Partial wrong may be done to both, but it is to the interest of society that it should be so. The system of voting, therefore, that excludes the lowly, the indigent, and the depraved, should be held in its integrity, and all other efforts at reforming the ballot should be abandoned. Half the population of America is suburban, yet the agricultural classes seldom elect a governor in any State. Under the cumulative and qualification system the rural vote would be increased ; that is, it would be decreased less than the city vote ; so that in the aggregate it would count almost two votes to one. *This is the remedy for the Farmers' Alliance.*

Prior to the inauguration of this system the Federal Congress will almost always be composed of about three fifths lawyers, and the upper branch of same will be about four fifths millionaires and upwards. This can be entirely changed. The rural classes can have largely increased representation, and the lawyers can be reduced to about one fifth the whole. Merchants and manufacturers, who have accumulated that amount beyond which the cumulative rate forbade them to go, will become what in France is called the *Rentier*, that is, a man retired from business and living on his income.

This class of citizens being then exempt from the cares of business could engage to a greater extent than heretofore in politics, and the result would be that almost all industries, as well as the agriculturists, would have very considerable representation. This would produce good legislation, and such as would be adapted to the multifarious wants of the country. The large cities would more frequently send lawyers than those situated in districts which were part rural and part urban. There would be no longer any question in political discussion as to tariffs, taxes, protection, and the like. All parties would recognize and admit that the general government has no power, either express or implied, to tax the people for any purpose whatsoever, save for revenue ; that all systems of protection, of subsidy, of bonuses, and the like are retroactive and discriminating, and since the mode and method of obtaining revenue would be positively fixed on the basis of the cumulative rate of all property, as assessed by the respective congressional collectors, there would remain nothing relative to or in any way bearing upon this subject for Congress to perform, save to impose a percentum of horizontal increase or decrease, as the annual report of the Secretary of the Treasury might indicate to be necessary. Thus the whole matter of taxes, tariff, and the like, that has for years occupied most all the attention of the federal legislature and caused widespread differences of opinion as to the special rate imposed on different ar-

ticles of import, and which has forced the Committee of
Ways and Means to listen to the tiresome and useless
harangues of representatives of special interests, would
be entirely set aside, so that the attention of the representatives could be with more deliberation directed to
matters of greater import. So universally recognized
also would become the principle that Congress should
deal less with individual affairs—that is, legislate less
with and as regards matters of individual determination,
that the sessions would usually be very much shorter.
In years gone by the average representative has begun
to look upon himself as the master or guardian of the
people, rather than as their agent, chosen to do their
bidding in conformity with his wisest discretion for the
greatest good to the greatest number. Members in former years have actually introduced bills not alone for
the prevention of the importation of 'merchandise, thus
preventing the people from availing themselves of the
world's cheapest and best markets and causing unjust
discrimination to certain individuals, but greater and
more ridiculous and presumptuous has been their folly
in endeavoring to pass laws forbidding individuals from
selling their lands to any one save a citizen of the
country. The people should become indignant, and
justly so, at such interference with the natural laws of
barter and exchange. "Why," it may be asked, "do
not these congressional idiots and fools let us alone?
Do they think we need guardians? If so our local
courts can appoint same, and we will apply for congressional aid to assist the local courts when we desire, and
not before. Do they think that because they are daft
we are also, on the theory that a drunken man thinks
everybody else drunk?" For years it has been recognized that a citizen could take up and occupy the public

domain, from which he is entitled to one hundred and sixty acres, and though efforts are frequently made, no law should be passed that will prevent citizens from selling whatever they own to whomsoever will pay them their price.

CHAPTER XI.

Trade, money, work, and wages—Convict labor no great harm to
honest labor—Corporal punishment should be resumed for small
crimes—Child labor—Eight-hour agitation—Scientific invention
no obstacle to labor—Causes of increased urban population—
Circulating medium : money ; gold coin the best—Qualities the
circulating medium should possess—Silver money, iron money—
Government "fiat" money as good as the government's sovereignty—Must be redeemable in something representing the
value of labor—Increased quantity not beneficial—Purchases
forced on the government wrong, and should be stopped—Gold,
and gold only, finally adopted ; no double standard—Banks and
banking—National banks continued.

THE supposed evil effects from immigration and other
incidental economic questions having been frequently
discussed, and the public mind also placed at rest on the
question of the over-population of a country capable of
sustaining one billion or more, when it has less than one
tenth that number ; and since protection tariffs have
been by many admitted to be useless and discriminating,
there naturally arise other questions, which should have
their full share of consideration, but it is useless to attempt to regulate everything by legislation directed to
each supposed wrong in its individual capacity. Some
people have brought forth the argument that the labor
of convicts in prisons causes such competition with free
and honest labor outside that this must be stopped ;
others have opposed by saying that it is better to make
them work than to maintain them in idleness. If it cost

one dollar per week to board and clothe a convict, he
had better be made to earn it than to be idling away his
time ; others have persisted in saying that a man boarded
and clothed at one dollar per week would interfere with
the work and wages of honest men, causing them to
suffer a reduction in pay, so that it would become only
a question how many men would become convicts and
work at one dollar per week until all outside labor would
be receiving the same insufficient pay, and that this condition is now alarming, and must be stopped. Others have
very wisely replied that the condition could not be alarming, because it is to be hoped that convicts would not be so
numerous, but, at any rate, if wages were forced down to
one dollar per week everybody would find that the said
dollar would buy a great deal more than a dollar now
does, if not quite as much as do their ordinary wages.
Still the question of convict labor is assuming some
scope.

The prisons are filling rapidly ; in fact it is said that
many residents of the slums of the large cities would, but
for the fact that they could not sell their votes, about as
soon be in the pen as any other residence, and about as
soon be called a convict as any other name (for if called
a rose he would smell as sweet), yet he does not like to
be deprived of his chance to sell his vote for a drink.
Thus universal suffrage has perhaps one argument in its
favor ; it does tend to prevent the drunkards from voluntarily entering the penitentiary.

However, the question as to what is the best thing to
be done with convicts calls for attention. Their labor
does not seriously interfere with outside labor because
many of the inmates have become defaulting bank
cashiers and they do little work, yet the prisons are
becoming crowded. The reason for this is that about

the only penalty for crime that the sentimentalists of the
country consider not barbarous is imprisonment, and this
has to be prescribed for all. Not so much by reason of
the fact that convict labor is interfering with outside
labor, but because many seem to have become so depraved that they care little for incarceration, is it found
absolutely necessary to alter the universally prevailing
plan of punishment by imprisonment. Thus for small
and petty offences—such as would put a culprit in jail
for from one to five months—notwithstanding the outcry
of the sentimentalists which hitherto has prevented many
a good alteration in the affairs of the state, corporal
punishment should be reinstated in all the States of the
Union ; that is, instead of sending a man to prison to
become worthless, from enforced idleness, more depraved, if possible, from evil association, confirmed in
his lowliness and dejection by being constantly in that
environment, and, to a certain extent, if occupied, to
compete with honest labor, *they should thrash him* for his
misdemeanors and then let him go. Some punishment
has to be inflicted and experience has shown this to
be the best. The culprit would then be no longer a
charge upon the state, he would earn his own bread,
or receive none, and the effect would be very wholesome. Many now serve a short sentence, are liberated,
and then return for a similar offence, but few who would
receive the lash would want it soon again. Thus could
the prisons be purged and the annoyance, slight as it is,
to outside labor settled and prevented.

Then comes the questions of child labor, eight-hour
day, and "kindred cries for kinder keep." It does not
look proper on the face of the papers to see little children forced to toil, but their parents must be able to care
for them otherwise or the state must take them in charge,

15

and then comes the old question "what can the state do?" "how far can it go?" without encouraging idleness and inviting malingery.

Would not many parents feign inability to provide so as to put their children on to the state for support? Such not only appears to be a reasonable probability but it certainly would be the case, so that public houses for the care of children can safely be maintained only to the extent of actual necessity and in cases of proven worth, so that able-bodied children cannot be admitted; hence some are obliged to work for the simple reason that their father, either by idleness, negligence, misfortune, stupidity, or for some other cause, has failed to provide for their sustenance in idleness. Either these children must bide these unavoidable results or they must be put aside with their mothers, and their mothers pensioned till they reach a self-sustaining age, and this appears to be impracticable, though much favored by many of the women of the world.

Then comes the eight-hour discussion. It looks well on the face of the papers. One third of the time for refreshment and ease, one third for labor, and one third for enjoyment and pleasure tickles the ear. Likewise does it look reasonable that if working hours are reduced more men could secure jobs. If 10 men do a certain job on the 10-hour basis in 10 days it would certainly require 1 man 100 days to do that job at 10 hours per day, and it would take 8 men 12½ days to do it at 10 hours per day; hence it must take at least 12½ men to do it at 8 hours per day, or if the hours of labor are reduced one fifth, or 20 per cent., that reduction is equivalent to an increase of 25 per cent., so that one fourth the number of men, in addition to those at first employed, would be required, and this alone would give employment to at least

from 1,000,000 to 2,000,000 men in America, frequently
doomed to perpetual idleness for at least one fourth of
their time. Hence great and widespread has been the support of the eight-hour day. People should reflect that if
an inch is cut off one end of a stick and then pasted on
to the other the stick is no shorter. How could an employer, in the general outcome of the thing, pay as much
for 8 hours' work as he formerly paid for 10 hours' work
without advancing the price of his product? or it is certainly clear that if he is obliged to pay 12½ men the same
price per day that he previously paid to 10, that excess
must be added to the price of his goods or he would soon
become bankrupt.

Ten men at $2.00 per day cost $20.00 per day. Twelve
and one half men at $2.00 cost $25.00, so that $5 has
been added to this cost of the product and must be added
to the price—why not? Thus it becomes self-evident
that the eight-hour law would mean in the end either one
of two things, to wit : Wages would be reduced 20 per
cent. or the price of products would be increased 20
per cent. What matters it to the workman whether he
receives $2.00 per day and to obtain the necessaries of
life he is obliged to spend 90 per cent. of that, or whether
he receives $1.80 and is obliged to spend 90 per cent. of
that? Thus it must be acknowledged that, it matters not
how plausible it looks on the outside, in the general wind-
up there would be nothing in it except the happy realization of the fancied dream, which is in itself considerable,
that " one third for work and one third for play and one
third to sleep the time away," is most conducive to
human happiness.

This division of the time might cause men to labor
more earnestly for the eight hours they toiled, but then
the eight hours of idleness would cause some to imbibe

too much grog, which they would not do if engaged for ten hours, and so on to the end. The eight-hour system would be a very nice division of the time, and for this reason might be better, but wages, or the purchasing power thereof, would not be relatively changed. The only way possible of maintaining a wage rate in excess of that warranted by demand is to control the supply by trades unions or otherwise, and this can only be temporary.

The eight-hour system resulting in no good, many reformers have begun to inveigh against the encouragement of scientific invention on the theory that each machine that is invented must have for its chief merit the fact that it is " labor-saving," otherwise it would be useless ; that every machine that can be operated by steam is necessarily a displacement of that much energy that the people would otherwise supply, and to that extent the laboring classes are said to be injured ; and that it remains only a question how much machinery that is " labor-saving " would be introduced until all the labor would be saved, or, in other words, till machinery would do it all. Formerly, it was claimed that it required many farm hands, at about $1.50 per day, in the harvest field to do what one man and a team of horses can now do with a self-binding reaper in less than half the time. This appears to be a direct interference with manual toil, as also do a thousand similar devices, from the manufacture of needles and pins to threshing machines and locomotives, and some hold that the only possible relief is to check the introduction of " labor-saving machinery." It appears to some reformers and their erudite (?) coterie of megatherium philosophers, that if one machine would save half the labor, then certainly two would save it all, and that enforced idleness and starvation would be the people's inevitable doom—a condition too utterly deplorable to be contemplated with composure, and "that we must arise, shake the dewdrops from our eyes, and stoutly bid defiance to the universal earth ! ! " Yes, 't is true and 't is a pity 't is true as it is. Superficially con sidered it does appear as though there might be an interference, and to the extent of changing or, as it were, to a certain degree, shifting the character of labor, there is an interference.

However, to the condition of mankind as a whole there is no injury, but, on the contrary, an advantage. In the first place, it certainly requires a certain amount of labor to make the machine, which, by reason of its previous non-existence, called for no labor. This of course has a tendency to convert farm labor into factory labor, and to the extent that the conversions could not be immediately accomplished there would be a dearth of mechanics—of factory employés—or, at least, a greater demand for same, and a corresponding plethora of farm labor, or, at least, a less demand for same, which will work a temporary inconvenience which time alone can adjust. This is one of the greatest causes for the increase of the population of cities or manufacturing centres in excess of or more rapidly than the out or rural districts. The introduction of machinery has, to a certain extent, diminished the demand for farm labor, but has increased the call for city labor, and the facts are that the urban population of America has for many years increased much more rapidly than the suburban, which condition, though natural and unavoidable, is not especially to be desired.

People, like grains of sand or drifting snow, will naturally gravitate to places of least resistance, and it is almost a safe conclusion to say that the apparently

crowded conditions of large manufacturing and commercial cities is not in fact a curse but a necessity
—rather that the demand for labor brings them there, or
that by reason of the demand they come there. There
are always thousands of avenues for occupation in large
cities that do not exist in the country, and whilst it is
not safe to say that that which is is always the best, it is
safe to say that it is the unavoidable result of certain
conditions, and can only be altered, if altered at all, by
a change of the conditions. Under present systems of
taxation, where it is not recognized that individuals
should contribute to the government in proportion to
their ability, and when it is held or supposed that the
right and proper thing to do is to permit them to contribute in exact *disproportion* to their ability—that is, that
all of a poor man's estate shall be taxed to full value and
at full rate while one tenth or less of a rich man's estate
is sufficient for a levy,—and when it is not admitted that
by increasing the rate proportionately to the property the
effects of secretiveness could be almost entirely counter-
acted even if more efficient means of assessment should
fail in its object, then and under these conditions one
man can become possessed of a million men's labor, and
it is but the natural result of the existing conditions.
This, however, can only be altered by altering the conditions, which can be done by "cumulative taxation,"
recognizing man's right to an abundance but not to a
redundance of the world's effects and property.

The result of operating agencies which cause the increased populations of cities results in no serious conse-
quences, as the operations of natural agencies seldom
do, but it has concentrated the poorer classes therein,
which makes their condition more glaring. The farmer,
with his horses, his machines, and a few boys, can handle

a large crop, thus making the labor of many farm hands useless, or at least reducing the demand for it.

Not only is the creation and manufacture of the machine an item of compensation as against the supposed interference with labor, but the increased facilities for production cheapens the article produced, either by increasing its excellence or by directly decreasing its price. Likewise also does increased facility for the performance of labor increase the amount of labor that will be performed, as, for example, before the hole was discovered to be in the wrong end of the needle, or rather, before sewing machines were invented, the number of ruffles and flounces on a woman's dress was not so numerous as afterwards. Neither when a single blacksmith forged a shaft with his hand, hammer, and anvil were such large shafts forged as when done by machinery, and thus throughout the list it will be found that increased facility either compensates by increased cheapness or increased energy the supposed loss to labor, and the temporary inconvenience experienced in converting that labor from one class into another is of little serious consequence. The entire discussion of such subjects as these presupposes a total lack of knowledge or comprehension of that fundamental law of nature which is "that energy cannot be conserved"; where there is a cause there is an effect—where there is energy and force apparent there is action and motion that is perceptible. A machine cannot be created that will supplant or destroy the exercise of energy without the use of energy in the construction of the machine, and so on to the end of time. If scientific inventions were in fact an interference with labor, the progress of all thought and development would of necessity stop. But there is—must be—a compensation. If some man would invent a machine that he could suspend in the air and attach a huge belt to a pulley and thence with his belt reach around the world so that the rotary motion of the latter would propel the machine, and then devise another machine that would supply the material required without the use of labor, and cause these machines to proceed to grind out victuals and clothing, they certainly would interfere with labor, but the people would get their wants supplied for nothing or without labor. In the general wind-up, in the end—the *ultima thule*,—labor is the thing that creates the value ; no machinery having value can be made without labor, and the more efficient its operations when made the more excellent or the cheaper its product. Successful men acquire their wealth because they make a profit off of other men's labor, as has been discussed, and by reason of causes wholly natural and unavoidable and entirely with the consent of the employé, who need not work for another if he prefers to idle away his time, and instead of earning his bread can try to use his wits and steal it.

This accumulated wealth does not always reduce the price of its compensation in the same ratio as the reduction in the competitive price of labor, and it is to the extent of this difference only that the prices of commodities that wages buy are not reduced identically the same as wages.

For the convenience of the world and for the expedition of its business—to facilitate exchanges,—there has been introduced in it the intermediary article called money. Trade is simply exchange—the boot-makers exchange boots for hats and the whole thing is illustrated ; both buy, both sell. The function of money is *only to facilitate exchanges.*

Since all men who want boots do not want hats, or not so many hats as boots, and so on throughout the lists, for convenience the said calculating medium (money) has been introduced in all civilized countries. This money either represents value in itself or there is behind it a guaranty that has value. In the most advanced trading nations of the world in 1890 (the United States and England) money is gold coin ; gold is the standard —the yard-stick—by which other things are measured. Gold is, and doubtless always will be the best metal for money. It has not intrinsic value in the sense that it can be eaten or worn, but men will expend considerable labor for a very small amount of it, and as the fondness of the people for its possession has existed for countless years, and since it appears as though the time will never come when men will not give their labor for a very small amount of it, it may be looked upon as a thing of reasonably reliable value, so that a gold coin, whether backed by the stamp of one nation or another, is equally good when of equal weight and fineness. In the progress of the world's affairs this facilitation of exchanges is necessary. The most perfect money would be something that has absolute value in itself—that is, a thing that requires no government backing, and which the world would accept,—a thing coined or fashioned in some convenient way, and such that all governments would recognize as a tender for a debt that could be enforced. However, all governments prefer to have their own coin, and each prefers to issue it and each to make its own coin a legal tender for debt. If John Smith owed Tom Jones value to the extent of one hundred dollars, he could not make him take a horse for it, but he could make him take money—say, one hundred dollars in American coin. Usually Jones would prefer the dollars because he would

know that some other fellow would give him for them a
horse or anything else he desired of no greater value.
Thus the wealth represented by money is the kind of
wealth that is most convenient to handle ; but since the
world's exchanges, or the exchanges of a nation, can be
accomplished with an amount of wealth in this shape of
much less value than the whole of its property, a very
small per cent. thereof exists in the shape of legal-ten-
der money, coin or its equivalent. The circulating
medium may be more or less, just as may be preferred
by the nation that issued it. Wealth in this shape would
not be required at all except to facilitate exchanges, but
since, for this purpose, it is absolutely necessary, it is
thought to be the proper province of the government to
provide it and regulate the character and amount.
Wealth in this shape, just like wealth in all shapes, represents the product of labor. Land, at least the ownership of it, is the product of labor, even if the title be
originally acquired by causing a crow to fly over it. So
much, therefore, of the labor of the nation must be
represented in that class of wealth which is most convenient for facilitating exchanges. The multiplication
of these facilities for exchanging human products is,
however, the chief cause for the great contrasts in the
ownership of those products, and why : because the
greater the facilities for exchanges, that is for *trade*, between men, the more frequent and the greater in magnitude will those exchanges become ; and since on
every exchange or *trade* there is a profit to somebody,
the faster the said trading can be done, the quicker the
shrewd man will become rich. If men did not exchange their products, then, aside from the gain from
unearned increment, no man would, in an entire life, become richer than another save to the extent that *he as*

an individual could perform more physical labor, which
would perhaps not be more to the strongest than twice
or thrice the maximum of the weakest. Some writers
therefore have proposed that the *great facilitator*—money
—or the circulating medium, should be abolished. Its
abolition would greatly retard the monstrous extremes
in earthly possession ; but civilization *demands* exchanges,
hence *it must maintain the medium*. Neither gold nor
silver make any better money than iron or copper or tin,
but they are better adapted to the purpose because they
exist in nature in such limited quantities (or at least
have done so) that a very small quantity—such as may
be conveniently carried—represents considerable labor.
Of silver, it is usually considered that one ounce of it
would almost represent the labor of a man for one day,
and that gold to the same amount would represent sixteen times as much labor, hence these can simply be put
into convenient shape, and suitable sizes and weights of
these shapes can be used as the circulating medium. If
gold and silver were dug out of the ground in the convenient shape that the government gives them in coinage,
the latter could simply say these shall be the legal tender
—the circulating medium—and would not be required to
place on them the government stamp or obligation to
give them value, yet they would go in any civilized land
on account of the value of the metal they contain ; and
so long as the supply is no greater than it has been, the
original size would exchange for similar value in current
productions, because the same amount of labor would
have to be expended in securing them. If, however, the
government could find no gold or silver, it would yet
have to provide its people with a circulating medium. If
it should select iron it would find that in amounts representing, say, one day's labor, it would be too heavy and

unwieldy for use, and the same objection would apply to
most other metals ; consequently if it selected iron it
would be obliged to coin it in convenient size and write
on the face of it something like the following : " The
government will pay for this the equivalent of a certain
amount of labor," or rather one dollar or one thousand
dollars.   In this case iron money might be of one size,
circulating not on account of the value of the particular
piece itself, but because of the promise of a responsible
government to pay that which is valuable for it, and as
long as the world was satisfied that the said government
could and would pay this value, so long would it go, and
people would be justified in including it in their estates
at the value of the " promise to pay."   The governments
of the world have not yet found any metals which, in
quantities suitable for use, can circulate as coin on their
own merits, except gold and silver, and since these are
obtainable, iron and the like are of course altogether
dispensed with.

These baser metals could only circulate upon the faith
of some good promise, and since that promise can be
expressed much better on a small piece of paper than
on a little coin of iron, and since the paper is more
convenient to handle than a little coin of iron, paper is
used whenever any government seeks to issue a promissory money.   Paper, being more convenient than either
gold or silver, is preferred even to these, and is in fact
the circulating medium of the world, though of no value
save as an evidence of the government's promise.   If a
government should have written on the face of a bill,
" For this will be paid one day's labor, or ten days'
labor," or some other definite and fixed value, that
would make it go if it were thought the government
could make good its promise, but since governments

cannot well deliver the value in this form, they usually
say that the bill will be redeemed in one or the other of
the metals which, in convenient quantities for circulation, represent in themselves the said amount of labor or
value. The only question, then, to be considered is :
Can the government procure, so as to have ready for all
bills that may be presented for redemption, the amounts
of these metals as nominated in the bond ? That is to say,
are its resources such that it can secure it ? and if so,
the bill is good for its face in that metal. When a government issues the coin direct the coin should go on its
own merit, but the possessor of it runs his own risk as
to its fluctuations in value. The experience of the world
has been that gold has fluctuated least, hence it has been
considered the safest and the best, and consequently has
been adopted as the metal out of which the circulating
medium is made by the greatest commercial nations of
the world. Gold, however, is subject to fluctuation in
value—that is to say, there might be a vast mine of it
discovered, or several large deposits might be found so
accessible that only one half the labor that has hitherto
been required to put it into marketable shape would be
necessary. If but one such mine should be discovered,
(or if several, if such there should be were found,) and
the whole consolidated into one man's hands, he would
receive the benefit of the discovery to the extent of all
the labor that was saved. If, however, mines should
become very numerous, competition would inevitably
reduce the price. The likelihood, however, judging
from centuries of experience, is that gold is not apt to
fluctuate greatly, and hence is safe in the hands of the
man who owns it, as a representation of that labor which
any particular quantity of it represented when first acquired, save the necessary loss from attrition and wear.

Silver is more liable to fluctuation, and hence is not as safe as gold. In the United States, in 1873, an ounce of silver was worth about $1.18—one sixteenth the value of gold ; in 1878 it was worth about $1.10 ; in 1880 it was worth about $1.04, and in 1886 it was worth only about 84 cents, on a loss since 1873, or in thirteen years, of 34 cents,—nearly one third of its value in gold, and why ? Principally if not wholly by reason of the fact that during said period it was found in larger quantities or in more accessible places, or because the facilities for putting it into marketable shape had increased such that it then required less labor to produce it, or because demand proportionate to supply was less, and not because of demonetization, save as this affected demand. Hence, any man who owned silver in 1873 and kept it till 1886 would have suffered a net loss of about 33 per cent. of his fortune, just as might have been the case with any other commodity, and any government or individual that had issued in 1873 a promissory note to be paid in silver would have been the gainer to the same extent. Such a catastrophe having occurred to silver might also to gold, but less likely.

It however illustrates that a government that obligates itself to pay its bonds or circulating currency in gold might be either the gainer or loser, and the holder the loser or gainer, as the case might be, so that it is in fact questionable, first, whether or not a government will be able to secure the precious metal, and if so whether or not it will be worth the same at the time of payment as when the obligation was incurred. Likewise are individuals who own gold subject to the same liability to fluctuation, but since as regards gold the changes have been and are likely ever to be small, but little risk is incurred by either. These conditions, however, lead to the question : Might not the circulating medium of a country be simply the promise of the government on paper to pay certain value as thereon expressed based on the value of human labor ?

This could certainly be done if it were practicable to receive, hold, and pay out the said labor, but since such is not practicable it is found necessary to receive that labor in some shape or form that is practicable (and gold and silver appears by experience to be the best of all commodities for the purpose), and to pay out that labor represented by the same commodities, leaving with the people the risk of all fluctuations in value. Imagine a great nation wholly without a circulating medium, and that no such substance as gold or silver existed, and no other metal suitable to the purpose of coinage—that is, none that would represent in a small, convenient shape the value of any considerable amount, say one day's labor—could be had. The labor of a common man might be worth a ton of iron ore, so that a circulating medium made of this metal in a highly refined state—that is, after much labor had been expended upon it—would have to be carried in a plate weighing about one hundred pounds, to represent intrinsically one common man's labor for a day, so that if carried in sizes convenient for use, the government would be obliged to put its promise to pay the product of labor for it in some other shape.

If this promise would be necessary with iron, why use iron when the promise would be quite as good and binding if expressed on paper—a more convenient article for the purpose than iron ? It is evident, there-fore, that in the absence of gold and silver the circu-lating medium (since civilized men do not value shells and beads) would have to be altogether a promissory one backed up by a government to give the value of labor for it, and this promise would likely be made on paper. Suppose the people of that government owned between them, when aggregated, property of divers kinds worth the labor of a billion men for a day, or say in the American standard one billion dollars, but had no circulating medium. In order to trade together to advantage they would have to secure a circulating medium, and how could they best secure it? Experience had shown that the circulating medium need not be over a small percentage of the total value of the property—even one or two per cent. may answer. Assuming that they determined on one per cent. (which is rather smaller than the average), and that they could secure no precious metal but had all other things of value known to civilization. In such a state of affairs it is obvious that some kind of a medium predicated upon the faith in and resources of the government would have to be devised, which leads to the conclusion that any medium—that is, any money that does not represent in itself such value as will command a certain amount of human labor—must be promissory or " fiat " money.

If, therefore, a government could not secure the value of labor with which to make good its promissory money in the shape of gold or silver—that is, could not secure gold and silver,—it might be difficult to determine in what shape or upon what basis the medium would be redeemed. To legislate that a piece of paper with certain figures, letters, and characters printed upon it is a dollar is an arbitrary creation of wealth—making something out of nothing, a task not successfully performed since the creation of the Great Whole, if indeed ever, and it might not work. The thing must be redeemable in some sort of value.

As long as everybody consented it would undoubtedly

go just as gold and silver go, because of universal consent, and for that reason alone.   If the desires, fancies,
and preferences of the people for these metals should
cease, then no man would be willing to give a day of his
labor for an ounce of silver or for one sixteenth of an
ounce of gold, even though the quantities of these metals
remained as secure as before.   The total taxable property of America in 1890 being sixty billion dollars, and
the circulating medium being less than two billion dollars, the latter represented but little over one per cent.
of the total wealth of the country, or say one dollar on
the average out of every hundred dollars that the people
owned.   If the government in its own capacity had possessed not one dollar of property, but simply had for its
backing its right to tax the people or, rather, to compel
them to yield up and give over certain parts of their
estates, that power alone with unquestioned ability to
enforce it would constitute resources of great magnitude
and extent, certainly largely beyond one per cent. of the
total property value.   It was suggested, therefore, that
the government abandon the policy of promising to
redeem its obligations in precious metals.   It has to
obtain these metals by means of its right to force its
people to yield up value which can be exchanged therefor,
and this is its only means, assuming that there was no
federal domain or other federal property that could be
exchanged outright or hypothecated for these valuable
metals ; so why pursue the intermediary step of taking
value from the people and with that value securing
these metals, and then when secured for the further convenience of the public issuing paper money redeemable
in same, but simply issue the paper money direct and
pledge for its redemption the government's sovereignty,
its right of eminent domain, its power to enforce its

16

people to yield up value in some shape. This, it was
claimed, or something akin thereto, would have to be
done if there were no precious metals to be had, or if
the fancy and fondness of the people for these metals
should for any reason cease ; and, furthermore, the identical power and process that enables the government to
secure these metals would operate with equal force in
the maintenance of the paper money at par.

Since, however, it has been for centuries possible to
obtain these precious metals, and since there appears
to be no reasonable possibility that either the supply or
the fondness of the people for them will be materially
diminished or in any way changed, this policy should be
continued ; but as both gold and silver are in use, there
arises much difference of opinion regarding the coinage
of same.   Some people want silver or paper redeemable
in same made the only standard, others prefer gold only,
and others still prefer both.   Some, again, think that the
more money there is in circulation, the better for the
people.   This class fail to consider that if the money
has intrinsic value, or, if not, is backed by an unquestioned support, it will be no cheaper and no easier to
obtain whether there should be one or two or ten per
cent. of the property value of the country represented
in the circulating medium, and that if it has not intrinsic value, or is not backed up by an unquestioned prop,
that the greater the volume the less the value and
consequently the purchasing power.   Notwithstanding
the fact that there is much silver produced in America,
and many of its citizens favor silver as the medium
and wish to have it unlimitedly coined, yet there is a
large element that favor gold only, to which England
and the greatest of commercial nations firmly adhere.
Silver, it is by this class argued, is more cumbersome,

more liable to fluctuation, and less suited than gold on general principles for the standard of money. The silver men claim that gold cannot be obtained in quantities sufficient for the requirements of the country (which proposition has never been fully proven), and that silver is a necessity. Aside from its *less suitableness*, there is no good reason why silver alone should not be the standard, except for the fact that the nations whose force in the financial world exceed all others prefer gold. There is, however, good reason why both should not be recognized, because their relative values will change, they cannot be kept together any easier than wheat and oats. Some years wheat will be worth one dollar per bushel and oats thirty cents, and other years wheat eighty cents and oats forty cents, and so likewise with gold and silver. In 1873 an ounce of silver being worth about one hundred and eighteen cents and in 1886 being worth only about eighty-four cents, proves conclusively that the metals cannot be kept together. Silver might be demonetized and remonetized, and yet the values would fluctuate and from causes entirely natural. Silver men may force the government to buy certain amounts of silver bullion per month (just because they have the votes to do it, not because there is any reason, justice, or benefit to the people in it), thus forcing the state to become a customer of certain private enterprises and interests to the extent of many millions of dollars. With equal reason might the government have been forced to buy a certain amount of iron, copper, cotton, or any other private article of production (which alone silver is) each month, thereby benefiting these interests, and, retroactively, as is the inevitable result, injuring others correspondingly. This class of legislation is discriminating and baneful, and, like protective tariffs, bounties, subsidies, and similar interferences with private business, *must ere long be stopped.* It can be of no possible benefit to the people (but considerable to silver producers) for the government to buy more silver than is required, and the people will become aware of that fact, and legislators will be elected who will put an end to the iniquity and firmly establish gold, and gold alone, as the standard of money. Trade wants only one yardstick, especially does it not want two when they will constantly vary in length. Coins may be minted containing enough silver to make them intrinsically equal to gold, and before the milling is in the slightest degree worn, and sometimes before the face of the piece is tarnished, the market value of the silver it contains might be less than gold, so that they could only be received at par, because of the fact that the government could make them so, or rather they are as much "fiat" dollars in principle as an irredeemable paper bill. Ere long the difference may become so great that the thing may become ridiculous, and people in making their trades will specify the kind of coin they will take, or rather the particular yard-stick with which they will have their cloth measured, which will ultimately force the adoption of gold, which is the least fluctuating, the most desirable, the most generally accepted, and the best. Silver should be coined only in small denominations for change, and should be a tender for small amounts, but no man should be forced to take any considerable amount contrary to or against his will. Paper redeemable in gold only should circulate almost exclusively, and the government would have no difficulty in securing all the gold it wanted, and it would require proportionately to the outstanding circulation a very small percentum.

No more bills should be introduced and passed forcing

the government to patronize individual miners, and the
effectual suppression of this class of discriminating legislation is about the first thing that the people, who have
long suffered from its effects, are called upon or will
find it necessary to do. The government should maintain a circulating medium redeemable in gold coin only
to such an amount per capita as Congress thinks advisa-
ble for the business of the people, and that medium will
be good the world over. In determining the volume of
money, nothing should be taken into consideration save
the question, *What does the trade of the country require*
for its proper facilitation? All else is irrelevant and in-
admissible. The idea that schemes of inflation, looking
either to cheap paper or cheap silver, will benefit the
people is not only shortsighted and barren, but indicates ignorance as to the proper function of money.
There can be little doubt as to the supply of gold being
sufficient, but if not, the scarcity would apply to the
world as well as to America, and the world will provide
a substitute, and even in such an event there exists no
fear lest the United States would be fully able to supply, instead of gold for the redemption of any promises,
that adequate value that they would have been able to
give to secure the gold if obtainable. There should,
therefore, be but one yard-stick—*gold*, or paper redeemable in gold. A circulating medium to trade is like oil to
an engine. It could run without it, but runs better with
it. Too much oil, or a poor quality of it, simply runs
off the slides and journals and is wasted, and just so with
money. Therefore let it be sufficient only in quantity,
the best in quality, *and absolutely invariable.*

Silver should be sold, as any other merchandise, for
what it is worth, without any discriminating and unjust
(if not unlawful) legislative stimulus.

The demonetization of silver in America in 1873 doubtless tended to widen the breach between the two metals, either by the depreciation of silver, caused by a curtailment of the demand, or by the appreciation of gold caused by an increased demand, but certain it is that by said act of demonetization nobody was injured except an owner of silver. The claim put forth by owners of silver mines, that said act caused the financial panic of that year, or that in subsequent years the relative increase of the wheat supply to Great Britain by India was likewise attributable thereto, which caused a corresponding decline in the demand for American wheat, cannot be sustained. America had an unquestioned right to demonetize silver, and in so doing not only did not violate the slightest faith, but, on the contrary, vindicated her national honor. Bonds and other obligations payable in coin should, when due, be paid in that coin which is equal in value to that expected by the buyer at the date of the obligation, otherwise, to the extent of the depreciation, there is virtual repudiation, which no government can afford to perform as to its own or render lawful as to private obligations.

Forcing silver on the government can only result in enabling its owners to secure a dollar at a depreciated price (which hope and desire alone prompts the movement), or in reducing *all* dollars to that depreciated price. The first would be governmental favoritism and rank discrimination, and the last governmental dishonor or downright disgrace.

The government was under no obligation *not* to demonetize silver, and if in the progress of the world's commerce and by the chief commercial nations of the world gold is preferred, why should America not likewise choose gold and gold only ? Who, by the depreciation of silver, or, to put it differently, by the increased price of other things in silver, is injured except the owner of silver, and what obligations could the government have been under to pursue a policy calculated to enhance the price of silver rather than of any other commodity, which alone and nothing more silver is and should always be so long as gold is obtainable, as it doubtless ever will be in sufficient quantity for coinage? If silver had been a self-sustaining commodity the price of silver would not have decreased, notwithstanding demonetization, and notwithstanding remonetization and unlimited coinage, unless an ounce of silver will command more labor than it does, the price of silver will not increase unless the latter is sustained artificially equal to gold by the government "fiat," which is wrong.

Where can be found reasonable support to the proposition that silver would be worth permanently any more if coined in little pieces called dollars (except the cost of minting, etc., etc.) than when in bars of equal fineness, unless by reason of some sort of governmental "fiat," which is unjust?

Who can successfully show that it is to the interest of any one, save an owner or producer of silver, that the price of that commodity should be increased by any cause, much less by governmental favoritism? It is clear to any reasonable man that the people at large would be in no sense benefited if by unlimited coinage all the silver that could be produced should be made into dollars, for just as certainly as those dollars circulated on their own merit, just that certainly would they be worth no more than bars plus the cost of minting, and if so, the price of all the requirements of life in this silver would increase. If made more valuable than bars, it would be by reason of some governmental protection

that is not just. The silver producers themselves would
therefore get no great benefit unless at the expense of
the people or by the protection of the government. To
put more silver into the dollar would be the only honest
remedy, and then its size would be variable as to the
labor, to the wants of life, or to the gold it would buy ;
hence justice to all, simplicity, certainty, and reliability
demand but one yard-stick, and efforts to make two are
prompted more in the interests of mine-owners than for
the good of the masses of the people. Cheap money is
like poor soil ; it is difficult to get a living if you own a
world of it. Farmers' alliances and tradesmen generally
should remember that a sow's ear is not a silk purse, and
legislation will never make it such.

Everything should be on a gold basis. He who possesses silver in bars should be as well off as he who possesses it in coin ; it should not be a legal tender, so that
there would be no special reason for putting it into the
shape of little round pieces. Any man who cared to
exchange a horse or anything else for silver could, of
course, do so, and he who had mines that were so rich
and accessible that he could produce it for less than it
would sell for in the market will be a fortunate man, just
as he who has iron, copper, tin, or lead mines that are
similarly located. Silver has its value—sometimes higher
and sometimes lower—just as other metals. Civilization
has, however, about ceased to call it "precious," because a man will not give a day's labor for a whole ounce
of it. It has, however, its commercial uses in the arts, in
trade, and the like. Rich men ornament their fire-places,
furniture, and door-knobs with it ; sometimes watch-
cases are made of it, but ladies do not care to wear it as
jewelry. Expectant benedicts will not insult their lady
loves by presenting engagement rings made of it ; yet it

has its uses. The government should buy what it wants
for subsidiary coinage ; and when England and the commercial world recognize it as the best metal for money—
that is, the metal least liable to fluctuations and of such
value as to make coins minted of it the most desirable
size and generally the most acceptable—of course it may
then answer the purpose of money. But so on this basis
would copper or iron ; but if silver or copper or iron,
then not gold—why two yard-sticks that must fluctuate
in value ? Silver has become so cheap—that is, a man's
labor will, with the appliances for mining it, produce so
much—that a piece of it worth twenty dollars is a burthen to the wearer, and it becomes a question as to how
much cheaper it may become, until the same objections
that apply to copper or iron could be directed against it
with equal force and effect.

The government should recognize both convenience
and value in the national banking system, and permit it
to be continued.

When any association of gentlemen wish to engage in
the banking business, if they take to the federal treasury
an amount of gold or its equivalent in any acceptable
shape equal to the circulating medium they desired,
the government should issue to them a two-per-cent.
bond running thirty or forty years, or if they secured
these bonds from any outside owner all the same. By
depositing these bonds as security the government should
permit the bank to issue circulating notes to the full face
value of the bonds, on which the banking institution
should be obliged to pay to the government one per cent.
annually, which would leave to the institution a gain of
one per cent., representing the interest on the bonds.
These banks should be, of course, subjected to govern-

ment supervision and control, and would stand as an
adjunct or a means, as it were, that the government
would adopt to better regulate the supply of the circulating medium.

Providing and maintaining a uniform and stable circulating medium should be one of the government's
chiefest functions acknowledged by all, and this system
of banking rather *localizes* even that important duty.
The bonds deposited as security (security bonds) should
not be subjected to the cumulative rate, being the property—assets—of the bank (a corporation), but the bank
stock representing these and such other assets as it
might own, would be, of course, cumulatively taxed in
the hands of the individual owners, just as the bonds
would have been in the hands of an individual owner.
The government, be it ever in mind, would receive its
tax exclusively from individuals, excepting this special
one-per-cent. circulation tax that applied to banks only
whilst they used the circulating medium that the government authorized them to issue. The government should
conclude that the one per cent. the bank would gain in
interest on its security bonds, notwithstanding the fact
that the institution would be authorized to issue a medium on which while circulating it could draw interest,
was no more than a fair inducement for the bank to enter
into business, and since it would be open to all, would
not be discriminating. The system insures a circulating
medium not only equally stable but *more flexible ;* that
is, when different localities of the great continent want
a circulating medium there would likely spring up a
national bank and issue new currency, which would be
better than taking that part of the medium that it would
require from the general fund already in the various
channels of trade. In other words, it is a means of
getting nearer to the wants of trade than the government

could well do unless by some similar system, and it would avoid, to a great extent, legislation in Congress on the supply of the circulating medium per capita. Furthermore, if there should be required an increase of say ten or twenty per cent. in the circulating medium, it could be accomplished through the bank at a net cost of but one per cent. to the government, whereas if it had been obliged to secure the gold in the market it would doubtless have had to give bonds therefor, which would bear at least two per cent., or procure the value with which to secure said circulation by an increase of tax on the people.

If it should issue an increased amount of paper notes, it must have an increased amount of gold with which to redeem the same on presentation, which would be the same thing in effect ; consequently, all things considered, the national banking system is worth what it costs, and should be continued. Its circulation is secured by bonds, and when surrendered up the bonds would be returned to the banking institution. This does not alter the feature of a circulating medium being redeemable in gold, for the bonds are and should always be payable in gold ; and it gives the government a chance to maintain a greater circulating medium with less ready gold at hand. If gold is demanded of the bank, it should be required to pay it for any of its own notes, and for this purpose should be required to keep a certain balance on hand. Any bank failing in this particular should have its charter cancelled, notes called in, on receipt of which the bonds would be returned, and the business of the association would be ended. All systems of national banking must of course undergo changes and modifications to meet the exigencies of the times, just as any other business. Likewise, the quantity of money must be subject to the variable conditions and expansions of trade, *but its quality should never be impaired.*

CHAPTER XII.

THE practical operation of the cumulative rate as applied to home property having been explained, and also the result of the qualification-for-suffrage system in its beneficent effects on the character of representatives and the purification and perfection of the balloting system having been illustrated, it may be well to look for a moment into the incalculable benefits that would result, and the increased conservatism that would be displayed by men who were chosen to public place by men, rather than blatherskites chosen by bribery and corruption.

Though America, by reason of her wondrous resources, her varied clime, and, by no means the least, her free institutions, has prospered so unprecedentedly in population, in wealth, and in power, notwithstanding the baneful and centralizing effects of some of her despicable policies, there has arisen quite a sentiment against foreign immigration.

This is but reasonable on the part of the hitherto ignorant workingmen, who at last begin to see that that system of " protection " which discriminated against labor's products and yet invited the laborer himself is, to say the least, rather a second-handed benefit, if, indeed, it is not an actual injury.

To maintain that a man who performed his day's work three thousand miles away in England, Germany, or in France or Belgium, was a greater interference—hence the object against which the protectionists should build their walls—than the thousands of the same class who were seeking positions at our very doors, does not look quite as forcible to wage-earners as it once did. It therefore appeared to the workmen as though it was simply a question how many would come over till competition would be quite as fierce, and hence wages as cheap, as in the least favored and most oppressed of any nation in Europe, and the thing to do was to keep out the *people* rather than their products—*i.e.*, stop immigration. That heretofore they had been skinning the cat from the wrong end ; they had been protecting the country against cheap goods, which they all wanted (save their employers), and filling it to overflowing with cheap labor, which none of them wanted (save their employers).

In fact, the more enlightened began to bump their heads together and ask themselves if they had not all along been goats ? The facts are that they had been goats. If there is anything to be gained by any system of protection it would certainly be in that which would protect the laborers directly, by avoiding competition with foreign or any other class of labor, and not in that which deprived them of the best and cheapest sources from which to obtain their supplies. If one hundred men were wanted to plow a certain field, they could certainly obtain a better rate per day if there were no competitive bystanders

ready to take the jobs, than could they if the price of
the potatoes which were to be grown in that field were
artificially enhanced by some discriminating legislation,
and a hundred other laborers were standing by ready to
take the job. The increased price of the potatoes would
inure to their employer and against themselves, whether
the competitive bystanders were ready or not, and to a
greater and more alarming extent would they be discriminated against and harmed if, by legislation, the
employer could make them pay the increased price for
the potatoes, pocketing the profit himself, and at the
same time be in a position to make available the cheap
competitive and by-standing laborers. Better a thousand
times, and from any view of the case, had the price of
the potatoes remained normal—the result of open competition,—so that they could buy them cheap, and keep
away the competitive by-standing laborer, so they could
sell their labor high. Thus the masses began to think
that curtailment of immigration was the remedy for their
ills. Keep out the laborers who compete with us and
let in the products that compete with our employers, and
things will even up better. That does look more reasonable, and soon there may not be found a laboring man
in the country but such as favors opening the ports to
cheap products, but not to cheap labor. The employers
have said well : "Cheap products mean cheaper wages."
"Yes," said the employé, "cheap labor means cheap
wages also, and we have failed to see many cases where
you would pay us $1.50 per day when you could get as
good a man for less ; the latter is a direct blow at us,
and the former is indirect. We have been trying protection against cheap goods, and you have got rich and
we become poor ; we now want to try protection against
cheap labor, and see how that will work." Therefore

there has been a great outcry against immigration.
America for Americans, cheap goods but no cheap men;
bring in your goods but keep out the men. These and
similar arguments may gain currency and receive support before the adoption of the cumulative scale. Congress will be appealed to to restrict immigration not
only as to character (which restriction is now made) but
as to numbers (which restriction should never be made).
The annual immigration is between five and six hundred
thousand, and Congress may be asked unconditionally
to reduce it to ten thousand per month. These impor-
tunities may cause long debates in Congress and much
discussion throughout the country. Whilst nearly every
other country in the civilized world is using its utmost
endeavors to prevent emigration, here America stands
opposing immigration—a very unusual and anomalous
position. The question may be much discussed and
thoroughly sifted. It may be asked of those who oppose
foreign immigration, foreign money, foreign goods, in
fact everything foreign that will make, and has made,
the country rich, if the prevention of immigration to the
extent of four to five hundred thousand able-bodied men
who desire to come is good, why would not the enforced
emigration of about the same number of able-bodied men
who are now in America be better? Which argument,
reduced to its natural sequence, would mean, at an early
day, the depopulation of the country.

If in scarcity there is plenty; if in vacuity there is
material; if in weakness there is strength; if Thersites
is Hercules; if a singed cat is a Bengal tiger, or a puling
puppet a roaring lion; if, in fact, a fool possesses wisdom,
then such policies would be wholesome—not otherwise.

It appears reasonable enough that the laboring man,
failing to be benefited by protection, in fact, contin-

uously, though for a long time unconsciously, being
worsted by it, should rush towards the proposition of
curtailment of immigration—on the surface the most
reasonable remedy—for the disproportionate condition
of affairs, of which they complain. Reflecting minds,
however, at once observe that a self-sustaining man is a
benefit rather than a curse to society ; that, if a country
with a population of 640 to the square mile, as is
Belgium, or one to the acre, could maintain itself at
all, certainly, increased population could not be oppressing America—on the average naturally richer—
with a population of less than twenty to the square
mile, or but one to every thirty-two acres.

The agitation of these questions in America is not by
reason of the greater oppression (which really, though
becoming the same, is as yet less than that elsewhere),
but on account of her free institutions. Here the populace can, and with some hope, discuss, proclaim, and
expound ; but elsewhere they cannot, with much hope.
In America the grievances of the entire world are discussed, and, naturally, a greater number of remedies for
wrongs are proposed.

To argue that the increase of population by immigration (provided that immigration is of a self-sustaining
character) is hurtful, is to argue against the increase of
population in the world at large in the natural manner,
and whilst it has to be admitted that many families
in moderate estate are too prolific for comfort, or too
numerous to enable them to provide their offspring with
the best of social conditions and opportunities, yet it is
by no means to be advocated that the biblical injunction
"be fruitful and multiply" should be summarily inter-
dicted. The inability to properly provide for a number
of little children during their infancy is one thing, and

the detriment to society supposed to be consequent upon immigration quite another. For the former there appears to be no feasible remedy. If as the result of the marriage of two healthy people there should be born into the world ten or a dozen children in as many or in a fewer number of years (as frequently happens), and then if by accident the father, hitherto a dutiful sire and husband and the main support of the family, should be taken off, leaving an indigent widow with the burden of the family, the condition would be of course not the most desirable, if, in fact, it is not actually deplorable, but how can it be remedied? Society has and does, to a very reasonable extent—perhaps quite as liberally as would neither encourage idleness nor invite malingery,— provide homes for widows and orphans.

Philanthropists likewise often have and yet do leave much of their estates for benevolent purposes, and it yet remains for some philosopher to suggest a better system. Nothing save the plan of making all mothers pensioners on the government could reach it effectually, and that would appear to disrupt the domestic relationship, and, though possibly for no good cause, be prejudicial to society.

At least it appears to shock the moral conscience, but possibly only because it is in conflict with long-established custom. Rather it appears to be one of the greater of the unanswered problems, just how far can charity or public care and protection extend without inflicting injury? Too much is taken advantage of, for thousands would prefer the care of the poorhouse or hospital—some, in fact, incarceration in jail—than the support their own energies would secure for them. It appears as though the infant and the growing child should have adequate support, even proper training and

17

education, to fit it for the duties and cares of life, when it shall have arrived at the age when it should be self-sustaining. There is scarce a domestic animal of the lowest type, even unto a dog, that is not thus cared for, not alone in infancy but in maturity as well.

It does look as though the young of the human species should be as well cared for in infancy as the colt, the pup, or the calf,—not only as well, but as much better as its estate when maturity is reached is superior to that of these animals ; yet there are thousands—yea, millions— of children in all thickly populated cities in Europe, America, in Asia—in fact, everywhere—that seldom have enough to eat and never enough to wear.

But, then, many children are born into the world, maimed, crippled, imbecile, and decrepit ; those of the rich are subjected to these misfortunes, whilst not to such an extent, yet likewise, as are those of the poor.

Therefore, since in keeping with what most people are disposed to term the will of Divine Providence, but what others consider rather the result of nature's active agen-cies (be it the one or the other, or both), it is manifestly true that disabilities and misfortune have existed (with both rich and poor, though oftener with the latter) from the very beginning ; and since they cannot be absolutely prevented nor controlled, what is left save to make the burthen as light as possible, by providing for the extreme, just as is necessary in poverty—the other apparently essential result or condition of society which cannot be absolutely prevented or controlled.

Consequently, mothers must be made pensioners on the state till their children have reached the self-sustain-ing age (which will relieve the poverty in the rearing of children, mitigate disease in same, though not absolutely avoid it), or some—yea, many—children must grow up

in a worse relative, if not worse actual, state than the
colt, the calf, the dog, or the hog. After man has
grown to be a self-sustaining individual, or after he has
reached the age say of fifteen years, when he ought to
be self-sustaining, it is no use to argue that the world is
too small, that time has not yet arrived, and it is not apt
soon to arrive, if ever.

Those who are affrighted by the Malthusian theory
may dispel their fears for the time. If the resources of
the world are ever to be too severely taxed, that time will
not be within the lives of our grandchildren, and they will
doubtless be producing all kinds of vegetable and other
food products out of earth, water, and heat in a few
hours, as they are now produced from the seed out of the
same essential substances in from four to six months.
But if it were actually at hand during the lives of the
present generation, the condition does not exist in
America, therefore it is useless to argue that increased
population here is in any sense injurious (rather is it a
blessing) ; and if increased population is not injurious,
then self-sustaining immigration is not injurious. But, it
is urged, let us have the increase native-born instead of
foreign-born. To this it may be replied that a good,
stout, and able-bodied foreigner is worth just as much to
the country as his productions would exceed his consumption—so why exclude him ? If the country is not
suffering from over-population, caused either by natural
increase or by immigration, what object would there be
in curtailing either ?

If a horse adds to the wealth of the country, so likewise does a man, if he be self-sustaining, to a greater
degree ; and if the world is being over-taxed with its increasing population (especially if America, with a population of sixty million in 1890, when, if then populated

as was Belgium, it would have contained six hundred million, is so), better begin the depopulation by killing off the horses, for they eat much that man can consume, and do much work that man could perform. In Belgium six hundred and forty people to the square mile live, and that too in a country a very large part of which was once sand dunes and deserts; how, therefore, could population have the slightest effect in America, with twenty people to the square mile, every acre of which, with less labor and care than reclaimed the Belgian sand dunes, could be made as fertile as a garden? But, since to admit a ridiculous proposition always results in a ridiculous conclusion, which usually shows up best the fallacy of an argument, we will accept it as settled that America is over-populated, and that immigration and then ere long fecundation must both be stopped. When attempting to carry the scheme practically into execution most supporters of the faith will be willing to shut out immigration, but before interdicting fecundation many will think it would be best to kill off a few thousand horses that were consuming the world's products and eating up its roots, herbs, and grasses; but why do this when the people can, if they choose, eat up the horses?

Thus does the admission of premises, to the vulgar apparently reasonable and sound, invariably lead to the same result—an absurd and ridiculous conclusion. It requires brains to build a boat, and brains to set a boat afloat; so also does it require brains to run a government, and brains (more than all men together possess) to properly regulate society and equitably (not equally) to distribute the blessings of the earth.

Consequently, great benefit will result in relegating the fools to the rear by qualified suffrage, for they belong nowhere else. Those who are guided by hyperbole and nonsense miss their calling when they try to reform the state, just as an ass would lose his beauty and but little increase his ferocity when he donned the lion's skin. Hence it is that attempts at reform amount to nothing— the masses have not the brains; they are rash and inconsiderate—moved by the incendiary utterances of some loquacious fool who knows nothing about the practical workings or the probable effect of any proposition; in fact, the best and wisest know but little and can prophesy not at all. If ever a wise and conservative leader appears, trivial and petty dissensions arise of no consequence or effect on the main issue, and he is either shorn of his utility or disgusted with the follies of his ignorant coadjutors; and it will not be until that conservative reform is proposed which looks for its following not from the ignorant, the vicious, and the depraved, but from among men who know the benefit of direct, consolidated, and prudent action, that things will begin to move.

This class of men can see through a grindstone when the hole is sufficiently large. These men can see that all talk regarding the decrease of population, either by anti-immigration or by the more natural and effectual method, anti-fecundation, is stupid nonsense. They know that every able-bodied and self-sustaining man is of value to the state; that he not only has labor to sell, but he has wants to supply, so that he not only occupies the position of supplying labor, but of creating a demand for it as well. He must have food and clothes and boots and shoes, and to the extent that he requires them causes just that much demand for labor which, to say the least, offsets the supply he furnishes with his strong muscles and rugged frame. There was scarce as much per capita demand for labor when the population of America was six million as when it is sixty million people, and there was certainly

not as much actual or aggregate demand. The reduction
of population curtails demand as well as supply, and increased population enlarges demand as well as supply,
so that the conditions in either case are relatively about
as before.   There are times when there is a greater supply of workmen for a particular class of work than there
is work for them to perform, but this may—in fact, will—
happen in a population of six million just as well as in
sixty million.   There are times when there is over-production, just as there are seasons when there is too much
rain, and over-production, just as over or excess of rain,
can as well and is quite as likely to happen when there
are six million as when there are sixty million.   The
only possible difference between that condition which
applies to six million and that which applies to sixty million lies in the fact that population creates wealth, and
without a regulating balance-wheel that wealth will concentrate, because the extremes can be and are greater in
a population of sixty million than of six million people ;
just as in a great desert like Sahara, where there is much
sand, the variable and shifting winds can amass greater
heaps in one spot, leaving others almost bare, whereas in
a small desert, where there is little sand, the difference is
scarcely noticeable.   It takes a big ocean to turn up a
big wave, so a big community to cause greater contrasts
in condition.   Apply the proper remedy (Phronocracy),
and the contrast will be no greater in sixty million than
in six million, but the nation will be ten times richer,
more powerful, and secure.

Prior to the curtailment of suffrage, however, the conservative people will utter many a lingering sigh. When,
oh, when will Congress quit legislating ; when will the
fool-killer actually be killed ? When will we be permitted to run our business on business principles, and

be relieved of the blatherskites who thwart our operations ; when will the fool who thinks it is a curse to the
country for a foreigner to invest his money in it, be sat
down upon and elected to stay at home ? When suffrage
is purified—it will be purified when curtailed,—not before.
Before then the vulgar representative will be in clover ;
but he will elicit only laughter, contempt, and scorn when
confronted by the wise. He now tells the people (especially the Irish) that some English subject owns land in
a certain State, and the American people are actually
paying money rent for the use of same, which appears to
be horrible. What a pity the benighted heathen cannot comprehend that the American who is paying the
one, ten, or one hundred thousand for the land, is in all
probability gaining two, twenty, or two hundred thousand
for the use of same, or at least a profit satisfactory to
himself ; if not so, then the American tenant is as great
a fool as his would-be protector, and should have been
tried at once for lunacy—a better remedy than discriminating legislation.

The Englishman can't force an American to pay any
fixed price for land, and it is a fair presumption that if
an American voluntarily pay a certain price he does so
to his own profit. The sophistical politician has annoyed the people with his nonsense for a time too long
to endure, but in the long run he will be suppressed.
Finally it will be an act of almost as much reproach as
treason to attempt to incite the populace to rash and
absurd doings. No public man or aspirant for public
trust should ever think of seeking popularity by frenzied
railings against the conservative institutions of the state.
Men of this kind will simply be called blatherskites—
Bombastes Furiosos—for full are they of sound and fury
that signifieth nothing. Verily are their arguments as

two grains of wheat in two bushels of chaff. One can seek all day ere he finds them, and when he has them they were not worthy of the search. One of the very greatest drawbacks to progress is the attempted legislation against foreign investment. Public land can only be taken up by a citizen, and of right so because he pays his citizenship for his title, and that is the government's only price for that which is exclusively its own ; but when the individual has acquired his title he should be permitted to sell it, as anything else he owns, to any man or set of men who would pay a satisfactory price. If he fritters it away for naught he is a fool, as would be the man who would pay rent for glory and to please the foreign land-owner. Legislation is not the remedy for these fools, and all efforts in that direction tend directly to depress the price of land—and why ? Because a good customer is taken away ! What matters it if John Jones, who happens to have his mail addressed London, England, owns ten thousand acres of land in every State of the Union, provided he pays his tax ? He cannot carry the land away, and the money he pays for it remains in this country, and to his rent he is entitled, and it usually happens that the tenant secures a better deal from a foreigner than from a home landlord, who keeps better apace with the rapidly advancing tendencies of all American properties than the foreigner.

Much wrong is done to foreign investors by unjust decrees of the courts, and as such discrimination is usually followed by unanswerable results, vast sums of foreign gold (principally British) have been diverted from America, where they would have preferred to have placed it, and been taken to remoter parts of the world. The Irish element in American politics has been very hurtful to English investment ; true, the money comes

in considerable lots notwithstanding all, but more by
many millions of pounds would gladly come if only
fairly treated. It is this very class that excites the
opposition to foreign ownership in America, or, rather,
their prejudice against England has almost ruined their
own island, and now they seek to ruin America too. It
is admitted by very many—in fact, some say by a
majority—of the resident property-holding Irishmen,
that the continuous agitation of the land question
and the legislation that has been passed in the futile
endeavor to satisfy the complainants, has actually
caused more harm to the island than half the property is
worth.

Man, as an individual, either has the natural right to
possess property or he has not. If he has (as the conservative people of the world admit, and which few, if
any, deny), then he is entitled to the possible enjoyment
of the usufruct of that property, and the state should
not only not interfere with said title, but should protect
the individual in its retention. It is not an argument
against the right to hold and enjoy property to say that
the owner once acquired it cheap, provided that ownership was secured by the highest and most equitable
means recognized at the time, any more than it would
be good logic to maintain that, if it was acquired by the
payment of an exorbitant price, the title would be secure
if not obtained in conformity with the highest recognized
authority at the time. It cannot be maintained, either,
that the sacrifice of excessive individual estates, as is
vouchsafed by the cumulative rate, is of itself absolutely
just, but this is a penalty of increased severity imposed
upon the excessively wealthy individual for the good
and well-being of society, just as the original sacrifice of
a part of his individual rights to the state was made for

the good of society. It is not claimed for the system that it is absolutely just to the individual, but it is frankly admitted that it is discriminating and socialistic, but it is supported on the ground that the discrimination is directed against the man who can best afford it, and not against those, as under all other systems, who can least afford it, and the socialistic feature of it is no actual harm, even to those whom it most oppresses. It cannot therefore be charged against the advocates of cumulative taxation that they are inconsistent, that they oppose legislation that forces a landlord to practically sacrifice his land, and yet favor a system that accomplishes the same thing in fact. There are wide distinctions and obvious differences between the two, even more than would be casually recognized by those who possess the ability to consider and the candor to confess. The one strikes directly at the right of property ownership in the abstract, the other at the same in the concrete; or, rather, the first recognizes that property has no rights that the community is bound to respect, and the latter that it has (till it has been amassed to an unreasonable, unwieldy, and useless extent) more rights even than has hitherto been granted to it. Furthermore, the adoption by the country of some such general system will relieve it of the necessity of considering the passage of special acts which are discriminating and oppressive in their effects, and which are usually the ebullitions for popularity of some blatherskite in legislative assemblies. Such representatives, however, are the inevitable product of the present debased suffrage system, and are very hurtful to wise and prudent legislation. Nevertheless, they are "duly chosen" as a result of the prejudice *and ignorance* of the "great unwashed," and are called "*honorable*" when *fool* would be far more appropriate. What signifies "*honor*" thus unworthily worn, thus prostituted, disgraced, defiled ?

> " The mere word 's a slave,
> Debauch'd on every tomb ; on every grave,
> A lying trophy, and as oft is dumb,
> *Where dust and damn'd oblivion is the tomb*
> *Of honored bones indeed.*"

CHAPTER XIII.

Desirableness and result of territorial annexation—Some opposition to extending the boundaries—Other land thought by some to be useless—Value to the countries themselves greater than to the States—Final preference of all for one flag over all—Detail of the discussion regarding annexation—Tropical lands needed by the States—Better acquire land suitable to tropical products than to produce them by taxation and bounties—North America adapted to one government over the whole continent—Likewise tend to make customs, language, and people alike—Local home-rule vital—Possibility of division in North America if local rule is molested.

THE United States of America having, after the acquisition of the Louisiana country, the Mexican conquest of 1846 and 1847, and the purchase of Alaska, acquired about three and one half million square miles of territory, and the entire amount, excepting Alaska, being joined and conterminous from ocean to ocean, and, as if chosen by design, within those parallels of latitude that are most desirable, and beyond which, either north or south, there is but little that is of great value, it appears as though the talk of extension of territory is the wildest bluster, and prompted solely by the desire for glory. Why should Canada be annexed to the American Union? it is asked. The States can produce anything that can be grown in Canada save icebergs, and they possess little value save beauty, and that only as a sunset or an aurora shows them to the observer to advantage. Why, likewise, should Mexico and Central America and Cuba be annexed to the American Union? That land, it is claimed, is too far south to be of any great value. The lakes on the north and the Rio Grande River on the south are the natural boundaries, it is claimed, and beyond these limitations either way there is nothing, some people claim, over which the Stars and Stripes could float and feel within the sphere of their accustomed conditions. This banner now waves, it is said, over about the only part of North America that is fit to be called the "land of the free and the home of the brave," so why extend it farther? Likewise is it claimed that the present limitations, well populated and well governed, are worth more and will be greater than the entire continent besides, for the reason that the remainder is either too far north or too far south to be of any profit, but must, on the contrary, be a constant source of trouble, annoyance, and expense ; that neither Canada, Mexico, nor Central America are more than self-sustaining, and, by reason of the natural conditions that afflict them, they never can become great, in the national sense of the word. Two thirds of Canada is ice-bound more than half the year, and consequently is practically uninhabitable. Mexico, likewise, is an elevated plateau in the centre, on which nothing will grow, a practical desert, as compared with the lands in the States, save along the coasts of the Pacific Ocean and Gulf of Mexico, where the land, though fertile, is subjected to an inhospitable clime, fatal to foreigners, scarce innocuous to natives, and if so, to say the least, so enervating and depressing that progress to any great extent, as the result of individual enterprise, is practically impossible.

It is also urged against Mexico that her population is composed of a different race of people, speaking a different language, with different wants, customs, desires, and inclinations ; that they would not affiliate with or become sympathetic with the people, and that the cost of administering justice and preserving domestic tranquillity would be greater than all the value that could be found in the country. It is claimed also that both Mexico and Canada are burdened with debt, which would have to be provided for, and that to make either of these countries a part of the great Union of States, in the benefits of which, co equally with any, they would share and participate, would be unjust, and that we would get practically in return, therefore, nothing save debt, disturbance, and discontent.

It is claimed, on the other hand, that both of these countries could be governed, if annexed to the States, at less than half the cost that is necessary for either independently ; that the maintenance of a complete system of administration, legislative, judicial, and executive—armies, navies, and internal and coast defences, would be but little more for one hundred million than for eighty million people, and practically the same for one hundred and fifty million as for one hundred and twenty million, so that the present expenditure by these separate powers for the maintenance and perpetuity of these civic and military institutions is no criterion as to the expense that need be incurred, if made a part of the Union, and that the only question to be determined is the mutual desirableness of the association. Both, of course, cherish national patriotism and pride, a fondness for their own flag and their national institutions, that no American cares to alter or disturb. All objections as to the remoteness of the country are entirely abandoned, for the boundary of Canada is scarce a stone's throw from the northern boundary of the States, and the city of Mexico, on the other extremity, can be

reached from Washington City in less time than is required to go from New York to San Francisco. Likewise is any desire to take either of these countries by
force absolutely suppressed. There arises, however,
throughout the entire continent what is termed the
"American sentiment"—that is, a pride in the greatness
and glory of this quarter of the whole world. Whether
he be Canadian or Mexican, he is yet an American, and
if each section could retain its local control, why not, for
the good and the pride of all, have the whole together
on matters exclusively and essentially national? If
seven tenths of the population and nine tenths the
wealth of this quarter of the world can not only be
governed, but prosper as no country in the entire world
had ever prospered, under one form and system of
government, why could not the other small fraction
participate equally in that prosperity and glory, not only
to the great advantage of their local institutions (which
would not only be retained to themselves, but solidified
and strengthened), but to the pride of each in the grandeur of—not the States, not Mexico, not Central America,
nor Canada—but of *America* from ocean to ocean, from
the Isthmus to the Pole, destined by the forces of
nature to be, not only one, but the greatest nation of
all? Since Canadians, Mexicans, and Central Americans
would participate in the general government precisely to
the same proportionate extent as any of the existing States
in the lower House, and exactly to the same extent State
for State in the Senate, and a resident of either of their
sections might become President, the same interest and
pride could be taken in the affairs of the country that is
manifested in any other section. The Mexican government, though more stable now, has been for years uncertain and despotic, and the educated property-holding

people, who are progressive in their instincts, and who
are not parties in the spoils of government, yearn for
such a condition of affairs as annexation would bring.
They have seen its effects in California and the West, and
can imagine no cause that would prevent a similar condition in Mexico.

Their lands, they are certain, would bring a very
greatly enhanced price ; the better classes can already
speak English and are capable of affiliation.   The whole
country, abandoning pauper suffrage, would remove the
objection heretofore urged against the Mexican peone
population, and there would remain no reason why
America should not be America nationally, especially
when there could be preserved a system, the value and
efficiency of which had been tested, whereby localities
could nevertheless control their domestic affairs.   Present non-office-holding, or non-political spoils Mexicans
would be eager to aspire for governorships of their
States, under such conditions as exist in the northern
sisterhood ; for senators in the upper house and for
representatives in the lower house of the American
Congress.   They would want to participate in what
would then be an American nation—in fact, as much
theirs in the ratio of numbers as any other man's ; and,
above all, they would want to effectually settle the
supremacy of the sword, under which alone they have so
long lived and suffered.

Deputations of prominent Mexicans may yet visit
Washington City and consult with the authorities on
some plan of annexation.   To this, of course, the Mexican government would at first be very hostile, so it
might have to be done secretly, but would afterwards be
more open.   The authorities at Washington could be
assured, as well as Americans on the border, that if any

aid or countenance would be given them, they could maintain a successful result ; that the brain and property of Mexico wanted to be annexed—knowing as they would its inestimable benefits,—but they dare not speak or act in any concerted direction without American sympathy. All know that there would be no disposition in the States to take Mexico by force, notwithstanding the earnest, though suppressed, desire of many of her very best citizens.

There is no question, of course, as to the ability of ten or twenty men to conquer one man, or that a thousand dollars would buy more and larger guns than one dollar ; but conquest would not be the thing. Many Americans have already invested their capital and are making their homes in Mexico ; large mining and smelting establishments have been built ; immense tracts of land irrigated and reclaimed and naturally these residents are sympathetic with that class of Mexicans who desire annexation (which will be the better class, almost to a man). Quite as enthusiastic for Mexican annexation to America as even the American residents of the country, would doubtless be the Englishmen who have settled there in charge of British investments. England cares but little even for Canada, and of course nothing for Mexico, save to trade with the people ; and since it looks probable that the whole of North America, if joined, would accept the free-trade policy, which is impossible with either Canada, Mexico, or Central America if separate ; and since the entire eight millions of square miles of country would then be accessible to British enterprise, it would be quite natural that England should at least urge no objection to the amalgamation of all American countries, which would in fact be to her interest and gain. Thus the Americans and Britishers, together with the Mexican

18

annexationists, which latter class would include practically all of the substantial citizens of the country who were not a part of or in sympathy with the dominant political power, could make common cause for annexation.   Finally, the feeling will wax so warm that meetings will be held for the discussion of the question right in the city of Mexico.   Allusion will be made to the likelihood of Canadian annexation and the beneficent results consequent thereon, which are now apparent ; the talk of " manifest destiny " and the like is now current and widespread, and the sentiment could move rapidly on until at last the hostile factions of the dominant Mexican party would find it necessary to institute measures of suppression, and might send messages of complaint to the administration at Washington. The government of the United States would take no part in the movement, which, if encouraged, would move over Mexico as naturally as would a prairie fire fanned by autumnal winds and fed upon the sun-dried grasses of her extensive plains.   Discussion would become lively in the States, the controversy doubtless drifting on to the general proposition as to whether or not annexation of territory is to the interest of the States.   Whilst there is apparently no particular reason for or special good to be subserved by the annexation of Canada—save perhaps the settlement of the seal and fisheries question, the control of the mouth of the St. Lawrence, and kindred controversies, none of which are of very great importance,—yet territorial domain extending to the north pole would be placed under one government, and with that once accomplished the desire to complete the job and extend the same flag to the Isthmus, would become the desire of almost all residents of the continent.   Annexation does not signify the subjugation of

Canada or Mexico by the United States, but their voluntary preference to become a part of one good government for the good of all.

This would relieve much of the sting which under other circumstances would pierce the patriotic breasts. As to Mexico, there are a great many reasons upon the part of its own and the people of the North why it should become a part. The States, as now constituted, practically end at latitude 30 north—this being about the last parallel running through the whole,—and there are very many tropical plants, vegetables, and fruits that cannot be produced so far from the equator.

Mexico and Central America are all south of this, and can, and if properly cultivated would, produce every tropical plant that civilization needs. The States cannot grow sugar to supply one tenth of the population, nor, in fact, any tropical product excepting oranges and lemons in Florida and California, and these are not essentially tropical, nor is the climate fully suited to their best development. The States have imported sugar to an extent that has produced under the useless tariff a revenue of over fifty million dollars annually, and under a proper system of cultivation, all that could be grown in Mexico, together with fruits and spices of an infinite quantity and variety, also coffee, tea, and, in fact, everything not grown in the States, that any part of the world could supply. On the other hand, Mexico is dependent on the States or other outside sources for all sorts of manufactured articles and implements for agriculture—cotton, woollens, and textile fabrics,—in fact, for almost everything not produced directly from the earth. What applies to Mexico is equally true as to Central America, and in both the land suitable for mineral developments is practically untouched. Mexico

needs the markets of the States for her silver-bearing
lead ores, and notwithstanding the fact that the States
need the ores, they are practically excluded by the prohibitory tariff. The progressive, non-official Mexicans
see these conditions, and Americans likewise see great
increased opportunity for selling machinery, and implements, and merchandise in general. In fact, in deciding
the question as to the desirableness of annexation, it
must be considered as any other business proposition—to
wit : is it worth what it will cost to the parties most interested ? That country is of course the most nationally
independent that can produce within the limits of its own
jurisdiction all the commodities required for civilized
life, but to attempt to accomplish this by legislation is
utterly impracticable as to many, and usually too costly
as to any that cannot be produced from nature's unaided
storehouses. Oranges cannot be made to grow practically in Greenland's icy mountains, nor even in the
vicinity of New York, and if orange culture is desirable
it is decidedly the most profitable, reasonable, and com-
mon-sense policy to secure, if possible, land on which
they will luxuriate and thrive by reason of its inherent
adaptability, than to seek to accomplish the purpose by
legislation. In the former case it shuts off a natural
source of supply and forces in an unnatural one, whereas
by the latter it is simply a matter of transportation. In
thirty years the States have to 1890 averaged fully forty
million per year in taxation on sugar, making one billion
two hundred million that her people have paid for that
commodity in excess of what it could have been secured
for, if land of sufficient quantity in a clime that was suitable had been procured by the nation. Likewise so with
coffee and all tropical productions, and this amount is
equal to the then value of all land and property south of

the Rio Grande. Without suitable territory there must exist a state of utter dependence on foreign lands for all exogenous productions, or there must be instituted a system of encouragement or support by protection that is invariably discriminating and expensive, if not altogether impracticable.

Hence the great necessity of a thoroughly equipped nation possessing territory, if such can be obtained, that will produce, naturally, all the commodities essential to the needs of the human being in a civilized state.

Mexico offers this supply to more than a sufficient extent, if the land therein along the coast of the Gulf as well as the Pacific Ocean is properly cared for and cultivated. That these lands should be made available is the great wish of the progressive Mexicans, who are almost always English-speaking Mexicans.

The two countries are becoming amalgamated by other ties than natural and commercial interest. The Mexicans are usually dark-complexioned, and, on the theory of contrast, admired the light skin and blue eyes of the more northern women, which results in many unions in marriage that are fruitful of good results to both. Likewise do the blue-eyed northern men become enamoured of the voluptuous Mexican ladies, and ere long there will exist a bond of domestic interest and affinity that will be stronger than commercial ties. When the belief is current, both in Canada and Mexico, that annexation is not sought by the States as a matter of subjugation or conquest, and, in fact, not cared for by the States at all, save for such motives as might as well prompt both Mexico and Canada—to wit : the naturalization of North America, in which all are interested, and should cherish just pride,—it will not be opposed.

The States are not only the most populous and richest of all the countries in North America, but their institutions are the most progressive, and by all thought to be the most desirable for the government of the great continent of America, especially when to their past practically working system is now proposed to be added an improvement in which all conservative minds sympathized—to wit : *increased security by the curtailment of suffrage, and increased opportunity by the extirpation of individual monopoly.* By all odds, therefore, if the systems of any one of the nations are to be chosen for all, to say nothing about the great superiority of the States in population, wealth, foreign credit, and the like, that of the American Union is preferable.

These considerations will effectually annihilate local antipathy, so that about the only opponents that will remain will be those who feast and fatten off the Mexican public crib—those who can, by the force of arms, perpetuate their own succession and that of their friends forever. The States have been, prior to 1890, sending into Mexico only about ten million dollars' worth of goods annually, when the total value of importations by that country has been in the neighborhood of forty millions annually, and is rapidly increasing.

Mexico had been prevented from sending to the States millions of tons of low-grade ore, and millions of dollars' worth of tropical products and valuable woods, which trade could not only be carried on to a largely increased extent, but the lands from which these commodities came would be more than quadrupled in value, as has been the case in California.

By retaining local government for their states, neither Canada, Mexico, nor Central America would yield much power that it would be desirable to retain ; in fact,

no more than the existing States of the Union, which
are not only richer but many times more extensive
than the whole of the latter or of the habitable portion of the former. Americans will be quick to grasp
the idea that the suffrage qualification would remove
the incubus of the peone vote of Mexico, as it will
do in the Southern States regarding the equally objectionable and equally unworthy negro vote, as well
as clear or rather wrest political power from the slums
of the large cities hitherto in the hands of the off-
scourings of the earth, and place it in the hands of the
conservative middle classes in the cities and the property-
holding residents of the country, all of whom know
something about government, and possess something to
be affected by it. These considerations remove the
objection which has been for a long time fatal to the
discussion of the annexation idea, and the commercial
feature will make the thing very popular. Instead of
selling ten million dollars into Mexico, there would be a
certainty of selling fifty, even on the existing basis of
population, and the possibilities of that country in min-
erals, mines, valuable woods, and all tropical products
are simply beyond computation. Of course, in the event
of annexation, every one understands that individual
property rights of all kinds would not only be preserved
inviolate, but confirmed by the strongest possible power—
to wit, the fiat of the property-holding people of a nation
governing one quarter of the entire globe, and that
quarter in climate and natural resources capable of sustaining ten times the population of all. It would extend,
not like Russia and Siberia, around the frozen regions of
the ice-bound north, but through all climes to perpetual
summer, and that, too, with uniform breadth, and populated by people suitable to their localities. Not like

England—a small gem in the Atlantic—governing most
of her domain over countless miles of trackless ocean,
but in one compact body, co-extensive, and conterminous, a world complete within itself, which neither the
United States (with all her resources for lack of tropical
country), nor Canada, nor Mexico, nor Central America
can ever be alone. Now that people have advanced sufficiently in civilization and intelligence to know that the
best possible means of making a nation great is to grant
to a central power only such concerns as are national in
their character, and leave to the localities all domestic
control, the question of distance, and territorial extent
does not figure in the calculation, especially in America,
where from the Capitol the extremes could be reached in
a week, though practically covering a fourth of the world.
Civilized men want the products of the earth ; they
require furs of the seal and the white bear, and likewise
do they want the banana, the mango, and the olive.
They travel from the boreal blasts of the ice-bound north
to the balmy zephyrs of the sunlit south. They will go
bounding over the billowy plain with antelope motion,
and climb the highest peak at early dawn, where the
crags and rocks stand out vividly, and are clothed with
glittering spangles of sunlit dew. They prefer to possess
all these varieties under their own flag, and not only do
personal pride and national glory prompt, but commerce
and complete independence demand, that "from land of
ice to land of sun the railway lines' through cars shall run."

Both Mexico and Canada, as well as Central America,
could be divided into states, the population of which
could be made equal to the average of existing American
States, which would be fair, just, and reasonable, and
thus said populations being small, would add altogether,
perhaps, not more than ten States to the existing galaxy

of sovereign stars. To Cuba, arguments for annexation apply with even greater force than to Mexico and Central America, and it is even more strongly desired by her property-holding citizens than by that class in the former ; but Cuba cannot revolt ; Spain will not voluntarily abdicate, and the States are neither ready to purchase nor to conquer. Ten additional States would add only twenty United States Senators, making one hundred and eight altogether, by no means an unwieldy number, and the remaining territories will add but few. Still better than all this, the suffrage-qualification feature of the Phronocratic creed would materially reduce the membership of the House of Representatives, now too unwieldy for either expedition in legislation or the proper consideration thereof. Representation could be based on about fifteen thousand, and the membership would not likely exceed two hundred on the present population, and its increase in quality would more than compensate for its decrease in quantity. The prevailing predilection to resist innovations has, perhaps, prevented many an error that might have been baneful, but on the contrary it has estopped many an improvement that would have bettered the conditions of men. "Let well enough alone," is a good maxim, but if never altered, the cave or a hole in the ground might to this day have been the habitations of the noblest animals of them all. The scoffer at suggestions for alteration, even though in his opinion they are not improvements, would be a great enemy to civilization and progress were it not for the fact that he is usually a fool and his utterances vapid. "An eagle soaring in all his height might be hooted at by a mouthing owl," but on he would soar, like "heaven's cherubim horsed upon the sightless couriers of the air," with head uplifted, and wings outspread, till he bathed

his plumage in the silvery vapors of a sunlit cloud, and
the owl might hoot till darkness—his element—shrouded
the world in gloom.   Thus with the progressive men and
the scoffers :

> " Poison, be the latter's drink !
> Gall, worse than gall, the daintiest that they taste !
> Their sweetest shade a grove of cypress trees !
> Their chiefest prospect, murdering basilisks !
> Their softest touch, as smart as lizard's stings !
> Their music frightful, as the serpents' hiss ;
> And boding screech-owls make the concert full of
> All the foul terrors in dark-seated Hell."

Next unworthy to the scoffers are those who are too
weak and timid for independent political action.   Many
a man doth hate the King, but preferreth rather

> " To bend the pregnant hinges of the knee
> That thrift may follow fawning,"

than to boldly assert his views, and act on his convic-
tions.   Hence it is that the multitudes must go together
almost at one great surge, else individuals will wait to
see how the cat may jump.   There existed scarce a man
in public life in 1890, who ever conceived or suggested
anything, and few who did suggest anything were ever
elected.   Most who were chosen were the result of a
combination between the contending factions of greater
or better men, who could and did conceive something, or
they were as logs floated in on the tide or down the
brooks in a freshet.

Apathy as to old matters, and cowardice as to new,
keeps real issues out, and puts money in to settle a
political controversy.   Party organization and party
discipline are both good things, but individual indepen-

dence of action, so as to put the party in the van of living issues, is the necessity of the day. The trite and oft repeated adage that " he serves his party best who serves his country best," should be ridiculed. A man becomes a member of a party, that is, a Republican or a Democrat, or a Phronocratic supporter of cumulative taxation, suffrage qualification, anti-centralization, and American federation, because he thinks that the principles advanced by these organizations are best suited to the greatest number of his countrymen, and, such being the case, how could he serve his country better than to serve his party faithfully and unconditionally ; for without organization there is bound to be discord, and where there is discord, there is no progress. Party organization, party fealty, and party discipline, are the means to a successful end, and when the Phronocratic avalanche shall once begin to move, for the very reason that its platform is conservative and unmistakable, there is no organization of men that will be so loyal, so united, and so true, as those who stand for cumulative taxation, suffrage qualification, American federation, and anti-centralization, with its typical insignia,—a four-leafed clover, and the significant name " Phronocracy."

It is universally admitted, that control of the government of North America as an entirety, from the Isthmus to the Arctic, under the improved conditions relative to suffrage, transportation, and the general administration of civil affairs, would be easier than was that of the original thirteen States, (void, as they were of facilities for transportation, etc., etc.,) or of the amount of country owned at any subsequent date. There is absolutely nothing in the way, or that would in the slightest degree prevent, save the abrogation of that all-essential principle—*local self-government*. This annulled and no tenth

part of North America as it is, would be content in
a Union, but with it fully recognized, all prefer fraternity
and indissolubility, concord and sympathy—"*union and
liberty, now and forever, one and inseparable.*" By reason
of the negro (forgotten be the day that his black face and
kinky hair was ever imported from the land of his sires !)
one rebellion has occurred in America, and even in 1899,
thirty years thereafter, fellow-feeling and good-will between the sections are still hampered by reason of that
same negro. The North wishes his vote, and the South
cannot and will not stand his rule, hence it appears that,
unless the suffrage-qualification movement is adopted
(which would forever settle all feeling), there might again
be another struggle on account of that same negro. If
such should ever come to pass, the result would probably
be that from the Ohio and Potomac Rivers, west to the
Pacific, and by the annexation of Mexico, Cuba, and
Central America, south to the Isthmus, there would be
established the "*Southern Republic of North America,*"
and from these rivers north to the Arctic Sea, the
"*Northern Republic of North America.*" In the former,
curtailed suffrage, on account of the ever present negro,
and of its general sound policy, together with restricted
individual accumulations, and with absolute free trade
with every nation of the earth ; and in the latter, Plutocracy to excess, and Democracy to excess, or communistic
tendencies, with universal suffrage, and a *protected au-
tocracy* with universal monopoly. However, the farmers
and conservative city residents, both north and south,
should resist and prevent the tendency towards interference with home rule, *destroy force bills forever*, and erect
on the ruins of all, the precepts of Phronocracy, which
will be the salvation of all. It is not claimed for the
propositions advanced that they are original or new.

The material substances of nature doubtless always existed and ever will exist ; so human thoughts, more or less forcible, have existed in the minds of men since men, as such, were evoluted from inanimate substance and crude material by cosmic energy. Thoughts doubtless have existed in incipient degree in all animated things, and possibly in stones and trees *as well as in every grade of men.* Granite has existed in the adamantine hills for countless millions of ages, and the matter of which it is composed is doubtless coëval with the universal whole. The question is not *have we discovered the quarry, but have we carved the statue?* So from the chaos of human thought it is not the question, have we originated the myriads of ideas that are scattered broadcast in limitless confusion and labyrinthian heterogeneity, but *have we winnowed the wheat from the chaff* and arranged the valuable material into systems from which practical results can be obtained ? Nature arranges few of its substances in right lines, and makes few of its surfaces smooth and ornamental. Its roads are rough, its paths tortuous, and its ways are winding. In native forests, trees are seldom arranged in exact geometrical figures ; and, just so, crude ideas are seldom grouped in practical propositions. A few integers are susceptible of many combinations, most all of which are rude, fantastical forms. The question is, does Phronocracy combine any of these so as to make an *ensemble* that will result in greater good to a greater number than existing outrageous and useless inequalities, and *if not what will ? If so, is it practicable, is it just, and if not what is ?*

CHAPTER XIV.

BECAUSE an absolute monarchy or a despotism is almost universally acknowledged among civilized people to be anti-progressive and inherently wrong, it does not follow that the radically and diametrically opposite system (universal suffrage) is absolutely progressive and inherently right. It is possible to err on the one side just the same as on the other. Doubtless among the wild beasts that roam in the forests nothing save cages or chains will guarantee any restraint, and that for insubordination it may be that death would be the only proper penalty. So among the higher order—that is, human brutes—a similar exercise of power would perhaps alone be available or in any way meet the requirements of the case.

It is evident, however, that as human beings cease to be brutes, that kind of government which was suitable for brutes ceases to be the thing for the human beings, and the greater divergence from the animal state, the greater must it be in the governmental state ; hence, eventually, if things mundane continue to progress as they have for the last fifty centuries, all absolute monarchies or despotisms must go, as, in the most enlightened portions of the earth, they have already gone. From a despotism, in which all power and absolute unrestraint is vested in the king, there is really no tenable position that can be assumed except such as places power practically with the people, but upon the people there should be placed a wholesome restraint. The limited monarchy represents a government in which the prerogatives of the king are proscribed. From the limited monarchy to a limited republic or a Phronocracy the step is very short ; in fact, the abolition of the image of sovereignty, and the creation in its stead of an actual entity, made so, for a certain time by the consent of the people, represents about the entire items of difference. Of popular forms of government there are two, with some distinctions, but little if any difference :

First—A democracy, derived from two Greek words, δῆμος, signifying "the people," and κράτος, "strength," or sovereignty *en masse*.

Second—A republic, derived from two Latin words *res*, signifying "a thing" or "an affair," and *publica*, "public."

Democracy really means "a government by the people ; a form of government in which the supreme power is in the hands of the people, and directly exercised by them ; hence, more usually, a form of government in which the power resides ultimately in the whole people, who conduct it by a system of representation and delegation of powers ; a constitutional and representative government ; a republic."

A *republic* signifies "a state in which the sovereign

power is exercised by representatives elected by the
people ; a commonwealth ; a democracy.

Hence, in the abstract, a republic is a democracy, and
a democracy a republic. In the concrete, however,
there may be considered to be a slight difference, to
wit : in a well-constituted republic, as the United States
of America, the government is administered by *representatives* chosen by the people, and in a democracy
by the people in a body, as in some of the ancient states
of Greece. The distinction, therefore, if there be any,
is that a republic is one step further from the people
than a democracy, yet the two terms are almost synony-
mous and interchangeable. Since, however, governments of great magnitude cannot be administered by
the people in a body, and must be operated by representatives thereof, chosen in an agreed manner, and
clothed with certain powers, the term "republic" is
closer to that condition which exists in America, and
which must exist in all large congregations of people
possessing popular governmental forms, than is the term
"democracy." In America, the party called Republican
is supposed to represent that portion of the population
that tends towards centralization—that is, the party that
favors a liberal construction of the powers conferred by
the federal Constitution on Congress, and is inclined
rather to enlarge the scope of federal jurisdiction ; and
the party called Democratic tends rather toward a strict
construction of the powers conferred upon Congress by
the Constitution, and opposes any enlargement of the
scope of the central power. Of the two positions the
latter is by far the more reasonable, since it is but right,
if there be a constitution, that it be construed with
absolute strictness, for if liberal, then how liberally, and
where is the limit ? If certain powers are delegated,

then beyond these powers the federal government should not go, until the said powers are enlarged in the manner prescribed, or until additional powers are granted in the form set forth and agreed to by the parties to the compact.

There are, however, some general clauses in the Constitution, as "for the purpose of carrying these provisions into effect," and the like, that give fair ground for the belief, that it was intended that in times of emergency the strict construction might be varied, or, rather, that Congress might do incidental things that would practically extend the scope of the specific powers. It comes, therefore, to a question of individual preference. Those who think the interests of the whole would be best subserved by increasing the scope of federal jurisdiction, call themselves Republicans; and those who think that the powers of the general government should be strictly confined, call themselves Democrats.

The tendency of the times being towards that principle which prefers "that nothing shall be done by the general government which the local authorities are competent to do, and nothing by any governmental power that individuals can do for themselves," it must soon be almost universally accepted, in fact tacitly agreed, that Congress shall do absolutely nothing save such things as are expressly set forth, and everything that may be done under general clauses should be made obligatory, if contested, only by the vote of two thirds of the congressional delegations and three fourths the State legislatures, which would leave no longer any room for discussion as to the proper limitations of the delegated powers of the federal Congress. Most of the political differences after the adoption of cumulative taxation and suffrage qualifi-

19

cation will doubtless rest on the question of a further
increase of the latter as the population becomes dense.
However, since it is not the amount of property or the
scope of his education that is to entitle a man to suffrage,
but simply a requirement that to participate in same he
must attain a certain standard of excellence, it will doubtless ✱
be unnecessary to increase the rate.   The very existence
of a republic pre-supposes intelligence, since for the
bestial and ignorant the despotism is the only proper
form, consequently strenuous effort should never be
abated until intelligence and property to proper limitations are made the conditions of republican citizenship
everywhere.   The distinction between a democracy and
a republic is so small that it is scarcely appreciable, and
Democrats, as they now exist, when really the only vital
question is free trade or protection, have in their ranks
many men who favor even a more concentrated governmental system than is advocated by the Republicans,
and the Republicans, a protective organization, have in
their ranks many free-trade sympathizers.   There are,
therefore, no absolute lines of demarcation.   Republicans
hate the name of Democrat, and a Democrat hates the
name of Republican.   He who has previously affiliated
with either will not change his political name to the
other, even though in principles he recognizes in the
organization of his opponents that which would be most
conducive to the interests of himself and his country.
Hence it is that those who advocate cumulative taxation,
free trade, suffrage qualification, and the other progressive tenets of political organizations are obliged to adopt
a name differing from either of the old organizations.
The control of excessive individual accumulations, free
trade, and increased opportunity to the individuals of
the masses is democratic enough for many Democrats,

and the curtailment of suffrage and the general concentration of power to within the qualified members of
society is centralizing enough for many Republicans, but
the position is neither all Democratic nor all Republican,
neither Plutocratic, nor Democratic, nor Aristocratic, nor
Autocratic, nor Gynecocratic, but, resting on judgment,
prudence, and sense, is " Phronocratic."

It involves a representative electoral system, which is
the proper signification of the word republic, but it
curtails the right of participation therein to those only
who can show certain excellence or fitness for the privilege, as is required for participation in all other channels
of civilized life. The advocates of these special views,
therefore, may sometimes be called "Conservatives" and
sometimes "Phronocrats," either being appropriate.
The difficulty of securing independent political action
will for a long time be discouraging, but it is known that
there already exists such an undercurrent of sympathy
that it must one day burst out with astounding strength
and fury. Party fealty is to be prized, yet parties void
of principles or of any direct object are useless both to
their members and the state, hence the lack of necessity
for that close adherence to name that is expected of an
advocate of any fixed purpose or principle.

The proposed system of government is not, as stated,
properly described by either of the names applied to the
two great existing parties. It is, of course, in all respects
a republic, but not, however, in the sense that the term
has been used, but one in which the representatives are
to be chosen not by the people absolute and unconditional, but by the people within certain limitations. It
cannot be considered a " Plutocracy," because, whilst
the wealth of the country had its share of consideration
and representation, yet against the government by

wealthy classes alone, which the term really signifies, there is a vigorous and effectual restraint in the cumulative tax.   It is to that degree socialistic that it looks toward a surrender to the state for community purposes of a certain portion of excessive individual property, yet it is not essentially a socialistic position.   It is, in fact, a compromise between excessive democracy or socialism and excessive republicanism or plutocracy, in the strict sense of these terms, yet, nevertheless, essentially a republican form.   The people as a whole will not rule as is especially signified by the term " Democracy," so that the term " Phronocracy," signifying a "limited republic," appears to cover the case better than anything else. Its policy expressly supports the republican or representative system, but proposes to " limit " same to within certain lines, representing moderate wealth and adequate knowledge.   Many Democrats will refrain from supporting such a party's candidates simply because the word Phronocracy is to be the name of the organization, but Democrats certainly favor republicanism, for what is a republic but the very form under which the Democrats live ?   A government that is a republic must be republican, and the fact is that the United States of America *is a Republic and not a Democracy*, which latter signifies a government by the people as a whole, which could not exist in a great country, and never existed, essentially, save in some of the ancient states of Greece.   The word republic signifies more properly that representative system in force in America, and to " limit " the selection of that representation certainly would constitute a "limited republic," or Phronocracy a "limited" electoral and representative system.

The right to be a representative would, of course, be " limited " to within the limited class of electors ; both are expected to reach a certain standard of excellence, and he who should vote should be capable to represent.

Under the present system, such is *not* the case, and monstrous mal-administration ofttimes results simply from downright incapacity. The Democrats of the South will not be alarmed by the term Phronocracy, nor, if any prefer it, by the equally applicable term "Conservative," which latter some Northern thin skins but thick skulls may think is a term signifying English oppression towards Ireland. The South has no enmity towards England ; it does not sympathize in the American-Irish agitation, knowing it to be both presumptuous and unreasonable ; the white element is for free trade almost to a man—at least such are the sympathies of the vast majority ; and the English position on that subject is thought by the South to be reasonable, proper, and in keeping with the advanced ideas of commerce and trade. The South sells England its cotton, and is quite willing that the United States government shall permit England to enable the people of the South to make an additional profit by buying England's cheap goods. A dollar saved in purchase is the same as a dollar made in sales, hence why not make both available ? The South favors the strongest possible system of local self-government, or the anti-centralization features of the proposed organization, which confines the federal government to within its strictly construed limitations, and above all the South could by the qualification feature, practically disfranchise the negro (being more anxious to utilize his work than his vote), and yet not decrease the proportionate representation in Congress or in the electoral college of that hitherto solid section—solid against the negro and discriminating paternal governments.

Most of the hide-bound Democrats who will object to

the term "Phronocrats" or "Conservatives" will be the
irresponsible foreigners of the lower wards, who would
be suppressed as they should long ere this have been,
by the qualification requirement. This class is not
wanted, except as the individuals thereof make themselves worthy by acquiring the necessary excellence.
Since in the propositions and creed of the Phronocrats
or "Conservatives" there appears nothing that aims at
the exercise of any power whatever by the federal government, other than such matters as cannot be performed by the localities, or rather yielding to it such
only as are essentially national, there exists no plank
from which to invite the support of those of the community who believe in "paternalism in government."

The American farmers having for years permitted themselves to be oppressed by discriminating
traffic and similar legislation calculated to enrich the
favored manufacturer, have of late, with that enthusiasm and unanimity that usually characterizes the oppressed when once aroused to the enormity of the
oppression, sought by the organization of the "Farmers'
Alliance" to obtain restitution for their long and well-
recognized grievances. They have submitted to too
much in the past, but in seeking to establish and secure
relief by asking that a most impracticable system of
"paternalism" be adopted by the government, their
position is as untenable as their patience has heretofore
been inexplicable. Collecting taxes for the purpose of
making land loans or for building storage warehouses
is not the province of the government, and if ever
adopted would result in the end in as much if not more
harm than good even to the farmers themselves.

No considerable part of the people can ever be
brought to an acknowledgment of the fact that the

general government should ever exercise this function, even if void of radical objections, that are absolutely insuperable. In the end nothing is gained to the nation by paternalism. Those who advocate it disregard the fact that a government must get its funds from the people by some plan of taxation. If it obtains funds from the people in excess of the requirements for its own support, and then pays back to the people in pro- portion as they contributed (which is the only just basis of return), then each man is in the same identical situa- tion as if he never had paid the excess ; but if it returns to John Jones $10.00 who contributed nothing, and to John Smith but $5.00 who contributed $50.00, then it has distinguished in favor of Jones and against Smith. To have this excess expended by any paternal device is but a system of refunding that is most liable to be unjust and discriminating ; so that the only safe and proper plan is to permit the government to collect only what it needs for the most economical administration of its legitimate functions. and cause these functions to be as few as possible. The Farmers' Alliance will find all the relief its members need in the principles of Phronocracy, and there are *four million farm owners* in America who should support it to a man, and if Phro- nocracy be "paternalism," say to the millionaire and the loafers, "*Make the most of it.*"

Through Phronocracy and through this alone can the *American farmer* ever accomplish much that will benefit his condition, for by this system *he can increase his pro- portionate representation and decrease his proportionate tax- ation.* He can then remove the existing governmental favoritism that he has participated in creating, and pre- vent its re-establishment. His remedy lies in *preventing favoritism to others* not in seeking it for himself. In other words he must *suppress existing evil, not seek to establish greater evil.* This is all he can ever do and all he should ever do, and the sooner he becomes mindful of this fact the better will be the condition of the *" oppressed American farmer."* Establish Phronocracy and let the details establish themselves as they will surely do. Class legislation should never be supported, no *never, never! never!!* Phronocracy is not class legislation for it applies to all alike whose conditions are alike.

It is thought by some that any new term, signifying the supposed object or intent of the movement, would be useless, and that no better designation could be applied than that of "Limited Republicanism," which, though offensive to Democrats who cherish affiliation to the organization on account of name rather than from principle, is yet more logical. America is a republic, and not a democracy, and the name of the organization whose precepts are best adapted to the perpetuation and purification of that republic, it is said, should be something in consonance therewith. However, Phronocracy expresses the idea and is independent of all others.

It is a fact of general knowledge that many of the ignorant voters who come to America and settle in the great Northwest, and who make good agricultural citizens, vote with the high-protective Republican party— diametrically opposed to their interests,—because they consider that in a republic they should be Republicans. This feature actually weighs to a very appreciable extent in those Granger States that so persistently vote for the preservation of that discriminating system.

The name Phronocracy is not suggested for the purpose of catching votes anywhere, but because it appears to be about the only proper expression for a government by representatives and electors, both "limited." A "limited republic" would have the same rank among popular representative governments that a limited monarchy has among nations recognizing the inherited right to rule ; that is, it will be the best of its kind, and the republic is undoubtedly the best kind for progressive and educated people and nations.

To one of the would-be supporters of the "Phronocratic" creed it was said by one of the blatherskites of his present political association : "Why, the curtailment of suffrage is anti-democratic." To which it was wisely replied : "My friend, I am democratic, but I am not too d—d democratic. I wish to be no more democratic in my political affiliation and association than I am in my personal and business association. I would not associate with nor sell my goods to a man who knew nothing nor possessed nothing, and I do not see why such a man should have it in his power to participate in legislation that affects my property, neither do I care to associate with a man who has in his possession two hundred million dollars in United States gold, for that man can indulge in useless extravagance that is not only beyond my power but beyond my desire ; he could if he chose sail over the sea in a ship of gold. I could not, nor do I desire to do so, and the only satisfaction that inures to him in being able to construct the hull of his ship of gold is, not the fact that gold is better or even as good for the purpose as iron, but simply because, in being able to do so, he has obtained something that other men cannot get, and to that extent is their superior in the estimation of the world. I prefer to say to him : 'You shall not enjoy this vain glory, for it is of no use to you, for by so doing you oppress the reasonable opportunity of other men. Rather than permit you to build your ship of gold (for glory, not for utility), I will force you to contribute a larger amount to the support of the state, which protects your property. I will give you a reasonable reward, but not an unreasonable one. I will protect your reasonable reward by putting in control of it men only of brains and property, of neither, perhaps, to the equal of yourself, but of enough of each to prove them to be men, and not brutes.' Yes, I am thoroughly democratic to the extent of curtailing excessive and useless individual accumulations, which are usually the result more of opportunity than design, and to the extent of bringing all government, first as near to the locality as possible, and then as near to the individual as possible, but I want that individual to be a man, and not a brute. I want him, in other words, to prove his worth before he can exercise the rights I possess and have acquired only by diligence and effort—that is, to come up to a certain standard of excellence, below which a man is but a brute ; and outside of these very reasonable limitations, to Hades with your democracy—it is a mockery and a farce. Yes, Phronocratic is the name to be applied to a proposed organization, to become a member of which, if such ever should exist, has been my life-long desire, because I have always believed in republican institutions as against monarchical institutions, but have always feared that the concentration of wealth and power on the one hand would paralyze its usefulness, and that hoodlumism on the other would render abortive its professions. The curtailment of the excess on the one hand and the extirpation of the mockery on the other leaves a conservative mean, which must one day be the government adopted by the civilized powers of the earth. King'scraft is the result of a lingering prejudice of the dark ages, and for the countries that are afflicted with it time alone can bring relief ; but it must come, and the sooner the better, for that which exists by prejudice or as the result of a lingering custom, and cannot be said to be supported by greater reason than are other systems directed to the same end, must perish, and perish it will. Whenever that system of government that maintains that 'all just power comes from the consent of the governed' can be considered absolutely and unquestionably stable and secure (such as is guaranteed by this Phronocratic, conservative creed), all civilized people will adopt it, and the powers of heaven, or of earth, or of hell will never prevail against it."

The supporters of monarchy having been driven from their position, that there is a lack of security to property and to civil institutions in all republican systems, even though purged by a suffrage qualification, yet claim that the necessity for frequent elections is a fruitful cause of complaint ; that the choice of representatives and of state and federal executives causes a condition of commercial insecurity and unrest that must of necessity create a temporary suspension of trade, and consequent loss to investors in all mercantile enterprises and business pursuits ; that the uncertainty of succession and the variableness of the policy of the victorious organizations must render it impossible to calculate with any degree of certainty upon any fixed principle of government as applied to the material interests of the country, and hence confusion will inevitably result. It is predicted that when the protective system is abolished, by reason of the change thereby created, that widespread ruin, bankruptcy, and universal dismay will follow in its wake, causing paralysis in business and distress to the people, and as in this, so in all conditions of society and trade that can be in any sense affected by the popular will.

This class are respectfully referred to the progress of

America and the stability of her institutions, even under
universal suffrage, which was begun when the population
was yet comparatively sparse and homogeneous. Now,
however, when the country is menaced by the vast congregations of the Eastern World, many of whom possess
anarchistic tendencies, and seek to divert from the lawful
custodians all the property they own, and by ruthless
violence either to distribute or to destroy, this evident
tendency toward a rapidly approaching storm must be
checked in its incipiency and strangled in the throes of
parturition by the "compromise between Democracy and
Plutocracy," which promises forever to place society not
only on a more liberal but on a more substantial foundation than ever has existed under any form of government.
The question of diminishing the frequency of elections
has been mooted, as has been absolute ineligibility for
re-election to office. Both, except as to the judiciary,
should be abandoned—that is, no change, in America,
from the existing condition should be made. The President should continue to serve four years, and should be
eligible to re-election. Being shorn or rather relieved of
the great patronage of his office by the election of collectors and postmasters by the people, he could not
control the civil service of the country for his own
personal aggrandizement or for succession to official
power. Being thus deprived of any opportunity of
utilizing the force of governmental patronage, a power
that had been most cogent and demoralizing when used
for forcing himself or his party on to the people, there
would remain no possible chance for re-election other
than by the uninfluenced and untrammelled popular
will, and if the populace willed, why should he not succeed himself as well as be succeeded by another? It
might be well, however, to lengthen the term and increase
the pay of all occupants of the bench.

The idea of extending the presidential term to six or eight years, and the congressional to three or four years, is opposed, and with reason, on the ground that the very substratum—the foundation-rock of popular government —is elections. And why elections? In order that the people may choose agents to perform those duties, curbed by constitutional limitations, that cannot be practically done by the people themselves. Of course, by these agents certain discretionary power must be used, but essentially they are supposed to *represent* the people—that is, to do the popular will. If, therefore, the expression of the popular will is delayed, to that extent are the people unrepresented, and if it is well to seek that plan by which the best and closest representation of the people—that most in keeping with their varying wants and preferences—*can be avoided*, then it would perhaps be better to abolish elections altogether and lapse into the despotic systems of the dark ages. Laws are supposed to be made for the people, not the people for the laws ; hence to the representatives who make the laws electors should have access, and as time passes, and as conditions change, the very essence of popular government and the operation of the system made possible by it are frustrated if the expression of popular opinion is needlessly delayed. Purify the electors and the system by which their votes are cast and counted, and there will be no harm in reasonable frequency. A man who is to a certain degree educated and who owns property is not a dangerous custodian of the franchise, and will seldom if ever use it for vicious or revolutionary purposes. If the incumbent of an office and the principles he espouses are satisfactory to a great majority of the people, the question of his succession or re-election will cause no excitement, and no doubt and no uncertainty as to the continuance of any specific policy. It is only when the people are about equally divided on a great question that there is any doubt or uncertainty as to the results, and if there is a large element opposed, why should the opportunity of expressing that opposition be needlessly delayed ?

One of the greatest possible arguments in favor of reasonably frequent elections, in addition to the fact that they are the proper concomitants of a Phronocratic government, is the ability that is then vouchsafed the people to eradicate *a bad law* from the statute-books and remove bad men from office. There is as much necessity, ofttimes, of eradicating a bad or of modifying a good law, as there is of creating a new enactment. If a law is good it will not be changed, unless the majority alter their opinions, and, if altered, certainly the government would be akin to, if not in fact, a despotism, that would withhold the opportunity for expression. It is right and proper, in a word it is necessary, that proper safeguards should be thrown around precipitate action in legislation, and it is for this reason that separate bodies are created. Lengthening the term of office will not be necessary, nor will political discussion, purged of the demoralizing influence of hoodlumism and bribery, be injurious to the country or oppressive to trade. As the cumulative and qualification principles begin to gain strength there will be, of course, manifested from certain capitalistic sources some evidences of anxiety, of insecurity, and distrust ; but by all, save the one-hundred millionaires and their dependencies, and the loafers of the lower wards, increased confidence will be manifested and greater enthusiasm displayed.

With Phronocracy in force in America the republic is complete. It has existed without any necessity for the regulation of the extremes for more than a century, because the extremes have not been so great. However, as

the population becomes dense, and as wealth becomes
concentrated, the same spirit of progress and opposition
to oppression that animated our revolutionary sires to
disavow allegiance to the British crown now prompts
vigorous energy against concentrated individual wealth
and benighted individual irresponsibility and ignorance.
It is not a fundamental, though a considerable, alteration
in American institutions. It is simply a new, a less
burdensome, and more reliable system of collecting
revenue, a curtailment of suffrage, as the only possible
system of ballot reform and of meeting conditions,
brought more glaringly forward by the increasing heterogeneity of the growing population, which are made
necessary for the guaranty of personal and property
rights. Rather is it a requirement of the times. When
universal suffrage was instituted the population of America was not over four millions, of which number none
were vicious, and most all possessed property. The
extremes were not so great ; the contrast between the
responsible and irresponsible was less. There did not
exist a few one-hundred millionaires and almost a hundred million who were not heirs at all ; hence, then, the
necessity for regulating either extreme was by no means
urgent. When the few who own the millions can buy up
and use the millions who own nothing, great has become
the necessity of rendering both powerless—the former by
curtailing his wealth to within a reasonable reward, and
the latter by cutting short his power till he acquired some
reward—that is, till he possesses some knowledge and
some property, for otherwise his ability to use power is
not only dangerous but a mockery. The territorial-
extension feature is to America an all-important issue
and should not be ignored. For many years the vast
domain of Alaska has been owned and has brought good

returns for the outlay necessary to procure it, and it is
the most remote of all possible North American acquisi-
tions.   It can, however, now be reached from San Francisco in a very short time, and, after the completion of a
Western Coast road, from Washington City in less than a
fortnight.   All other habitable portions of North America
could be reached from Washington in a week.   In other
words, annexation simply means the union of territory
far less remote from the centre than that which has been
owned for a third of a century.

This inter-relationship between and co-dependence of
countries upon each other become greater as civilization advances and as facilities for transportation multiply.
Wants are more varied, and where transportation is adequate there is usually an ability to supply.   This condition renders necessary closer trade relations, and closer
trade relations bring closer personal relations ; closer
personal relations bring closer personal association,
which tends inevitably to lessen the differences, the desires, the appetites, the natures, and prejudices of the
people of the whole world ; they are more uniformly
dressed and more uniformly fed ; in their exchanges
they will use more uniform coin and more uniform
standards of measures and weights, and they will speak
to each other in a more uniform tongue—all of which is
attributable to the increasing wants of civilized life and
to increased facilities for the transportation of commodities to supply those wants, and of intercommunication
necessary to negotiate these interchanges.   The tendency
of all this is that people will be more uniformly governed.
Uniformity in government can best be obtained by dele-
gating to a central power such concerns as are essentially national and reserving to the state those essentially
local.

Civilized and progressive society will ere long yield to nothing else ; no other system will ever peaceably withstand the varying needs of progressive man.

National prerogatives solely and alone for national concerns specifically defined and closely restricted. It is to this grand principle, and to this alone, that is surely attributable the union of the North American States, and by which, to the pride, glory, and grandeur of every part, that quarter of the world can fly one flag, but by the abrogation of which dismemberment could only be prevented, if at all, by the reverberating thunders of the American cannon and by the unsheathed sword of brother against brother, father against son ; and even then the South, the West, the North, the East, would seek the Union bonds to sunder.

When in 1890 efforts were inaugurated to throttle federal elections by the interpositions of force, many portentous prophecies were made, by the ablest thinkers of the time, from all sections, that persistence in that policy would ultimately destroy the Union, for the reason that it is a total subversion of the spirit of the federal Constitution, an abrogation of the principle of local self-government, State autonomy, and personal rights—all not only near and dear to the heart of every free American (North or South), but vital to the perpetuation of domestic civil liberty. It is no dream, no fancy. What signifies delegated national powers if they are to be ruthlessly and violently transcended or enlarged ? The continent of North America is very large, it contains many physical conditions and many climes, also many people with room for many more, and just as certainly as the federal power asserts right of interference with these local conditions, just that certainly when the offence becomes too great, the Northwest or the Southeast—one

20

just as likely as the other—will object.   Men who have
sacrificed both blood and treasures to suppress one rebellion, bottomed on slavery, will be the most eager in
their readiness and desire to encourage and abet another
against federal interference and usurpation of power.
The tendency, however, to extend federal supervision
into and over local affairs will soon be entirely stopped.
When it becomes evident to the people of all sections
that suffrage is to be curtailed, then there will exist not
the faintest pretext for such legislation, for the negro of
the South will be practically disfranchised, and the hoodlum of the North would need no military supervision or
police control.   His name would not appear on the books
of the collector, in the hands of the judges of election at
the polls, hence the place that he has so long monopolized
around the voting booths to the disgust and vexation
of all good citizens, will be void of his presence, and
elections will be conducted in harmony and peace.

No section of North America, when the whole can be
traversed from the Isthmus to the Arctic in ten or twelve
days, and from ocean to ocean in about one third that
time, would care for anything save local government and
federal non-interference.   All would cherish pride in
one nation, one currency, one coin, one weight, one
measure, one language, and one people, provided the
federal power would there stop, and permit the inestimable blessing of local home rule—the only practicable
government for a great country—to prevail in all its
excellence, simplicity, and beauty.   Otherwise there may
again be trouble, and grim-visaged war may again present
his horrid front.   Then again might ripe and waving
grain be trampled beneath the hoof of the war horse ;
then may these fields of cotton or of corn be furrowed
by the wheels of advancing artillery ; then may the

stately forest trees again be blazed with cannon-balls and
grapeshot ; then may the blood-soaked earth be lapped
by thirsty hounds, and then may yelping wolves and
prowling scavengers of the night make the eyes of heaven
weep at sights of beastly carnival on the ghastly fields of
slaughter, where howling and in hideous gluttony they
might lick from their satiate, gaping jaws quivering
strands of human flesh—all but a fitting retribution for
useless fratricidal hate, and for the interference by the
nation with the proper functions of the *State*.

> " Ere the bat hath flown
> His cloister'd flight ; ere to black Hecate's summons,
> The shard-borne beetle, with his drowsy hums,
> Hath rung night's yawning peal, there shall be done
> A deed of dreadful note."

CHAPTER XV.

THE discussion of the propositions involved in "Phronocracy" based upon "cumulative taxation and suffrage qualification," proceeds on these hypotheses, viz :

First. That all men are or doubtless should be born free, but that all positively *are not* born equal ; that such as are or may be born equal become unequal by the variable degrees in which they exert themselves, in which they conserve their energies and make available their opportunities.

Second. That a man is entitled to a reasonable reward for his labor, his energy, and his opportunity ; that any man who possesses greater force (by which is meant excellence in any particular) than another man, is entitled to the result of that force.

Third. That it is not the proper province or prerogative of the state or of society to attempt to make all men equal, because equality in men is not only in conflict with nature, but impracticable in society. Multifarious duties must be performed in any civilized state, and it requires multifarious men with multifarious adaptabilities to perform these multifarious duties and requirements ; hence any interposition of the state that seeks to create an artificial equality (except such as is, in practice, found to be absolutely necessary) is not only unwarranted but absolutely injurious.

Fourth. That beyond a certain reasonable limit the accumulation of individual property ceases to be the result of individual effort and energy, but is in fact a contribution of society (which, however, is absolutely unavoidable), and that beyond this reasonable limit, individual accumulations are not only useless but harmful, hence should not be permitted to extend.

Fortunes, or the aggregations of wealth, beget fortunes, or the aggregation of wealth, and to this aggregation, for the greatest good to the greatest number, there should be some reasonable limit, because man's requirements can not possibly increase proportionately with the possible increase of his accumulations of wealth.

Fifth. It is admitted that even the curtailment of individual accumulations which are abnormally and uselessly excessive is an interference with individual rights and opportunities ; but it is maintained that, since for the good of society or for the practical execution of its laws, usages, and customs certain restraints or interferences with natural rights are necessary, it cannot be more equitably or less injuriously applied than to useless and excessive individual accumulations.

Sixth. That no man should participate in government who does not possess a certain amount of that which governments are established to protect and which alone can support government, to wit: property. The simple possession of life, which can be sustained without government, does not entitle a living being to the exercise of any authority regarding the disposition or regulation of that which is the result of inherent force (excellence) or the reward of its energies or opportunities.

Seventh. That it is useless to attempt to make men equal by legislation, and that an equal distribution of the products of labor would be detrimental to society, encouraging idleness and malingery, and that efforts in that direction are not the proper prerogative of the state (except to such a limited extent as practice proves to be necessary) and should not be encouraged.

These are a few of the simple but fundamental principles from which is derived the basis for the compromise between Democracy, which, by the exigencies of the times, is growing socialistic, and Plutocracy, which, by the accessions of individual wealth, has begun to paralyze the world's affairs. Accretions to population make it not only possible but usual for the increment of society to add to the value of properties by nature monopolistic (of which class there are many) an amount greater than the possible increase of the requirements of the individual, greater than any reasonable reward for industry or opportunity, greater than an adequate compensation for cupidity and greed, greater in fact than is possible of accurate computation or of human comprehension.

Many men become so wealthy, not wholly by their own energies, but by the necessary accessions caused by the increase of population and the demands of society, that they cannot compute to within ten to a dozen million dollars what they are actually worth. In other words, they own the equivalent of the labor of so many men that they cannot count to within an amount equal to the

labor of 10,000 to 15,000 men (a good-sized army) just
what they do own, and this unknown quantity is perhaps
not more than five to ten per cent. of their actual wealth.
It is estimated that if the Lord Almighty had contracted
with Adam to superintend the Garden of Eden at a salary of $40,000 per year (an amount almost equal to
the salary of the American President), and guaranteed
him uninterrupted occupancy without the possibility of
discharge or ejectment for the consumption of fruit that
was forbidden, at the solicitation of a woman, or for any
other crime of kindred nature or more glaring atrocity,
he would not have paid, from the date that he first
breathed into the inanimate element the breath of life
and from a rib of it created the consort and tempter, an
amount equal to that possessed by several of the millionaires of America.

Five thousand years at $40,000 per year would be
but two hundred million ; and if Adam had been subjected to that fierce competition and unrelenting strife
that characterize the struggles of most of his progeny
for a comfortable terrestrial existence in climates where
the leaves of figs are not an adequate protection from
the penetrating blasts of the boreal winds, the pay would
have been reduced to at least $5,000 per year (an amount
largely exceeding the average compensation for this class
of service), in which case it would have required forty
thousand years for the aggregate outlay to have equalled
the amounts possessed by several American capitalists ;
or if the price had been reduced to that which is actually
considered reasonable for an ordinary American gar-
dener—that is, one not especially skilled in the most re-
cent botanical discoveries or capable of delivering the
most learned discourses on dicotyledonous or deciduous
plants (in which Adam was not supposed to be especially

proficient)—to wit, about $500 per year, then it would
have required four hundred thousand years for an expenditure to have been made equal to the fortunes of
several American capitalists, or about eighty times as
long as the period of time that is supposed to have elapsed
since our primeval ancestor, tempted by a woman who
was beguiled by a snake, proved himself so utterly unworthy of the trust reposed, and was doomed to a life of
drudgery and toil, in which his innocent and unoffending
offspring must "root, hog, or die." Is it not absolutely
ridiculous that any single man (who at best is but little
better than the worst) should be able to possess wealth
equal to a very liberal compensation for the labor of a
fellow-man for four hundred thousand years ? Is it not
a mockery upon humanity itself that society should
countenance such a thing (when the life of a man averages
less than forty years) as a salary to one man for ten
thousand times as many years as the average man can
live ? It is claimed that this condition of affairs is
neither right nor just to society or of any benefit to
the fortunate (or unfortunate) individuals themselves.
It is, however, likewise claimed that there is but one
remedy that is not subject to insuperable objection, and
that is, to cause a man's contribution to the state, that
is, to the governmental system that protects and makes
individual titles to any property practicable, to be so
adjusted that outgo will equal income when a reasonable
reward for individual excellence and opportunity has
been acquired ; and that this contribution shall be so
rigidly applied to individuals only as to cause no barrier
to the concentration of capital in corporate enterprises
for the construction of great works otherwise impossible ;
and furthermore and finally, that increased security shall
be given to that curtailed individual property by placing

all governmental power into the hands of those only who
possess property, for

" An habitation giddy and unsure
Hath he, that buildeth on the vulgar heart."

It is claimed that no other system is practicable, and
that none other is just, even if practicable. Individual
excellence does exist, and conformable to nature as we
find it, should exist. Any law or system seeking to
nullify this individual excellence that does not provide
for its adequate compensation is unjust and a barrier to
social progress and enterprise. Equal divisions of property are not only unjust—for all are not equally worthy,
—but utterly abortive of the slightest permanent relief ;
and if just, and if productive of apparent relief, the
earth would have to turn backwards or humanity would
starve. That is to say, if all men were equally excellent
and all men equally circumstanced, every man who lived
in the present civilized state would have to be a community unto himself, for under these conditions there would
be no practical division of labor. The irksome duties
would be shunned by all, and the desirable duties sought
by all. It would not do to say that the thing would soon
become self-regulating, that is, that an overplus of appli-
cants for the good avocations would drive the required
number into the bad, for if such should be the case, those
driven into the bad, that is, into occupations that are
menial and lowly, would soon cease to be the equals, by
the very force of the situation itself, of those who remained in positions of development and growth. Neither
will it do to say that the menial occupations would command increased compensation commensurate with their
undesirableness, for that opportunity now exists and fails
of realization. If every man who now scrapes the streets

should suddenly be made the equal of any professor in any college, his usefulness as a street sweeper would as likely be diminished as increased, and if not increased, in the general panning out of the thing, the compensation for his labor would remain practically the same, or the strange anomaly would exist of making something nothing and nothing something, which is contrary to nature.   Even if it were admitted that, in the event all men were equal, increased compensation for menial occupation would cause the same to command a sufficient number of votaries, the practical fact remains that all men are not equal, and no earthly power, much less supposition, will ever make them so.   If all men's heads and feet were the same size they could all wear with comfort the same hat or shoe ; but these sizes differ, radically differ, but less by far than their individual characteristics or intellectual endowments.   By reason of these differences in men any law that bears upon all alike will leave the previously existing excellence the same as it was before.   Such efforts at reform are useless.

> And all attempts of kindred kind,
>   That emanate from mortal mind,
> Will be "like this insubstantial pageant faded
>   And leave not a track behind."
> As well a mermaid with her song,
>   Should seek to calm the raging sea,
> When curling tops of crested waves
>   Froth and foam in frightful glee,
> And lash the very stars in Heaven
>   As if in wild hilarity.

The feeble, sentimental, and impotent opposition that may be urged against the cumulative tax leveller is bottomed, firstly, upon what is called injustice, and secondly, on the assumption that all mankind would thrive as well, if not better, if the whole earth was owned by a few who could direct and control its energies and husband its opportunities. " Whilst our remedies oft in themselves do lie which we ascribe to Heaven," yet, as to the first, no man claims that it is possible for any one individual to amass as the result alone of his individual energy, sagacity, or opportunity, disassociated from and wholly unaided by the unavoidable increment of society, a fortune equal to the salary of an ordinary man for four hundred thousand years. All such estates are the result largely of fortuitous combinations and forces wholly unanticipated, and of course absolutely uncontrolled by the fortunate individual ; and if any possessor of a two-hundred-million dollar estate should begin life anew with all his faculties and powers intact, it is no more probable that he would ever again amass such fabulous properties, than it is that he would be twice the victim of a thunderbolt from heaven ; and inheritors of those fabulous sums are not entitled, by any excellence of their own, even to the very liberal remainder that cumulative taxation in no sense disturbs ; and finally, even admitting that there is exercised a palpable injustice, yet its oppressions are not severe, and it certainly accomplishes in a more effectual manner than any other system the grand *desideratum* of obtaining the revenues for the support of government (for which purpose alone taxation should be imposed) from the source which is least burdensome to the people and most certain to the government, effecting thereby a better, though not an unjust distribution of property—both objects long sought but never found.

Of those who believe that the world would be better if everything was owned by a few, it is simply asked : " Had you rather Cæsar were living, and die all slaves, than that Cæsar were dead, to live all freemen?" In the proposition to curtail excessive individual accumulations, the existence of which means practical commercial slavery for the many, there is no intent of killing Cæsar nor of depriving him of reasonable reward for his worth, but it might be quite as well for Cæsar himself if he be shorn of some of his power and live as to be possessed of it all and die, and so with the monopolists—*a fortiori.* When, by reason of these extraordinary accumulations, men of brains but of moderate means can neither profitably engage in any individual enterprise or safely invest in any corporate institution, not only loud will become the murmurs, but most cogent the power of conservative disquietude and unrest.

Men hitherto patient, long-suffering, and as calm as are the zephyrs that blow beneath the violets, scarce nodding their fair heads, will be, when once enraged, as fierce as are the boreal blasts that by the tops doth snatch the mountain pines and bend them to the vale. It will no longer be the childish and impotent whimperings of the thinly clad, or the blatant ebullitions of ignorant and impracticable orators of anarchistic mobs; but the calm, considerate, and thoughtful resolutions of brains in the counsel backed by valor in the field; and until then tall towers will ne'er tremble; but it now becomes obvious that, unless some reasonable compromise is effected, the stoutest buttresses may totter if not tumble into shapeless ruin; hence, not a few of the most philosophical and clear-headed of the monopolistic class have already begun to give heed to the distant rumbling of the approaching storm, to inquire into the details and determine as to the praticability of the plans proposed for relief and their operating effect. "*The people be d——d*" will hereafter be uttered more cautiously, if at all.

"Men want but little here below," but some want that
little "*strong*," and the most patient and prudent may yet
conclude that,

> "If it were done, when 't is done, then 't were well
> It were done quickly : If the assassination
> Could trammel upon the consequence, and catch
> With his surcease, success ; that but this blow
> Might be the be-all and the end-all here,
> But here, upon this bank and shoal of time,—
> We 'd jump the life to come."

It is not probable that monopolists will have "borne
their faculties so meek" "that their virtues will plead
like angels, trumpet-tongued, against the deep damnation
of their taking-off "; but rather that "this even-handed
justice will commend the ingredients of their poisoned
chalice to their own lips."

Why not then cease this unremitting strife, seek joy
and mirth, traverse the earth, or "leap astride some lazy-
pacing cloud and sail upon the bosom of the air "?

The argument has been advanced that "cumulative
taxation" would be abortive of good results for the reason that opulent individuals would demand for the use
of their capital or for rent of their estates an increased
compensation commensurate with their increased contribution to the government, to which it is answered : The
opulent individual might demand, but it is questionable
whether or not he could secure any greater compensation
for the use of his aggregated wealth than could a less
opulent individual receive. Would any borrower of
money pay eight per cent. to a man worth four millions
when the amount that he desired could be obtained from
a man worth but one million for a rate not exceeding
six ? Would any man pay fifty dollars per month for a

house that happened to belong to a man who owned a
hundred houses when a man who owned but ten houses
would rent him the same or its equivalent for forty
dollars per month ?   If so the renter is a fool and legislation cannot cure his complaint.   Certain fixed and
well-defined governmental limitations must be recognized
and adopted, otherwise there will be an endless confusion
and a chaos of uncertainty and doubt.   " The greatest
individual and personal liberty consistent with social
order " is the proper maxim for men who are guided by
sight—that is, by penetration and research—rather than
by sound—that is, by highly colored but meaningless
and impracticable epigrams and sophisms.   It is also
urged that " Phronocracy " is too complicated and intri-
cate for comprehension by the ordinary intellect.   If by
" ordinary " is meant the most depraved class on the earth
(which class alone would be unable to comprehend the
pronunciamento that signifies that knowledge and property alone shall determine man's right to participation in
government), then fortunate is it that the system is too
recondite and incomprehensible ; for this class is not
only not desidered, but it is absolutely spurned—that is,
looked upon with loathing and contempt, for he who is
so base as to be without the necessary qualification or
bereft of the required excellence, when but for a meagre
effort he can obtain both, is too utterly lowly and depraved to be of any consequence or worthy of any respect.   Hence, such men do not belong with the
" Phronocratic " class and would be ill at ease in their
association.   There will, in fact must, always be a class
lowly and degenerate, if not absolutely depraved, because
the natural forces and agencies operative upon the earth
appear to render it absolutely unavoidable.   It is the
height of folly, however, to permit this class to partici-

pate in that of which they have but little genuine comprehension, and to which they are not fitted, neither
regarding which can they assume any responsibility
either in knowledge or property. Nothing could possibly be more thoroughly supererogatory than further
effort at a quasi-ratiocinative dissertation on the truth of
the principle that *reason, knowledge, and property* should
rule this land. All else is but a vision conceived in
rashness, maintained in error, and can result in nothing
—a sounding brass and a tinkling cymbal. But the *glut
of wealth* must be entombed on some dark sepulchral
shore, returning to curse the world and enslave its owners,
as quoth the raven, *nevermore, nevermore!*

Many people, of course, otherwise or by natural inclinations favorable to the principles of the Phronocratic
organization, will be debarred from lending active
sympathy and support thereto, because they will think
the success of the issues impossible. This is always,
and reasonably, the fate of most reforms. Many thinking men will recognize and admit both the reasonableness
and justice of the proposition, but will be disposed to
say : "It is well if it could be brought about, *but it
can't.*"

There is always more difficulty in doing than in con-
ceiving a thing, more in execution than in planning ; but
that which is in accord with a man's judgment should not
be shunned because of the difficulties at first apparent,
provided there exists a reasonable probability of success,
for by failure nothing is lost, since the existing condition
is maintained. The monstrous and useless accretions of
individual wealth are not increased, nor the iniquity or
folly of universal suffrage aggravated by an honorable
effort to eradicate both. Reasonable probability of success, or certainly a reasonable groundwork for effort,

does exist. The white people of the South *en masse* are opposed to universal suffrage, especially as it applies to the negro, in which opinion many of the people of the North most heartily concur. If by the disfranchisement of the negro, and likewise a proportionate part of the degraded population of the North, the South could retain its proportionate representation in Congress and in the electoral college, there is greater cause for support of the system than of a proposition for the exclusion of the negro alone, and consequent curtailment of representation. That something has to be done as to the negro is manifest, because the North is restive and the South determined—the former that he shall count to the extent of his numbers, and the latter that he shall not control their sections, hence that he shall not count to the extent of his numbers. The rural population of all the States can see in the proposition a plan by which the municipalities would lose more votes in proportion to their population than would the country, and hence in this there appears an enticing allurement to the latter. It is well known that most all the corruption and prostitution of the ballot occurs in large cities, hence the conservative classes therein will look with favor on the idea.

Therefore, there appears to be a reasonable probability of support from the entire South, the ruralists of the North, and the conservative middle classes of all municipal centres. This support, too, is prompted largely on the ground of purifying the electoral system, to say nothing regarding the inestimable benefit and relief from oppression that would result from the removal of prohibitive and centralizing tariff duties and restrictions and the transfer of the burden of governmental support from the heads of the poor on to shoulders of the rich. From these three sources, coupled with the simi-

larity of the interests of the South with the younger
States of the West, which for years had been hostile
because of the absence of any issue sufficiently forcible
and vital to overcome the prejudices of the war, there
can be developed a very respectable following, which
will need but to be properly conserved and handled to
become very cogent and formidable.

> " Nor will its voice as angels' whispers,
>   Vanish in the heavenly choir,
> Nor as the music of the billows
>   Be lost upon some distant shore ;
> But rather like the lute of Orpheus,
>   Which with poets' sinews strung,
> Would soften stones and tame the tigress
>   Whene'er its music was begun."

In reasoning as to the possibility of success, it is most
important to remember that throughout the entire Union
the rural population numbers about one half the whole,
and in 1890 *comprised four million farm owners.* If a
majority of this half could be obtained, it is evident that
half the representatives could be chosen outside of the
occasional success of those seeking election from municipal districts in which, where the loafer element is not
too strong, there will be very reasonable prospects.
With these elements of support, and the almost universal
Southern sympathy, it appears quite reasonable that the
ultimate end can be accomplished as outlined in the
preceding pages.

Aside from the arguments, which are direct and unmistakable, wholly void of evasion or dissimulation,
there is a very decided conviction that the population of
America has become so great that suffrage must be curtailed or, to preserve order, peace, property, rights, and
domestic tranquillity, popular government might have to

15

be abolished and an empire or a despotism be erected upon the ruins of a system that respects the inalienable rights of men. Prudence must prevail or all is chaos, for a mob uncontrolled wreaks naught save wrath and crimson blood.

> "Look, as I blow this feather from my face,
> And as the air blows it to me again,
> Obeying with my wind when I do blow
> And yielding to another when he blows,
> Commanded always by the greatest gust,
> Such is the likeness of you common men.
>   He that trusts you,
> Where he should find you lions, finds you hares ;
> Where foxes, geese ; you are no surer, no,
> Than is the coal of fire upon the ice,
> Or hailstones in the sun. Your virtue is,
> To make him worthy whose offence subdues him,
> And curse that justice did it. Who deserves greatness,
> Deserves your hate, and your affections are
> A sick man's appetite, who desires most that
> Which would increase his evil. He that depends
> Upon your favors, swims with fins of lead,
> And hews down oaks with rushes. Hang ye ! Trust ye ?
> With every minute you do change a mind ;
> And call him noble, that was now your hate,
> Him vile that was your garland."

And thus it is and e'er will be, if into the hands of wretches is consigned the ship of state. The acknowledgment of every man's right to live does not carry with it every man's inherent right of supervision and control. The former is acknowledged and provided for, when all individual effort fails, to an extent that will not mar that effort ; but the latter can and should only be secured by individual excellence. In the strife of individuals to better their worldly state each should remember that when his efforts are successful he will desire the same uninterrupted possession and peaceful enjoyment of the fruits of his labor, his skill, or his opportunity that those who have already acquired it are entitled to receive.

This class should remember, too, that compensation for human exertion, whether by muscle or brain, is a thing of relative and comparative significance.

Aside from unearned increment, the only way one individual can excel another is to profit by the labor of another which results from employment. If in the beginning, or if a new start in civilization could be begun and all men made equal in worldly possession, it is evident that in this civilized state, where wants are many and of great variety and diversification, a division or classification of industrial occupation would follow ; and it is likewise evident that by increased energy, skill, and opportunity some men would excel other men in the same avocations. This increased excellence would bring increased facility, which would command the preference in all exchanges and markets either by cheapness or betterment.

This advantage once acquired necessarily drives the less fortunate out of business or compels him to sell his labor to his more fortunate rival. Rather than pursue said avocation on his own account and independently, at a loss (which loss is the natural result of the increased facility of the more energetic and fortunate), the less fortunate *prefers* (is not forced), but actually seeks, to sell his labor for a definite sum to the man who possesses the facilities, or, in other words, the accumulated capital in some shape, and hence naturally, by his own volition and consent, he becomes an *employé* and the other an *employer*. The latter, in other words—not by force, but by consent —secures the labor of the former at a rate that will yield to himself a profit, and hence the more men he can em-

ploy on these terms the richer he will become, and all by
mutual consent.   It is certainly clear, therefore, that the
employer is as much entitled to his profit as the employé
is to his wages, for both are matters of agreement and
consent.   It is likewise clear, as has been stated, that a
universal advance in wages would cause a universal advance in prices, so that primarily the only possible way
in which one man can acquire earthly possessions in
excess of another is first to secure the usufruct of his own
labor, then that of the labor of as many other men as
possible ; and to do this he must be possessed primarily
of increased energy, excellence, or opportunity, and then
conserve and utilize the results of same for the purpose
of acquiring increased facility ; and as all men are not
equal in the possession of these attributes, and not similarly favored by opportunity or hampered by adversity,
the acquirement of equal facility by all is impossible, *by
the very force of nature itself*, hence some must go up and
others must go down.   Nothing can be done that will not
wrongfully interfere with individual rights, except to
curb and prevent unreasonable excesses, *just because they
are unreasonable*, and because they are wholly disproportionate to individual requirements either as a reward for
excellence or as compensation for cupidity and greed.

Thus it is that all schemes and plans of socialism and
communism fail.   Nothing of the kind can ever succeed,
and simply because they seek to crush the very system
which upholds the very thing they seek in crushing.

Permit a man's reward for excellence, energy, and opportunity to be compensated to an extent adequate and
sufficient, or all daylight had as well be darkness, all
fertile fields arid plains, all summers winters, all genial
rays nipping frosts, all good evil, and all order chaos ;
for, else, naught save death and damned oblivion would

be the tomb of *all mortal* bones, indeed. Seek not by legislation or force to make either men or the results of their labors equal, for 't would be as useless and as ridiculous as

" To gild refined gold, to paint the lily,
    To throw a perfume on the violet,
    To smooth the ice, or add another hue
    Unto the rainbow, or with taper light
    To seek the beauteous eye of heaven to garnish."

Seek not to increase the relative compensation of labor either by prohibiting uninterrupted and absolutely free importation of labor's products, or by general increases in its apparent pay, for both must as certainly bring a retroactive effect as that motion follows energy— both, if not general, are discriminating; and both, if general, increase the price of commodities more than they augment the pay of labor. Do not seek to confiscate landed property, not to tax it disproportionately to other property, for this is both futile and unjust. Do not seek to give every man equal right to natural opportunity, for the inherent differences in men's individual excellence and force would still leave the relative condition the same. Do two things only : First. Discriminate against unreasonable and excessive individual fortunes ; that is, pass laws that *do not* bear upon all men alike, yet . leave just reward for them who are oppressed the most.

Second. Conserve your own energies ; that is, make the profit on your own labor to the greatest extent possible, and as you gain in possessions you increase your facility. Make available and useful any opportunity, and, when so done, do not squander.

It may be said that this is impossible, and to such as so think, be it answered in defiance of disproof—*then you will never rise.* In this manner and in this alone (that is, excellence and opportunity) did some men originally get the start of other men, and they are entitled to it, to within reason, by any and by all justice that the human mind can conceive.   It may be said that opportunity does not come to all, to which be it answered : *Then that is your misfortune and no man's fault.* Just as, should you accidentally discover a mine of gold, it would be your *good-fortune* and no man's design.   All men are not stricken down by the lightning, all are not born blind or hopelessly maimed and diseased.   Some are—why ?   Ask the winds to answer.   Are all men to suffer equally the pangs of those unfortunately stricken ? Certainly not.   Are all men, therefore, to enjoy equally the ecstasy of those fortunately blessed ?   Certainly not.

Hence necessarily, and by the very laws of nature ever immutable, is forced upon society that condition which has existed since the very earliest dawn, and which will exist till the latest crack of doom—to wit : social gradations and inequality, without which all would be confusion, if, indeed, the earth and its accessories being as and what they are, society could exist at all.

On the very same principle, however, that society steps in and provides hospitals, almshouses, asylums, and the like for those who are abnormally poor and destitute and helpless (which many will always be by the natural force of natural occurrences), to an extent that will not cause their abuse, so likewise it is perfectly competent and proper for society to step in and provide against those who are abnormally and uselessly rich (which some will be by the natural force of natural things), to an extent that will not interfere with their natural right to reasonable reward.   The wants and needs of any man, it matters not in what sphere he may desire to exist, cannot possibly exceed the income of four or five

million dollars, and if they do he had better be compelled
to curtail his personal expenditures and contribute more
to the state. It is said that a rich man pays to society
his increased tribute in the increased cost of his maintenance. Scarcely any man worth over five millions can
possibly contribute proportionately in this manner, even
if this could be called a contribution, which, of course,
it cannot be, for rich men usually expect the persons
from whom they buy to give value for their expenditures,
which therefore are available to society only to the
extent of a profit, just as are the purchases of any other
man. A two-hundred millionaire will not pay any more
for an article than a one-hundred millionaire, and the
latter no more than a five-hundred millionaire, but when
subjected to the cumulative rate, such contributions in
exact proportion to ability *are forced*. No one can deny
that abnormally large estates do in many cases augment
more rapidly by accretion and gain than they decrease
by division among heirs, and even if they do not so
increase, the simple principle of placing the burthen of
society and government upon those who can best afford
to bear it is not only not unjust to that class, but is really
a debt they can well afford to assume, especially if they
are still permitted to enjoy adequate, sufficient, yes,
redundant, personal possessions.

No one can deny that assessments would be more
thorough and complete under the cumulative system, in
which means and laws would be provided for increased
scrutiny, and where both the local and the federal assessor passed upon the estate, it would be more correctly
assessed than where the local official only, as under the
present system, had entire supervision and control.
But admitting that it would not be more thorough or,
more inconceivable yet, that it would be less thorough

than the present system, even then the increasing cumulative rate would necessarily compensate for any loss in the aggregate.

The facts are, as a matter of course, that it would be much more complete than the present system, and whilst not perfect would be nearly so. All the trees and undergrowth in a dense forest cannot be easily enumerated, but accuracy can be closely approached if the proper effort is put forth, and so with the proper effort under the cumulative system would assessments be far more complete and satisfactory than they have ever been before.

Those who would be shorn of their colossal accumulations would become reconciled to the situation much more readily than would be at first supposed, and, being guaranteed increased security, many would really enjoy the relief from the anxiety and care of such vast and burthensome estates, and would begin to realize that there are other things to live for save money ; other avenues for the exercise of intellect than through the stock exchanges ; other means of deriving pleasure than by cornering the market and forcing some competitor to the wall to die perhaps in agony and sorrow ; in a word, that greater absolute contentment could be vouchsafed from moderation than from excess.

Many men are now obliged to deprive themselves of much pleasure and relaxation, though their fortunes are ample to warrant both, simply because of the absolute necessity of devoting their time, their thoughts, and their energy, by night at times as often as by day, to the protection and conservation of their properties, or, rather, to be slaves to the master mammon—a beastly tyrant—a fiend than which there is none more remorseless or cruel. Phronocracy counsels moderation ; it

appeals to reason and to understanding; it will elevate
human hope and temper human passion ; it will cause
every thinking man to cherish one scale of prudent reflection to poise another of ruinous ambition ; and, above
all, it will check the interference of government with the
proper functions of the people, leaving localities and
states to control their own domestic affairs, and the
individual to pursue the enterprises of the earth untrammelled by any federal interference, and as the seven bright
pointers of the Major Bear blaze forth the brightest of
myriads shining there, and while to each other they are
motionless and fixed, yet, as in annual revolution they do
sweep the vaulted dome of heaven, first to the east, then
south, then west, though aiming always to the north, so
the Phronocratic creed, with equal certainty and truth,
will lead all persons who will it proclaim to the only
polar star of rest that mortal man can ever gain.

Strive on, thou virtuous and ever blessed reformer ;
strive, for in thy efforts lie weary mortals' proudest
hopes ; but when all is done nothing is done save to
check extremes in life, temper the severity and moderate
the effect of nature's operating forces, the result of
which, and nothing more nor less, are the things we see
around us ; and neither the wealth of high resolves, the
martyrdom of generous sacrifices, the theories of social
reformers, the deductions of eminent casuists, nor the
lapse of time, the progress of science, the penetration of
thought, the mutations of earth and fortune, nor the appeals of man to man—of misery to wealth—nor prayers
to all the gods at once, will ever make things equal.
Strive for this and you but seek the shadow of fancy,
and will lose the substance of practicality, stifle energy,
curb or crush enterprise, thwart the motives of life, and
war with nature itself—a foe that can't be conquered.

Remember, as well in the storms of adversity as in the height of glory, to be at all times prudent, temperate, and reliable, for

> " In the reproof of chance
> Lies the true proof of man ; the sea being smooth,
> How many shallow bauble boats dare sail
> Upon her patient breast, making their way
> With those of nobler bulk ?
> But let the ruffian Boreas once enrage
> The gentle Thetis, and, anon, behold
> The strong-ribbed bark through liquid mountains cuts,
> Bounding between the two moist elements
> Like Perseus' horse : where 's then the saucy boat,
> Whose weak untimbered sides but even now
> Co-rivalled greatness ? either to harbor fled
> Or made a toast for Neptune.   Even so
> Doth valor's show and valor's worth divide
> In storms of fortune ! "

Let all men to themselves and the world be true, remembering that

> " Corruption wins not more than honesty :
> Still in thy right hand carry gentle peace,
> To silence envious tongues, be thou just and fear not,
> Let all the ends thou aimest at be thy country's,
> Thy God's, and truth's, then if thou fallest, O Cromwell !
> Thou fallest a blessed Martyr."

PHRONOCRATIC PRECEPTS.

1st. Want is a necessary result of the operating agencies of nature.

2d. Want prompts acquisitiveness, and acquisitiveness prompts accumulation.

3d. Men have a natural right to possess and enjoy property.

4th. The progress of civilization and the occupancy by mankind of lands and climes differing from those in which the race most likely had its origin, causes both the multiplication and diversification of wants.

5th. Trade and exchange are a necessary result of diversified wants, and from these result profits and losses; hence the rich and the poor.

6th. Excessive individual accumulation is useless to the possessor and hurtful to the community.

7th. Man has a right to "unearned increment" the same as to property in the abstract.

8th. A nation gains nothing by interfering with the natural laws of trade and exchange.

9th. Protection in any form must impoverish as much as it enriches—something cannot come of nothing.

10th. To be able to "protect" the classes a government must tax the masses; nothing can be builded up without tearing something down.

11th. No tax should be levied save for *revenue*, and

that should be derived from a source least burdensome to the people and most certain to the government.

12th. Governments should operate no enterprise and do nothing whatsoever that can possibly be done by individuals.

13th. The operation of enterprises by government is simply giving to agents the proper functions of the principals.

14th. Individual excellence should be fully recognized and adequately recompensed.

15th. The world should belong in usufruct to the people, but the vast majority would fritter away their allotments either by improvidence or misfortune—neither the fault of any man or men.

16th. No law applicable to all men alike will alter the relative condition or estate of men.

17th. Schemes for relief must, to avail anything, " oppress the favored and favor the oppressed."

18th. Many enterprises must always be " monopolistic in their nature."

19th. Enterprises by nature monopolistic should be, to the greatest extent possible, popularly owned.

20th. Taxes should be borne rather in the ratio of ability than of property.

21st. It is probable that a hundred men own one dollar where one man owns one hundred dollars.

22d. Suffrage should only be exercised by men possessing a certain degree of excellence and capacity.

23d. Governments are instituted for and are supported by property, hence those possessing nothing should not participate in government.

24th. Women should neither vote nor fight.

25th. Genuine ballot reform can only be secured by its curtailment.

26th. The curtailment of the ballot is the only practicable solution of the race question in the South.

27th. Immigration of self-sustaining foreigners is beneficial to the country.

28th. Money simply facilitates trade and cannot create or enlarge it. Cheapening the standard benefits nobody.

29th. There should be but one standard of money, weight, and measure.

30th. As soon as possible all land from the Isthmus to the Arctic should be under one flag.

31st. A nation to be truly independent should own land in all climes.

32d. All of North America could be governed, if suffrage was curtailed, better than any part with suffrage universal.

33d. Because a despotism is the worst it does not follow that excess of liberty is the best form of government.

34th. The United States Government is a Republic, not a Democracy, and should be a " Limited Republic," or a Phronocracy.

35th. Excessive individual suffrage is as useless and unwise as excessive individual property ; hence, both should be curtailed, and, if not both, then neither.

36th. All schemes of governmental paternalism are foolish, abortive, and wrong.

37th. All government should be as near the individual as possible—that is, *Home Rule should be universal.*

38th. There should be greater opportunity for individual participation in business and less in government.

39th. Special privileges should be made general and general restraints special.

40th. Phronocracy signifies the rule of Prudence, Conservatism, and Understanding. There are about four

million farm owners and two million moderately circumstanced city residents now in America.   To these two
classes especially would it be very beneficial, and their
strength, united, would win.   Each year there will be
more millionaires and more paupers, hence fewer of the
conservative middle classes.

41st. *They are as sick, that surfeit with too much, as
they that starve with nothing : It is no mean happiness,
therefore, to be seated in the mean ; superfluity comes sooner
by white hairs, but competency lives longer.*"—SHAKESPERE.

THE END.

www.ingramcontent.com/pod-product-compliance
Lightning Source LLC
Chambersburg PA
CBHW021114270326
41929CB00009B/870